GENDER EQUALITY AND SOCIAL INCLUSION DIAGNOSTIC OF SELECTED SECTORS IN
NEPAL

OCTOBER 2020

ASIAN DEVELOPMENT BANK

ADB

Notes:
In this publication, "$" refers to United States dollars, "€" for euros, and "NRs" refers to Nepalese rupees.

Cover design by Kookie Trivino.

On the cover: Marginalized women and men empowered to achieve gender equality and social inclusion in different spheres of society.

CONTENTS

TABLES, FIGURES, AND BOXES

FIGURES

BOXES

The Asian Development Bank has prepared the *Gender Equality and Social Inclusion Diagnostic of Selected Sectors in Nepal* to assist itself, the government, and development partners in Nepal to identify ways to incorporate approaches for gender equality, social inclusion, and women's empowerment in selected sectors. These sectors involve agriculture and natural resource management; energy; skills development; transport; urban development; and water, sanitation, and hygiene. Gender equality and social inclusion consultant Chhaya Jha prepared this publication in close collaboration with Senior Social Development Officer Suman Subba of the Nepal Resident Mission. Principal Social Development Specialist Francesco Tornieri of the South Asia Department provided overall guidance throughout the process.

ABBREVIATIONS

ADB	Asian Development Bank
CBS	Central Bureau of Statistics
CGD	Child, Gender and Disabled
CTEVT	Council for Technical Education and Vocational Training
DFID	Department for International Development
DOLI	Department of Local Infrastructure Development
ESMF	Environmental and Social Management Framework
EVENT	Enhanced Vocational Education and Training Project
GDP	gross domestic product
GESI	gender equality and social inclusion
HDI	human development index
kWh	kilowatt-hour
LAHURNIP	Lawyers' Association for Human Rights of Nepalese Indigenous Peoples
LGOA	Local Government Operation Act
MHM	menstrual hygiene management
MOPIT	Ministry of Physical Infrastructure and Transport
MOUD	Ministry of Urban Development
NDHS	Nepal Demographic Health Survey
NEA	Nepal Electricity Authority
NGO	nongovernment organization
NLSS	Nepal Living Standard Survey
NSTB	National Skills Testing Board
NWSC	Nepal Water Supply Corporation
ODA	Official Development Assistance
OBA	output-based aid
OBC	other backward class
ODF	open defecation free
PPP	public–private partnership
PWD	person with disability
RUDP	Regional Urban Development Project
SDC	Swiss Agency for Development and Cooperation
SDGs	Sustainable Development Goals
SDR	special drawing rights
STWSSSP	Small Towns Water Supply and Sanitation Support Program
TESP	Training and Employment Service Providers
TEVT	Technical Education and Vocational Training
TSLC	Technical School Leaving Certificate
UNDP	United Nations Development Programme
USAID	United States Agency for International Development
WASH	Water, Sanitation and Hygiene
WSS	Water Supply and Sanitation
WUA	Water Users' Associations
WUSC	Water Users and Sanitation Committees

1

OVERALL CONTEXT

Introduction

This introductory chapter provides a brief background and highlights key points about gender equality and social inclusion (GESI) in Nepal.[1] The subsequent chapters focus on sectors and subsectors of cooperation between ADB and the Government of Nepal and provide practical resources for GESI mainstreaming in project operations.

Country context

The development indicators of Nepal have improved over the last two decades. Overall poverty levels have declined, but disparities still exist based on location and social background.

Nepal is heavily dependent on remittances. Agriculture is the mainstay of the economy. Industrial activity mainly involves the processing of agricultural products. Nepal is planning to graduate from the least developed country status by 2022 and transform into a middle-income country by 2030.

The Constitution of Nepal (2015) established a new federal structure with three tiers of government—federal, provincial, and local. For the first time, local governments have exercised executive, legislative, and judicial powers. The separation of roles and powers at the three levels is evolving.

Key points about gender equality and social inclusion in Nepal

Political representation of women and excluded groups has significantly improved after the restructuring of Nepal.

Despite progress, development indicators are lower for women and excluded groups. Gender-, caste- and ethnicity-based inequality and violence are still prevalent. In general, women across Nepal have a weaker role in decision-making compared to men. Caste-based and language-based discriminations are experienced by the Dalits[2] and Adivasi Janajatis are disadvantaged by caste- and language-based bias.[3] The Madhesis[4] are also prone to political, economic, and social marginalization. The Government of Nepal recognizes people of third gender, and official documents have provided space to identify their sex as "Others."[5] However, the lack of social acceptance of different sexual orientation, gender identities, expressions and sexual characteristics (SOGIESC) marginalizes people of the lesbian, gay, bisexual, transgender, and intersexual (LGBTI+) community.

Policy commitments	The Constitution is committed to ending discrimination related to class, caste, region, language, religion, and gender. Eight sectoral ministries have their own GESI guidelines. The Local Government Operation Act (LGOA) 2017 has several provisions for promoting GESI, which have been included in the functions of the local government. Nepal has ratified as many as 23 international human rights instruments that include international conventions and covenants on women, ethnic minorities, and persons with disability (PWD), and against racial discrimination. Nepal is committed to the UN Sustainable Development Goals and to "leaving no one behind."
Institutional structures	The location of GESI responsibility is spread over various institutional mechanisms and structures, from the federal to ward levels of the government, including the constitutionally established National Commissions for specific groups. There are many non-state actors and identity-based organizations working on GESI-related issues at all the three tiers of the government: federal, provincial, and local. However, they have lesser visibility in remote and backward areas.

GESI = gender equality and social inclusion, LGBTI+ = lesbian, gay, bisexual, transgender, and intersexual.

[1] Gender equality and social inclusion (GESI) is a concept that addresses unequal power relations between women and men and between different social groups (GESI Working Group IDPG Nepal. 2017. *A Common GESI Framework*. Kathmandu). Gender refers to the social, behavioral, and cultural attributes, and expectations and norms associated with being male or female. Gender equality refers to how these factors determine the way in which women and men relate to each other and to the resulting differences in power between them. Social inclusion is defined as the process of improving the ability, opportunity, and dignity of people, disadvantaged on the basis of their identity, to take part in society (Inclusion Matters: The Foundation for Shared Prosperity. Washington, DC: World Bank).

[2] Dalits refer to "communities who, by virtue of atrocities of caste-based discrimination and untouchability, are most backward in social, economic, educational, political and religious fields, and deprived of human dignity and social justice" (National Dalit Commission. 2008. Nepal).

[3] The indigenous people of Nepal are officially described as Indigenous Nationalities (Adivasi Janajati). The Adivasi Janajatis are defined as distinct communities having their own mother tongues, traditional cultures, written and unwritten histories, traditional homeland and geographical areas, and egalitarian social structures (Government of Nepal. 2002. *National Foundation for Development of Indigenous Nationalities Act–2002*. Kathmandu).

[4] The Madhesis are people of the plains (Tarai) having non-Nepali languages as their mother tongue. Many of these groups share cultural traditions and educational and family ties with people living in the Indian states of Bihar, Uttar Pradesh, and West Bengal (International Crisis Group. 2007. Nepal's Troubled Tarai Region Crisis Group Asia Report N°136. Kathmandu/Brussels).

[5] "The third gender refers to people whose gender identity (or self-identification and expression) or sexual orientation (or emotional and sexual attraction to individuals of same or different sex) does not match or does not conform with conventional notions of their "assigned sex" (male or female usually at birth and based on their genitals). These include lesbians, gays, bisexuals, transgender people, and intersexuals, who are known as LGBTI+ in abbreviated form" (Supreme Court Division Bench Honorable Justice Balram K.C. and Honorable Justice Pawan Kumar Ojha Order [*Writ No. 917 of the year 2064 BS (2007 AD)*] on *Case of Sunil Babu Pant et al. vs. Nepal Government on 21 December 2007*.) Translated by the National Judicial Academy Law Journal. 2008 (2). pp. 261–286.

Introduction

This introductory chapter provides a brief review of the country context, highlights key points about gender equality and social inclusion (GESI), and provides a brief overview of policy commitments and institutional structures to promote action on GESI. Each subsequent chapter focuses on agriculture and natural resource management; energy; skills development; transport; urban development; and water, sanitation, and hygiene, respectively. The selected sectors and subsectors reflect the major areas of cooperation between the Asian Development Bank (ADB) and the Government of Nepal.

The sector-focused chapters provide practical resources for ADB and its government partners. They aim to assist with GESI mainstreaming in each sector, in accordance with the commitments made by both ADB and the government. Each sector-focused chapter starts with a brief summary of the major themes or subsectors of ADB–government cooperation, and then provides a brief overview of sector characteristics and challenges. Government commitments to support GESI and institutional mechanisms responsible for GESI in the sector are briefly summarized. GESI issues relevant to sector activities and outcomes are then set out, substantiated with data and evidence, where possible. Each chapter concludes with a list of issues and opportunities to consider in sector and project analyses, and discussions with development partners. At the end of each chapter, a tip sheet is added summarizing sectoral barriers and possible measures to address them.

Country Context

Nepal is a mountainous, landlocked, and least developed country with a total area of 147,181 square kilometers, 26.41 million population, 125 ethnic groups, and 123 languages, according to the 2011 census. Ecologically, the country is divided into three eco-regions: the mountain, hills, and lowland (plains) Tarai. The Constitution of Nepal (2015) established a federal structure with three tiers of government—federal, provincial, and local—with local governments exercising executive, legislative, and judicial powers. Administratively, Nepal is divided into 7 provinces and 753 village and urban municipalities, which include 6 metropolitan cities (Mahanagarpalika), 11 sub-metropolitan cities (Upamahanagarpalika), 276 municipalities (Nagarpalika), and 460 rural municipalities (Gaunpalika). A mayor and deputy mayor (municipalities) and a chairperson and vice chairperson (rural municipalities) head the local governments. Local units are subdivided into wards, represented by a ward chairperson and four ward members. Out of the four ward members, two must be women and one of the two women must be a Dalit. All locally elected representatives comprise the village or municipality assemblies, with local legislative power. Each of the country's 77 districts has a district assembly comprising of the mayors, deputy mayors, chairpersons, and vice chairpersons. The district assembly elects a district coordination committee to act in behalf of the executive branch at the district level. The district coordination committee is comprised of a maximum of nine members chosen from among the members of municipal or rural municipal assemblies, and include a head, a deputy head, at least three women, and at least one person from the Dalit or minority community.[6]

---

[6] Australian Government, Department of Foreign Affairs and Trade and Asia Foundation Partnership on Subnational Governance in Nepal. 2017. *Diagnostic Study of Local Governance in Federal Nepal*. Kathmandu.

The development indicators of Nepal have improved over the last 2 decades. Nepal's Human Development Index (HDI) value for 2019 was 0.579, positioning it at 147 out of 189 countries and territories. However, when the value is discounted for inequality, the HDI falls to 0.430, a loss of 26% due to inequality in the distribution of the HDI dimension indices.[7] Poverty incidence decreased from 42% in 1996 to 25% in 2011 and to 21.6% in 2015.[8] Despite the decline in overall poverty levels, disparities based on location and social background have persisted. Around 42% Dalits (Hill Dalits 44% and Madhesi Dalits 38%) and 10% Newars (historical ethnic group inhabitants of the Kathmandu Valley) were below the poverty line in 2011;[9] and there was about 16% poverty incidence in urban and 27% in rural areas.[10]

The situation in the provinces varies according to their level of development. Most of Nepal's population resides in Provinces 1 and 2, each with more than 20% of the total population. Province 6 is the least populated, with about 6% of the total population. Population under absolute poverty is highest in Province 7 at 34% and the lowest in Province 1 at 12%. But multidimensional poverty rate is highest in Province 6 at 51% followed by Province 2 at 48%. (Figure 1.1).[11]

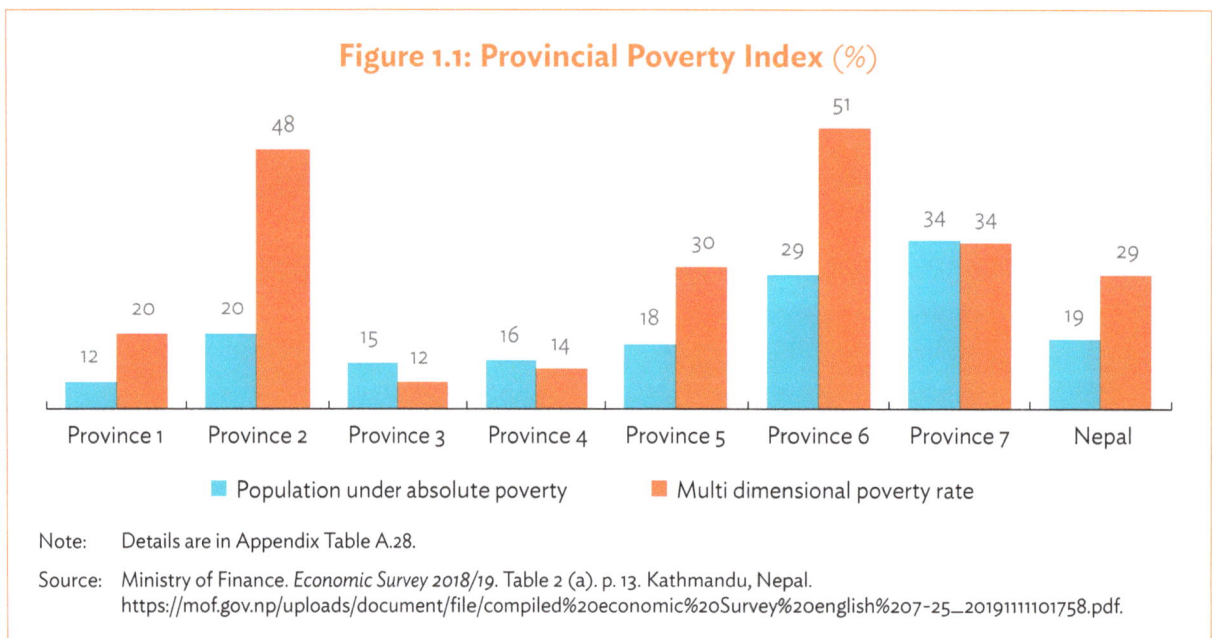

Figure 1.1: Provincial Poverty Index (%)

Note: Details are in Appendix Table A.28.

Source: Ministry of Finance. *Economic Survey 2018/19*. Table 2 (a). p. 13. Kathmandu, Nepal. https://mof.gov.np/uploads/document/file/compiled%20economic%20Survey%20english%207-25_20191111101758.pdf.

7   United Nations Development Programme (UNDP). 2019. Beyond Income, Beyond Averages, Beyond Today: Inequalities in Human Development in the 21st Century. *Human Development Report 2019*. http://hdr.undp.org/en/content/2019-human-development-index-ranking.
8   UNDP. 2018. *Poverty Reduction: Our Focus*. http://www.np.undp.org/content/nepal/en/home/poverty-reduction.html.
9   Lawyers' Association for Human Rights of Nepalese Indigenous Peoples (LAHURNIP). 2014. *A Study on the Socio-Economic Status of Indigenous Peoples in Nepal*. Kathmandu. https://www.iwgia.org/images/publications//0712_social-economic-status-of-indigenous-peoples-of-nepal.pdf.
10   Central Bureau of Statistics. 2011. *Nepal Living Standard Survey*. https://cbs.gov.np/nepal-living-standard-survey-2010-11/.
11   Nepal Rastra Bank, Research Department. 2017. *Nepal's Demographic, Social, Economic and Fiscal Situation (Provincial Profile)*. Kathmandu. p. 14. https://www.nrb.org.np/red/publications/study_reports/Study_Reports.

The population of Nepal is composed of approximately 31% Khas Arya (dominant hill caste), 27% Hill Janajati, 8% Tarai Janajati, 13% Dalit, 15% Madhesi, and 4% Muslims.[12] Percentages of social groups indicate that Province 3 has the highest percentage of Hill Adivasi Janajati group (including Newars, the most advantaged ethnic group in Nepal) at 53% followed by Province 1 at 40%. Provinces 7 and 2 have low population of Hill Adivasi Janajati. Presence of Dalits is highest in Province 6 at 23% followed by Provinces 2, 4, and 7 with around 17%. Madhesi, Muslims, and "other backward class" (OBC) reside mainly in Province 2.[13] Khas Arya is highest in Provinces 6 and 7, followed by Provinces 3 and 4. The literacy rate is highest in Province 3 at 69% with 82% men being literate. The lowest literacy rate is in Province 2 with 41% and women having the least literacy at 39% (Figure 1.2).

Figure 1.2: Percentage of Literate Women and Men by Province

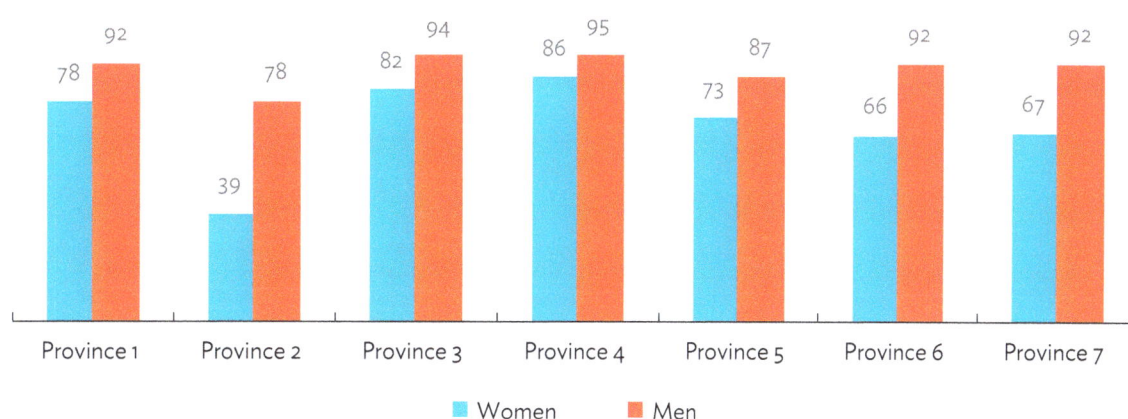

Note: Details are in Appendix Table A.1 and A.2 of this document.

Source: Government of Nepal, Ministry of Health. 2016. *Demographic and Health Survey*. Kathmandu
         (Table 3.4.1 and Table 3.4.2, pp. 54–55).

Nepal is heavily dependent on remittances, which amount to as much as 30% of its gross domestic product (GDP). Agriculture is the mainstay of the economy, providing a livelihood for almost two-thirds of the population but accounting for only one-third of GDP. Industrial activity mainly involves the processing of agricultural products, including pulses, jute, sugarcane, tobacco, and grain.[14] Nepal is planning to graduate from the least developed country (LDC) status by 2022 and transform into a middle-income country by 2030.

---

[12]   Khas Arya, as defined by the Constitution of Nepal 2015, refers to the Chhetri, Brahmin, Thakuri, and Sanyasi (Dashnami) community. See footnotes 2, 3, and 4 for definitions of Dalits, Adivasi Janajatis, and Madhesis.

[13]   "OBC" are one caste group of Madhesi people covering more than 35 sub-caste groups, some of whom are economically well-off, while others are among the poorest in Nepal. Socially, all the OBC groups typically practice gender-based discriminatory practices. They have a federation and have chosen to call themselves "other backward class." Government documents have accepted the terminology.

[14]   Index Mundi. 2018. *Nepal Economy Profile 2018*. https://www.indexmundi.com/nepal/economy_profile.html.

The Official Development Assistance (ODA) disbursement in fiscal year (FY) 2017–2018 reached $1,623 million, which was 16% higher than the disbursement in FY2016–2017. The share of foreign aid in the national budget was about 22% in FY2017–2018. The United Kingdom through its Department for International Development (DFID) disbursed the highest amount ($123.9 million) among bilateral development partners followed by the United States Agency for International Development (USAID). The World Bank Group disbursed the highest amount ($533.5 million) among multilateral development partners, followed by ADB ($291.7 million), the European Union ($116.2 million), the United Nations Country Team ($65.6 million), and the International Fund for Agricultural Development ($15.8 million).[15]

From 1966 to 2018, ADB approved a total lending reaching $592 million, and technical assistance at $8.01 million (including $5.31 million in cofinancing) for projects in transport, urban development and water supply, energy, rural roads, agriculture, and natural resources. In partnership with the government and other stakeholders, ADB has helped reduce poverty and raise incomes of subsistence farmers, marginalized women, and socially excluded Dalit and other indigenous communities.[16] A total of $727 million (45%) of ODA disbursement in FY2017–2018 was through projects directly or indirectly supportive of gender-related goals.[17]

Key Points about Gender Equality and Social Inclusion in Nepal

Gender equality and social inclusion is a top policy priority of government agencies and development partners in Nepal

The new constitution, which was promulgated in 2015, is committed to "ending discriminations relating to class, caste, region, language, religion and gender."[18] The 2015 Sustainable Development Goals (SDGs) called for the commitment of world leaders and 193 countries, including Nepal, to working together toward "a just, equitable, tolerant, open, and socially inclusive world in which the needs of the most vulnerable are met," ensuring that "no one is left behind."[19]

Various plans and programs, such as the three-and five-year plans (including the Approach Paper of the 15th Five-Year Plan covering FY2020–2024), address GESI issues. The 6th Five-Year Plan includes gender, while the 10th Three-Year Plan identifies social inclusion as a separate pillar. Eight ministries have developed their operational guidelines to mainstream GESI in their sector. National Action Plans on addressing gender-based violence and human rights are in place. Since 2007, the Government of Nepal's

---

[15]   Ministry of Finance, International Economic Cooperation Coordination Division, Nepal. 2018. *Development Cooperation Report.* Kathmandu. p. xii.

[16]   ADB. 2018. *Asian Development Bank and Nepal: Fact Sheet.* Manila. https://www.adb.org/publications/nepal-fact-sheet.

[17]   Ministry of Finance, International Economic Cooperation Coordination Division, Nepal. 2018. *Development Cooperation Report.* Kathmandu. p. xiii.

[18]   The Preamble of the Constitution states, "Ending all forms of discrimination and oppression created by the feudalistic, autocratic, centralized, unitary system of governance, recognizing the multi-ethnic, multi-lingual, multi-religious, multi-cultural and diverse regional characteristics, resolving to build an egalitarian society founded on the proportional inclusive and participatory principles in order to ensure economic equality, prosperity and social justice, by eliminating discrimination based on class, caste, region, language, religion and gender and all forms of caste-based untouchability." The Fundamental Rights under Right to Equality states, "No discrimination shall be made in the application of general laws on grounds of origin, religion, race, caste, tribe, sex, physical condition, condition of health, marital status, pregnancy, economic condition, language or region, ideology or on similar other grounds. The State shall not discriminate citizens on grounds of origin, religion, race, caste, tribe, sex, economic condition, language, region, ideology or on similar other grounds." See Government of Nepal. 2015. *Constitution of Nepal.* Kathmandu.

[19]   United Nations. 2015. Transforming our World: The 2030 Agenda for Sustainable Development. *Sustainable Development Goals.* New York (paragraphs 8 and 9).

gender-responsive budgeting demands all government interventions to be gender marked as directly or indirectly responsive to women's progress. The LGOA also has mandated provisions to address GESI.

Political representation of women and excluded groups has significantly improved after restructuring of Nepal

For the first time in 20 years, nearly 40,000 officials were elected in local, provincial, and federal parliaments. Women made up nearly 41% (14,352) of those elected in the local governments and more than 33% in the state and federal assemblies, which is higher than the global average of women's representation in parliaments (24%).[20] A high percentage of women (91%) are in the deputy leadership position (deputy mayor and vice chair) of the local governments. Dalit representation in the current House of Representatives is 7% compared to 0.48% in 1991. Madhesis and Janajatis have made significant gains in the first ever provincial elections held in 2017, winning seats above or almost at par with their national population shares.[21]

Gender-, caste- and ethnicity-based inequality and violence are still prevalent

Despite decades of progress in Nepal, patriarchal attitudes and stereotypes that perpetrate inequality against women and excluded groups remain entrenched.[22] These have resulted in multiple forms of disadvantage against women and excluded groups.

Due to gender inequality within the family, women in general across Nepal have a weaker role in decision-making compared to men, less control over resources, and often have restrictions on their physical movements as a measure to control them. Even among women, differences in position within the family (mother-in-law, daughters, older or younger daughters-in-law) affect roles, responsibilities, and decision-making opportunities.[23]

About 22% of women in Nepal (aged 15 to 49) have experienced physical violence since age 15. The percentage of ever-married women who have experienced spousal physical, sexual, or emotional violence is 26%. Of the women who have experienced any type of physical or sexual violence, 66% have not sought any help or talked with anyone about resisting or stopping the violence they experience, indicating silence or passiveness on such forms of violence. Approximately 30% women and 23% men agree that wife beating is justified under specific circumstances (if wives burn the food, argue with their husbands, go out without telling them, neglect the children, and refuse to have sex with them) (Figure 1.3).[24]

[20]   Inter-Parliamentary Union. 2017. *Women in National Parliaments, 2017*. http://archive.ipu.org/wmn-e/world.htm.
[21]   Governance Facility, Nepal and LAHURNIP. 2018. *Federal Nepal, The Provinces, Socio-Cultural Profiles of the Seven Provinces*. Kathmandu.
[22]   Individuals and groups are excluded or included based on their identity. Among the most common group identities resulting in exclusion are gender, caste, ethnicity, religion, sexual orientation, and disability status. Hence, excluded groups refer to communities of people who are systematically blocked from (or denied full access to) various rights, opportunities, and resources and are significantly less likely to receive the benefits of development investments because of their gender, caste, ethnicity, religion, sexual orientation, gender identity, and disability (World Bank. 2013. *Inclusion Matters: The Foundation for Shared Prosperity*. Washington, DC. p. 5). The terms excluded and marginalized are used interchangeably in this document. This document differentiates between the "excluded groups" (those who are historically excluded and have experienced inter-general exclusion) and "vulnerable groups" (those who are temporarily vulnerable due to the prevailing situation). See GESI Working Group, International Development Partner's Group Nepal. 2017. *A Common GESI Framework*. March.
[23]   M. Lama and O. Gurung. 2012. *Social Inclusion Survey, Caste, Ethnic and Gender Dimensions of Socio-Economic Development, Governance, and Social Solidarity*. Kathmandu: Central Department of Sociology/Anthropology, Tribhuvan University. p. 167.
[24]   Ministry of Health, Nepal. 2016. *Nepal Demographic and Health Survey*. Kathmandu. p. 16.

Figure 1.3: Attitude Toward Wife Beating
(% who agree with at least one specified reason)

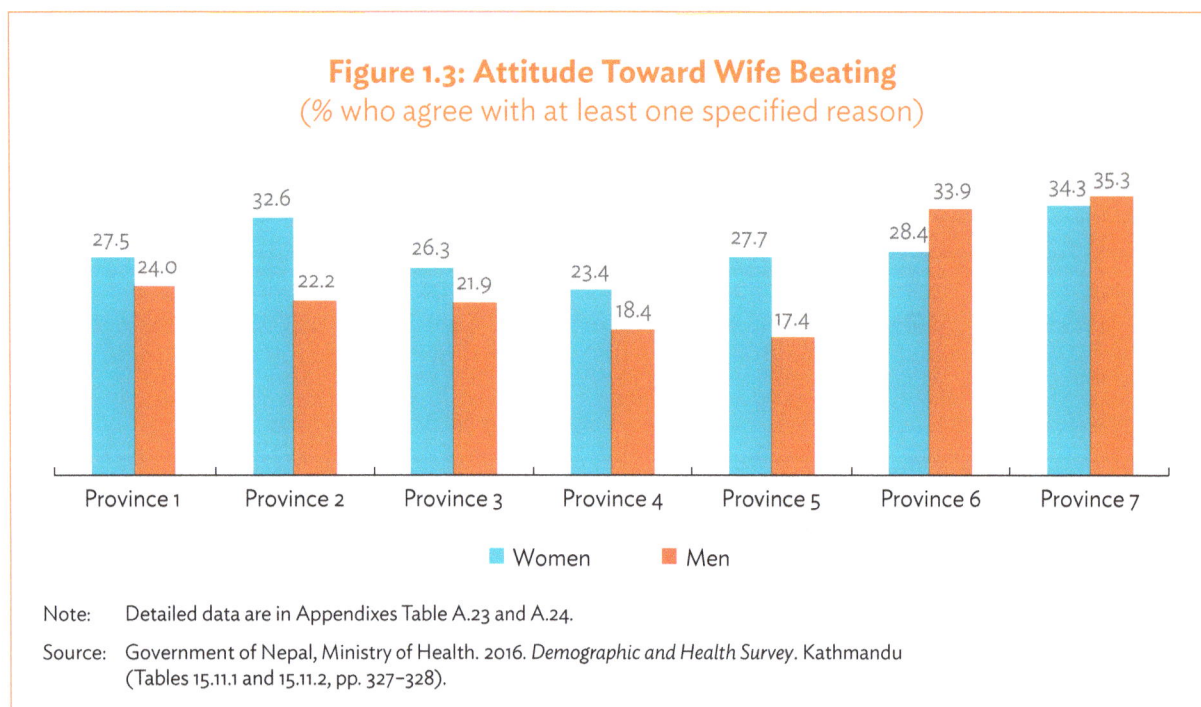

	Province 1	Province 2	Province 3	Province 4	Province 5	Province 6	Province 7
Women	27.5	32.6	26.3	23.4	27.7	28.4	34.3
Men	24.0	22.2	21.9	18.4	17.4	33.9	35.3

Note: Detailed data are in Appendixes Table A.23 and A.24.

Source: Government of Nepal, Ministry of Health. 2016. *Demographic and Health Survey*. Kathmandu
(Tables 15.11.1 and 15.11.2, pp. 327–328).

Bias against the most vulnerable population of Nepal can constrain growth and equitable distribution of the benefits of development interventions. Dalits are restricted on what they can touch, where they can enter, and which sectors they can work in. Language, geographical isolation or remoteness, and lack of education and information limit the Janajatis' access to development benefits. The Madhesis experience political, economic, and social marginalization. While Nepal has recognized people of third gender and acknowledges their existence in official state documents by indicating a space for "Others," the social unacceptance of different sexual orientations remains.[25] The bias against sexual orientation, gender identity and expression, and sex characteristics (SOGIESC) that do not conform with dominant norms marginalizes the lesbian, gay, bisexual, transgender, and intersexual (LGBTI+) community,[26] consisting of an estimated 8% to 10% of Nepal's population.[27]

Persons with disability experience stark marginalization

In Nepal, about 2% (513,321) of the total population (2.18% men and 1.71% women) have disabilities. The prevalence is highest in the age group of 60 and above. Persons with physical disability are the highest among those with disabilities (36%), followed by people with no or poor vision (18.4%), and those with hearing problems (15%). Mental disabilities are experienced by 6% of persons with disabilities (PWDs). Women with vision, hearing, and mental disabilities are higher than men with such physical disabilities (footnote 10).

---

[25]   The term "third gender" is not preferred by the LGBTI+ community who advocate for trans woman or trans man terminology for the transgender.

[26]   "SOGIESC" refers to general categorizations—all people have a sexual orientation, gender identity, gender expression, and sex characteristics. "LGBTI+" refers to people who have a marginalized sexual orientation, gender identity, expression, or set of sex characteristics (UNDP LGBTI Inclusion Index 2017).

[27]   UN WOMEN, UNCT. 2017. *Nepal Gender Equality and Social Inclusion (GESI) Profile for Humanitarian Action and Disaster Risk Reduction.* Kathmandu (Updated 31 August 2017).

Households with PWDs are more economically challenged in terms of their ability for and access to well-paid employment. The household is burdened by high costs of caring and living with PWDs, as well as limited PWD-friendly facilities and services within their communities. Women with disabilities are subject to more vulnerabilities and experience greater marginalization throughout their lifecycle, including barriers to access of services and fulfillment of their rights to health, education, and decent work. Literacy of PWDs is lower than of those without disabilities (40% PWDs are literate compared to 61% of those without). There are about 35% of children (aged 5 to 10 years) with disabilities who are out of school compared to the 5% without disabilities, with higher percentage of boys attending than girls with disabilities.[28]

According to government statistics, only about 200,000 have received the disability identity card, which enables them to access government support.[29] Disability is a cross-cutting issue that can impact people at any point across their lifespan. Its intersectionality with gender, race, ethnicity, indigenous group identity, migrant worker status, and other characteristics can lead to unique and multiple forms of disadvantage.[30]

Despite progress, development indicators are lower for women and excluded groups

Disaggregated data indicates that women and excluded groups have been unable to benefit equally from Nepal's development progress.[31] The Nepal Demographic Health Survey (NDHS) 2016 found that 33% of women in Nepal are illiterate, in comparison to only 10% men; and that 40% of Tarai women are illiterate or have no formal education, compared to 20% of women in the Hills and 36% in the Mountains. The literacy rate of women and men 15 years and older is 56%, with 45% women and 72% men being literate. Hill Brahmins have the highest literacy rate (75.64% with almost 90% literate men) followed by Newars at 72%. Tarai Dalits have the lowest literacy rate at 28% with only 11% women being literate.

A high percentage of women of Hill Dalit (66%) and Hill Brahmin (64%) do paid work while only 37% women of "other backward class" and 35% of Tarai Brahmin and Chhetri do so, indicating the conservative social norms of the Tarai which control women's abilities to access opportunities. More women (71%) than men (52%) are not paid for the agriculture related work they perform. More than 60% of Hill Chhetri and Dalit women work without receiving any cash remuneration. Due to prevailing gender norms, women continue to undertake a disproportionate level of unpaid care tasks which in turn constrain their choices of paid work, including type and location of work.

Dalits, Adivasi Janajatis (excluding the advantaged category), "other backward class," and Muslims have consistently shown low education and health indicators, including higher stunting among children and higher vulnerability to multiple communicable diseases.[32] The population with access to

---

[28] United Nations Children's Fund Nepal. 2017. *Disability in Nepal, Taking Stock and Forging: A Way Forward.* Kathmandu. https://www.unicef.org/nepal/reports/disability-nepal.

[29] G. Budhathoki. 2017. *Disability Sensitive Concept of Local Government.* Kathmandu. http://www.sarokar.com.np/?tag=status-of-disability-in-nepal.

[30] World Bank. 2017. *Including Persons with Disabilities in Water Sector Operations: A Guidance Note.* https://openknowledge.worldbank.org/bitstream/handle/10986/27542/117306-WP-P161461-PUBLIC-Disabilities.pdf?sequence=5&isAllowed=y.

[31] World Bank. 2018. *Reanalysis of NLSS 2011 and NDHS 2016 data for the GESI Diagnostic Paper.* Kathmandu (The data was prepared to inform World Bank's country partnership framework).

[32] Adivasi Janajatis are categorized into five groups based on literacy rate, housing unit, landholding and other economic assets, educational level, and population size: (i) endangered, (ii) highly marginalized, (iii) marginalized, (iv) disadvantaged, and (v) advanced. See Nepal Federation of Indigenous Nationalities. 2011. *Categorization of Adivasi Janajatis According to their Marginalisation.* Kathmandu.

any toilets in Nepal in 2011 was 56%. There was wide disparity, with 90% Newars and only 11% Madhesis having this access. Piped water supply systems coverage was 52.3%. There was high income disparity as 63% of the richest quintile households and 28% of the poorest had this access (footnote 10).

The 2011 census showed that about 83% of the population still resided in rural areas, and the Nepal Living Standard Survey III (NLSS) showed that 76% of households depended on agriculture for livelihood, and 84% of the labor force involved in agriculture are women. The land holdings of Dalits are small, and landlessness is extreme among Dalits (15% Hill and 44% Madhesi). Of Hill Dalits, 45% are marginal farmers. Access to land, credit, information, representation and participation, and geographical isolation are major issues in access to resources of women and excluded group farmers.

There is low representation of women and excluded groups in government services

Government records show low levels of representation of women and excluded groups in public life. In gazetted positions, there are 10% women and in non-gazetted, 17%.[33] In Special Class (which is the highest class among the civil service positions), there are only 3% women. The Chief Secretary, the highest position within the bureaucracy, has always been held by men. Representation of Dalits and of other ethnic groups (excluding Newars) is also minimal. Among the 83,000 personnel in Nepal's civil service, only 0.8% are Dalits, a disproportionate figure considering that they make up 13.8% of the national population. Most Dalit employees serve as non-gazetted lower level staff with limited power and authority. Among these Dalit service holders, nearly 90% are Hill Dalits.[34] Among Janajatis, the Newar subgroup are 7.21% of civil servants, which is more than their 5% share in the population. Other Janajati groups collectively constitute about 12% (Tharus are 3%, others 9%) representation in civil service though they are 32% of the population.[35]

High migration levels contribute to labor shortages, and have both empowering and disempowering effects on women

From 2008 to 2017, Nepal issued 3.5 million labor permits to migrant workers, predominantly for travel to Malaysia and nations of the Gulf Cooperation Council (GCC). Remittances comprise more than one-quarter (NRs699 billion [$6.56 billion]) of national GDP which is the fourth-highest proportion in the world in FY2016–2017. About 95% of Nepal's labor migrants are men and 5% are women (Figure 1.4). Women migrants primarily work as general cleaning laborers, factory workers, and restaurant and hotel workers, while men work as security guards, construction workers, and agriculture laborers.[36]

With high male migration, there is a shortage of workers in agricultural fields or in infrastructure projects. Poverty, limited employment opportunities, and lack of employable skills in rural settings are fueling unsafe internal and external migration and human trafficking. There is an increasing migration of women from villages to cities—84% of women migrated within Nepal. Nearly two-thirds (64%) of women migrated due to marriage, 11% for studies, 10% for work, and 14% to accompany their family.[37]

---

33   A gazetted officer is published in the official gazette by the government upon direct recruitment or by promotion.
34   The Kathmandu Post. 2017. *Dalits in Civil Service.* Kathmandu.
      http://kathmandupost.ekantipur.com/news/2017-03-28/dalits-in-civil-service.html.
35   Samabeshi Foundation. 2017. *Inclusion Watch.*
      http://www.samabeshifoundation.org/wp-content/uploads/2017/07/Inclusion-Watch_English.pdf.
36   N. Baruah and N. Arjal. 2018. *Nepalese Labor Migration—A Status Report.* Kathmandu. Asiafoundation.org/2018/06/06/nepalese-labor-migration-a-status-report/.
37   Ministry of Health and Population. 2016. *Nepal Demographic Health Survey.* Kathmandu.

Women going through irregular or illegal channels of migration are mostly from indigenous groups. Meanwhile, the women who are left in the villages experience greater responsibilities, autonomy in everyday household decision-making, heightened mobility, and exposure to the outside world. As they participated more in agriculture and economic activities, they became more empowered.[38] However, their time poverty and stress levels have also increased. Social norms are more strictly enforced on them limiting their engagement in the community. These have impacted their social mobility and level of participation in different sectoral committees and other decision-making forums.

Figure 1.4: Share of Total Labor Migrants by Sex, Fiscal Year 2008–2009 to Fiscal Year 2016–2017

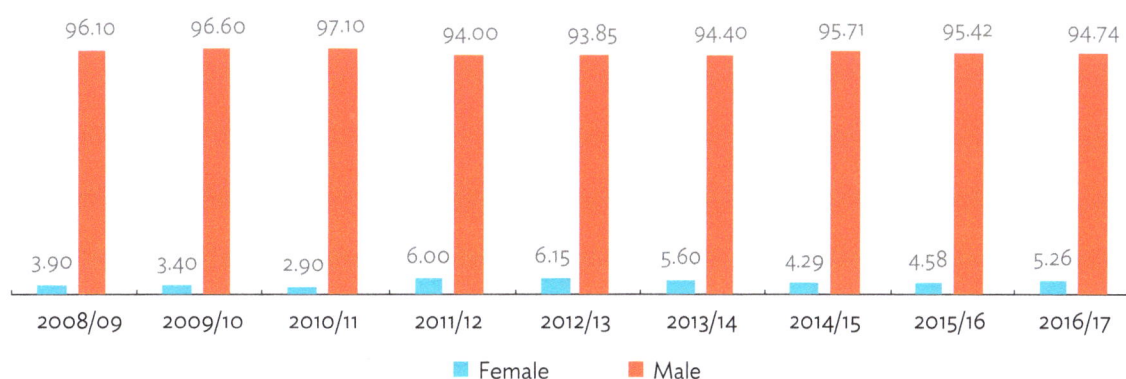

Source: Government of Nepal, Ministry of Labour and Employment. 2018. *Labour Migration for Employment: A Status Report for Nepal: 2015/16–2016/17*. Kathmandu. p. 10.

Policy Commitments

National Commitments

The Constitution, the 14th Three-Year Plan, and the 15th Five-Year Plan have strong commitments for GESI. Eight sectoral ministries have their own GESI guidelines.[39] The Civil Service Amendment Act 2014 embraces inclusivity and provides that 45% of the employees must comprise 33% women, and 27% Adivasi Janajatis, 22% Madhesis, 9% Dalits, 5% PWDs, and 4% from "other backward class."

The LGOA of 2017 incorporated provisions to promote GESI and recognize it as a function of the local government. It stipulates that planning processes should be participatory, and projects directly benefiting women and excluded groups should be recognized as those promoting GESI. Also, the Parliament passed the Disability Rights Act in 2017 establishing constitutional directives specifically to protect and support PWDs.

---

[38] Multidisciplinary Digital Publishing Institute. 2019. *Labour Migration in the Middle Hills of Nepal: Consequences on Land Management Strategies*. Geneva. https://www.mdpi.com/2071-1050/11/5/1349/pdf.

[39] The eight ministries which have approved GESI guidelines for their sectors include: (i) Federal Affairs and General Administration, GESI Policy, 2010; (ii) Urban Development GESI Operational Guidelines, 2012; (iii) Forest and Soil Conservation GESI Strategy, 2010; (iv) Education Consolidated Equity Strategy; (v) Health GESI Operational Guidelines, 2012; (vi) Agriculture GESI Strategy; (vii) Irrigation GESI Guidelines; and (viii) Physical Infrastructure and Transport GESI Operational Guidelines, 2017.

Under the Intergovernmental Fiscal Arrangement Act of 2017, the Government of Nepal can provide grants to the state and local governments, including a special grant to uplift or develop the class or community discriminated economically, socially, or in any other form.[40]

The Ministry of Women, Children and Senior Citizens (MOWCSC) prioritizes the economic empowerment of women by ensuring their meaningful participation in project processes, and the elimination of gender-based violence and harmful practices. The Ministry of Federal Affairs and General Administration has issued various model Acts for local governments integrating GESI.[41] These model acts have been used by the local governments to develop their own policies, regulations, and guidelines.

International Commitments

Nepal has ratified 23 international human rights instruments that include international conventions, covenants, and declarations on women, such as Convention on the Elimination of All Forms of Discrimination Against Women, Beijing Platform for Action, UN Security Council Resolutions (UNSCR 1325 and 1820), child rights (Convention on the Rights of the Child), ethnic minorities or indigenous peoples' rights (International Labour Organization 169), elimination of racial discrimination (Convention on the Elimination of All Forms of Racial Discrimination), and welfare and rights of PWDs (Convention for the Rights of Persons with Disability [CRPD]). Nepal has also committed to the SDGs.

These international treaties and commitments require Nepal to promote legal, economic, social, political, civic, and constitutional equality. UNSCR 1325 calls for women's equal participation in the peace process and in all decision-making positions in a post-conflict situation. The International Labour Organization Convention No. 169, endorsed by the government in 2007, promotes the rights of Janajatis. The CRPD also provides guidelines for ending all discrimination against PWDs. Similarly, many other international agreements, such as International Conference on Population and Development (ICPD) on reproductive health, Education for All, and the SDGs have called for Nepal's commitment toward achieving targets regarding gender equality and women's empowerment (SDG 5) and reducing inequalities (SDG 10). Thus, Nepal has an enabling policy environment, but the challenge remains in terms of effective implementation and bringing about gender equality and inclusive transformations.

Institutional Structures to Promote Action on Gender Equality and Social Inclusion Issues

The responsibility to work on GESI is spread over various institutional mechanisms and structures, from the federal to ward levels of the government (Table 1.1). Apart from the state, there are many non-state actors and identity-based organizations working on GESI-related issues at all the three tiers of government—federal, provincial, and local. However, they have lesser presence in remote and backward areas.

---

[40]   Government of Nepal. 2017. *An Act Made for Intergovernmental Fiscal Arrangement*. Kathmandu.
[41]   Ministry of Women, Children and Senior Citizens. 2018. *Meeting Notes* (Joint Secretary, MWCSC, 20 June). Kathmandu. Some of the model acts serve as guidelines for budgeting for programs against child marriage. See also Program Implementation Guidelines for Micro-Enterprise Development for Poverty Reduction, Regulation for Municipality Work Performance. https://mowcsc.gov.np/acts-regulations.

Table 1.1: Mechanisms to Achieve Gender Equality and Social Inclusion in Nepal

Level	Agency	Responsibility
Federal	Ministry of Women, Children and Senior Citizens	Empower women, children, and senior citizens, especially those who are economically disadvantaged, socially deprived, or otherwise underserved.
	Ministry of Federal Affairs and General Administration	Enhance access of socially and economically disadvantaged groups, region and community to the service and facility delivered.
		Empower Dalit, indigenous, Madhesi, Muslim, persons with disability, and ultra-poor people through social mobilization.
		Ensure inclusive development by enhancing peoples' participation in decision-making and planning process.
		Oversee Social Inclusion and Social Security Section and the different commissions.
	Ministry of Finance, Gender Responsive Budgeting Committee	Issue guidance on gender-responsive budgeting to be followed by different ministries.
	National Commissions for specific interest groups	Formulate and monitor policies and programs concerning the rights and interests of specific groups: women, Dalits, indigenous nationalities, Madhesis, Muslims, and Tharus.[a]
	National Inclusion Commission	Protect the rights of Khas Arya, Pichardiaka ("backward") class, PWDs, senior citizens, laborers, peasants, minority and marginalized communities, people of the Karnali, and the indigent class.
	The National Human Rights Commission, Election Commission, Public Service Commission, National Natural Resources and Fiscal Commission	Recognize GESI as a cross-cutting theme in all activities.
Provincial	Ministry of Social Development	Address GESI-related issues and integrate GESI in the formulation, implementation, and regulation of provincial level plans, rules, standards, policies, workplan, rehabilitation, monitoring and evaluation, gender-responsive budgeting, and gender audit.
Local level	Municipality/Rural Municipality	Develop and implement programs for the welfare and overall management of PWDs.[b]
	Social Development Section	Design, formulate and prioritize policy and plans.
		Implement GESI-responsive activities; social security schemes; data and information management; and operation and management of care and rehabilitation centers for senior citizens, children, and PWDs.

GESI = gender equality and social inclusion, PWD = person with disability.

[a]   The Tharu people are an ethnic group (a subgroup of Adivasi Janajati) living in the Tarai of South Nepal.
[b]   Buddhathoki. 2017. *Disability Sensitive Concept of Local Government*. http://www.sarokar.com.np/?tag=status-of-disability-in-nepal.

Sources: Nepal Constitution 2015, Local Government Operation Act 2015, Provincial Business Allocation Regulation 2018. In *A Common GESI Framework*. 2017. GESI Working Group of IDPG (updated in 2019).

2

AGRICULTURE AND NATURAL RESOURCE MANAGEMENT

Area of collaboration	ADB projects have supported agricultural credit, irrigation, hill agriculture, crop intensification, and commercialization of agriculture, and provided modern tools, techniques, and technology to farmers through community-based cooperatives and water users' associations (WUAs). ADB has provided broad-based assistance to the government for the agriculture, natural resources, and rural development sector, worth $1,086.59 million, through 176 projects, which is 19% of its cumulative lending, grant, and technical assistance commitments to Nepal.
Sector context	Agriculture is the backbone of Nepal's economy, providing livelihood for approximately two-thirds of the population. Agriculture is largely based on low-value crops and subsistence production, with only about 17% of output traded in markets.

About 66% of Nepal's total population are employed in agro-based activities. Women are far more likely to be employed in agriculture than men. About 14% women and 34% men are paid in cash in agriculture work but more than 71% women and 52% men are not paid at all.[1]

Technology constraints, a dysfunctional marketing chain, lack of product standardization, subsistence and traditional farming, limited knowledge, and inadequate rural infrastructure are among the key challenges in the agriculture sector.

The Government of Nepal and its development partners (i.e., USAID, DFID, World Bank, and ADB) have been promoting the value chain approach to increase production, income, and employment of farmers, including women and excluded group farmers.

Low availability of agricultural workers has resulted in reduced farming. |
| **Gender equality and social inclusion considerations relevant to sector planning and outcomes** | Limited land is available to women and the excluded groups for agriculture due to high landlessness among them and low land ownership.

Year-round irrigation facilities are limited to less than 25% of the arable land. Irrigation technologies are generally not designed for women's needs. Efficiency of its use is not optimized. Access to credit for the installation of irrigation systems can be very difficult, particularly for the income poor, unless collateral-free loans are available. |

Lower income farmers, including women and excluded group farmers, highly depend on the quality, quantity, and timely availability of production inputs such as seeds, fertilizer, high quality livestock, and forage seeds. Extension services are inadequate for these farmers.

Agriculture value chains have limited recognition of gender and social differences.

Climate change has more adverse impact on women and excluded groups.

Home- and community-based barriers constrain women and excluded groups from sectoral benefits and hinder them from assuming leadership roles.

Good practices and lessons

Policy directives are important for inclusion of the target group in agriculture related forums and services and should be accompanied with social mobilization.

In-depth poverty and social analysis of the sectoral issues enable identification of appropriate strategies for different social groups.

Specific measures to address the barriers of women and excluded groups enhance their access to benefits to production inputs, irrigation facilities, and benefits.

Climate change investment has positive socioeconomic impacts on women and excluded groups.

Looking forward: Issues and opportunities to consider

Limited access to production inputs by women and excluded groups.

Low levels of meaningful participation among farmers, particularly women of small and marginal landholdings.

Lack of understanding of existing gender- and social-based power relations for specific crops.

Gender and caste/ethnicity differentiated participation and benefits, and disaggregated data for different stages of the value chain.

Further resources

ADB tip sheet on addressing barriers experienced by women and excluded group farmers and integrating GESI in the agriculture sector (Table 2.2).

DFID = Department for International Development, GESI = gender equality and social inclusion, USAID = United States Agency for International Development.

[1] Ministry of Health and Population. 2016. *Nepal Demographic Health Survey*. Kathmandu.

Area of Collaboration

ADB has provided broad-based assistance to the government for the agriculture, natural resources, and rural development sector, worth $1,086.59 million, through 176 projects, which is 19% of its cumulative lending, grant, and technical assistance commitments to Nepal.[2] ADB projects have supported agricultural credit, irrigation, hill agriculture, crop intensification, and commercialization of agriculture, and provided modern tools, techniques, and technology to farmers through community-based cooperatives. Farmers are encouraged to engage largely on agricultural value chains and high-value crops (e.g., apple, medicinal and aromatic plants, potato and vegetable seeds, off-season vegetables, wool, and cheese). Collection centers for the distribution and efficient marketing of the produce and processing of surplus vegetables were established.

Sector Context

Agriculture is the backbone of Nepal's economy, providing livelihood for approximately two-thirds of the population, contributing one-third of the country's GDP, and constituting more than half of its exports.[3] Women are more likely to be employed in agriculture than men (70% women and 30% men; more than 80% women farmers in Provinces 6 and 7). Compared with men, women have minimal presence in professional, technical, and managerial positions (Figure 2.1).

Figure 2.1: Occupation by Profession and Sex (%)

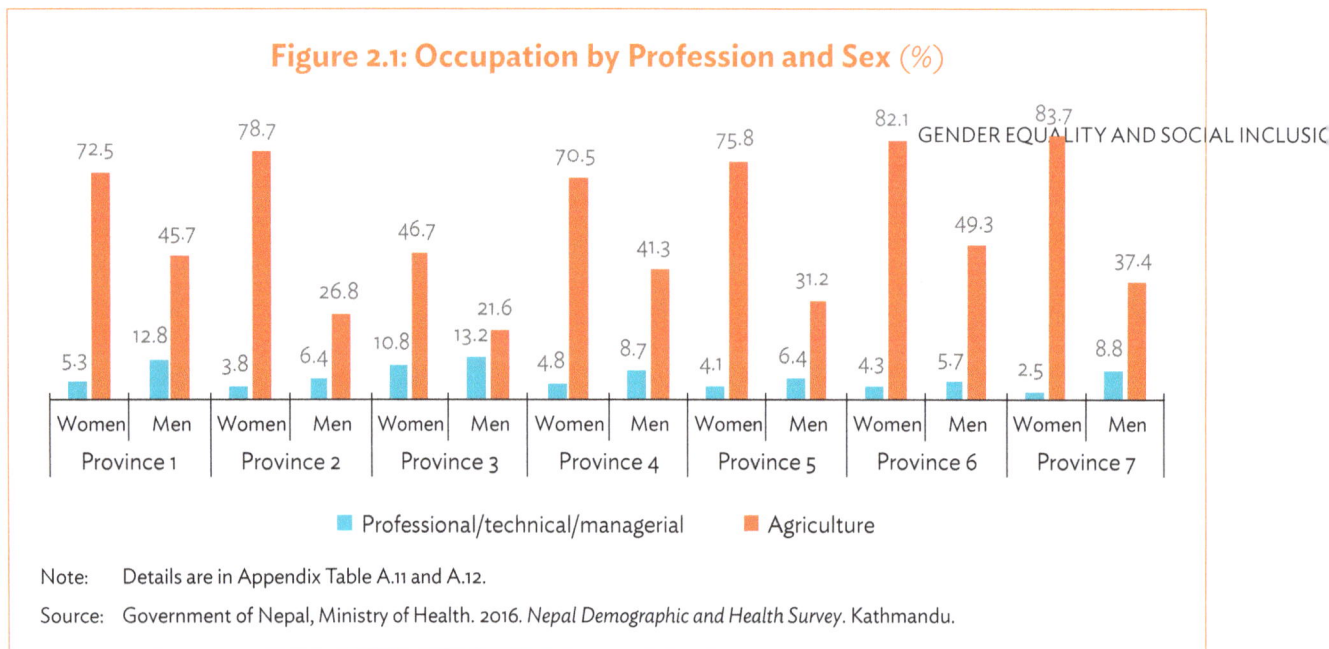

	Province 1		Province 2		Province 3		Province 4		Province 5		Province 6		Province 7	
	Women	Men	Women	Men	Women	Men	Women	Men	Women	Men	Women	Men	Women	Men
Professional/technical/managerial	5.3	12.8	3.8	6.4	10.8	13.2	4.8	8.7	4.1	6.4	4.3	5.7	2.5	8.8
Agriculture	72.5	45.7	78.7	26.8	46.7	21.6	70.5	41.3	75.8	31.2	82.1	49.3	83.7	37.4

Note: Details are in Appendix Table A.11 and A.12.

Source: Government of Nepal, Ministry of Health. 2016. *Nepal Demographic and Health Survey*. Kathmandu.

GENDER EQUALITY AND SOCIAL INCLUSIO

---

[2]   ADB. 2017. *Nepal: By the Numbers*. ADB Data Library. https://data.adb.org/dashboard/nepal-numbers (accessed 25 June 2018). Data about projects and funds are cumulative from 19 December 1996 to 31 December 2017 and cover all assistance.

[3]   J. Kyle and D. Resnick. 2016. Nepal's 2072 Federal Constitution: Implications for the Governance of the Agricultural Sector. *IFPRI Discussion Paper 1589*. Washington, DC: International Food Policy Research Institute (IFPRI). http://ebrary.ifpri.org/cdm/ref/collection/p15738coll2/id/131009.

Cereal production (primarily rice and wheat, pulses, minor grains, and maize) contributes about 50% of sector GDP, and livestock accounts for an additional 25%. Agriculture is largely based on low-value crops and subsistence production, with only about 17% of outputs being traded in markets.[4] This is also because there is no year-round irrigation to enhance agricultural productivity and commercialization in the agriculture sector. About 66% of the total population of Nepal is employed in agro-based activities (footnote 3). About 14% women and 34% men are paid in cash in agricultural work but more than 71% women and 52% men are not paid at all. Comparatively payment is better in non-agricultural work where only 8% women and 3% men are unpaid (Figure 2.2).[5]

Figure 2.2: Income Levels from Agricultural and Nonagricultural Work (%)

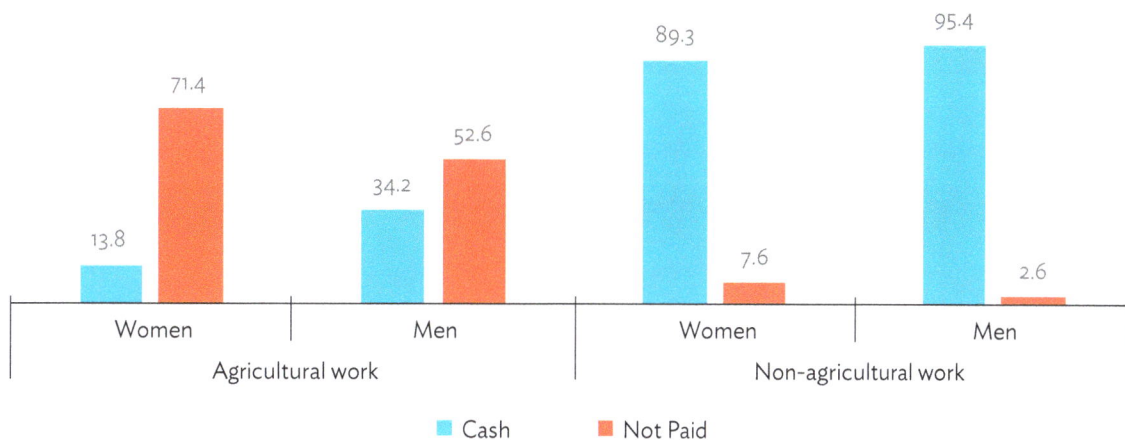

Note: Details are in Appendix Table A.8 and A.9 of this document.

Source: Government of Nepal, Ministry of Health. 2016. *Demographic and Health Survey*. Kathmandu (Table 3.10.1 and 3.10.2, p. 66).

Technology constraints, a dysfunctional marketing chain, lack of product standardization and quality control, lack of knowledge, and insufficient rural infrastructure are key challenges faced by the agriculture sector. The value chain approach is being promoted by the government and development partners like USAID, DFID, the World Bank, and ADB, with the aim to increase production, income, and employment of farmers, including women and excluded group farmers.

Policy Commitments

The Constitution of Nepal mandated policies on agriculture and land reform to increase production and productivity, commercialization, industrialization, diversification and modernization, and protection and promotion of the rights and interests of farmers. Agriculture is listed as a concurrent function across all tiers (federal, provincial, and local) of the government. The Right to Food is recognized as a

---

[4]   ADB. 2014. *Sector Assessment (Irrigation) Summary*. Community Managed Irrigated Agriculture Project. http://adb.org/Documents/RRPs/?id=33209-014-3.

[5]   The Labour Law of 2018 sets the minimum wage at NRs517. About 73.9% of the population employed in agriculture comprises 84.3% of all working women compared to 62.2% for men. Women, on average, are paid 30% less salary compared to men, regardless of profession. See *Nepal Labour Market Update*. 2017. ILO country office for Nepal. Kathmandu. January.

fundamental right. The 14th Three-Year Plan (2016–2017 and 2018–2019) targeted a 5% annual average agricultural growth rate; and the Government of Nepal has allocated NRs33.71 billion to this sector for FY2018–2019.[6] A budget of NRs4.77 billion was allocated as grant to improve seeds and plants of tea, coffee, cardamom, areca nuts, potato, banana, and lemon.[7] The budget included plans on increasing export of high-value agricultural products, establishment of agricultural knowledge center, increasing the subsidies on agricultural and livestock production and fertilizers, and use of modern technology for agricultural production.[8] Promotion of competitive agricultural value chains to add value and benefits to smallholder farmers and agro-enterprises are included in the plan. The 15th Five-Year Plan aims to (i) ensure food and nutrition security by increasing agricultural production and productivity; (ii) increase employment and income by developing agro-based industries; and (iii) balance the trade of the agricultural sector by developing commercialization and competitiveness.[9]

The Agriculture Development Strategy (ADS), 2015–2035 of the then Ministry of Agricultural Development is a 20-year vision with four leading programs: (i) value chain development of agriculture products, (ii) food and nutrition security, (iii) agriculture service extension, and (iv) agriculture research and technology. The main goals of the ADS are to expand access of farmers to agriculture programs, increase investment, reduce poverty, and improve food sufficiency. Provinces 1, 3, and 4 have more than 50% food security while Province 6 has the lowest food security at 23%. Province 6 also has the highest food insecurity at 18% (Figure 2.3).

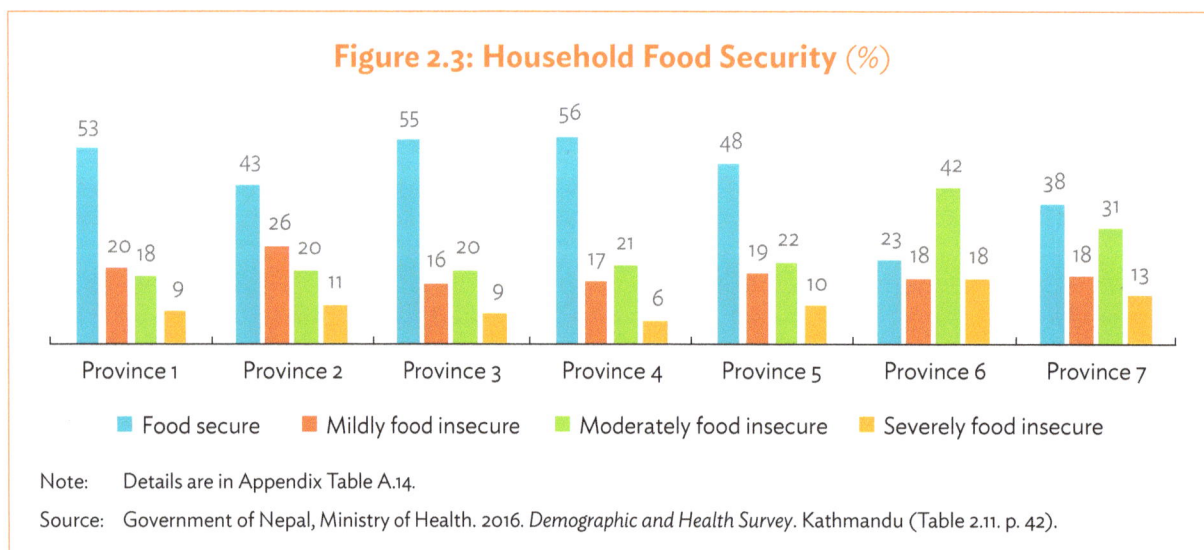

Figure 2.3: Household Food Security (%)

Note: Details are in Appendix Table A.14.

Source: Government of Nepal, Ministry of Health. 2016. *Demographic and Health Survey.* Kathmandu (Table 2.11. p. 42).

---

6   Government of Nepal, Ministry of Finance. 2018. *Budget Speech of Fiscal Year 2017–2018.*
     http://mof.gov.np/ uploads/document/file/Budget_Speech_207475_20170530011441.pdf.
7   The Prime Minister Agriculture Modernization Project was expanded to cover these grants.
8   Government of Nepal, Ministry of Finance. 2018. *Budget Speech of Fiscal Year 2017/18.* p. 20.
     http://mof.gov.np/uploads/document/file/Budget_Speech_207475_20170530011441.pdf.
9   Government of Nepal. *15th Periodic Plan of Nepal.* https://hamrolibrary.com/current-15th-periodic-plan-of-nepal-in-english/.

Food insecurity can lead to disability through poor living conditions, malnutrition, and lack of access to health services. Food insecurity and poverty are driven by lack of education and employment opportunities, inadequate access to social services, and unavailability of assistive technologies.[10] Hence the agriculture sector should be strengthened continually to ensure food security. One of the core outputs of the ADS is to establish mechanisms for gender equality and social and geographic inclusion.[11] The government enacted the National Agriculture Policy in 2004 as an umbrella policy in the agriculture sector to guide all sectoral policies. Also, the National Water Plan (2005) aims to provide irrigation facilities and increase: (i) the area of irrigable land from the current 65% to 97% by 2027, (ii) the year-round irrigation coverage from the current 38% of irrigated area to 67%, and (iii) the average cropping intensity within year-round irrigated areas from the current 140% to 193%.[12] Broader policies provide the policy framework for the sector, such as the Agribusiness Promotion Policy (2006); Commercial Agriculture Policy (2007); Trade Policy (2009); Irrigation Master Plan (2015–2035); and subsector policies, such as the National Seed Policy (1999), the National Fertilizer Policy (2002), and National Irrigation Policy (2003).

Institutional Framework

With the government system's shift to federalism, the responsibility for agriculture is mainly with the Ministry of Agriculture and Land Development and irrigation is with the Ministry of Energy, Water Resources and Irrigation. The Planning and Development Cooperation Coordination Division of the Ministry has been mandated to institutionalize the principles of gender mainstreaming and inclusion in the agricultural programs run by the Ministry and its agencies and projects and function as the point of contact related to gender and social inclusion.[13] The Department of Water Resources and Irrigation has a mandate to plan, develop, maintain, operate, manage, and monitor different modes of environmentally sustainable and socially acceptable irrigation and drainage systems from small to larger scale surface systems and from individual to community groundwater schemes. GESI focal persons are nominated in donor funded projects and the government also has institutional arrangements of GESI focal persons in the Ministry and department levels.[14] However, this position lacks authority and resources to function effectively.

At the provincial level, the Ministry of Land Management, Agriculture and Cooperatives is responsible for the agriculture sector while the Ministry of Infrastructure is in charge of the irrigation sector.

Each municipality and rural municipality has an Economy Development Section with an agriculture, livestock, and cooperatives office. Irrigation is under the infrastructure section. GESI responsibilities are with the Social Section of the Ministry of Social Development at the provincial level and the Social Development Section at the municipality level (Figure 2.4).

---

[10] International Disability Alliance, Food and Agriculture Organization. 2018. *Disability and Food Security: An Unfinished Policy Agenda*. http://www.internationaldisabilityalliance.org/fao-food-insecurity.

[11] Government of Nepal, Ministry of Agriculture and Development. 2014. *Agriculture Development Strategy*. Kathmandu. Activities for Output 1.5 on "Mechanisms Established for Gender Equality and Social and Geographic Inclusion in the ADS."

[12] ADB. 2012. *Report and Recommendation of the President to the Board of Directors, Proposed Grant—Nepal: Water Resources Project Preparatory Facility*. Manila.

[13] Planning and Development Cooperation Coordination Division. 2020. Job Description. Kathmandu. https://www.moald.gov.np/department/planning-and-development-cooperation-coordination-division.

[14] Nepal Rastra Bank, Research Department. 2017. *Nepal's Demographic, Social, Economic and Fiscal Situation (Provincial Profile)*. Kathmandu. p. 14. https://www.nrb.org.np/red/publications/study_reports/Study_Reports.

Figure 2.4: Provincial and Local Level Institutional Framework— Social Development

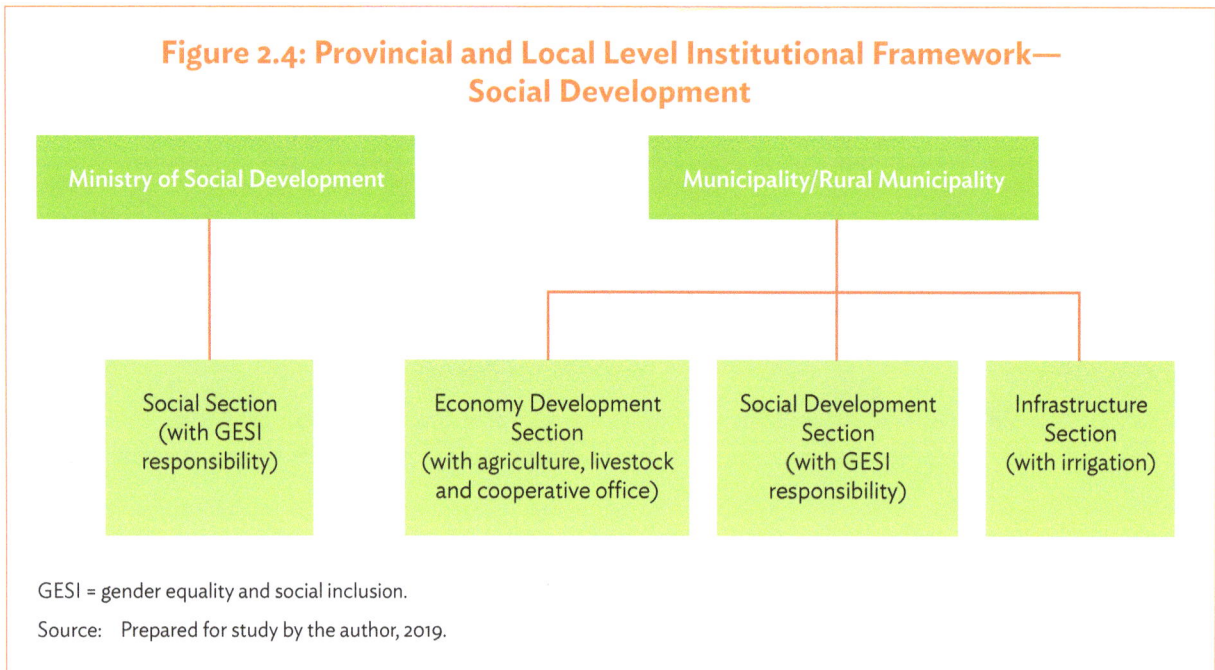

GESI = gender equality and social inclusion.

Source: Prepared for study by the author, 2019.

Gender Equality and Social Inclusion Considerations Relevant to Sector Planning and Outcomes

There is limited land available to women and excluded groups

Limited land is available to the excluded groups, particularly women, in agriculture due to high landlessness among the excluded groups and low land ownership. In Nepal, only 19% of women have some form of legal ownership rights over land.[15] The majority of Dalits are dependent on land for their survival, but 15% of Hill Dalits and 44% of Madhesi Dalits own no land. Of Hill Dalits, 45% are farmers of small and marginal landholdings. Less than 50% of Tarai Janajatis have land of their own, majority of them are renting the land they cultivate. On the account of leasing land, Tharu farmers mention, "We have taken land on lease from landlords but can cultivate one crop of potato each year only since the landlords grow their cereals in other months of the year."[16] At the provincial level, Province 7 has the poorest ownership of house and land among women (Figure 2.5).

---

[15]   Government of Nepal, National Planning Commission Secretariat, Central Bureau of Statistics. 2012. *National Population and Housing Census 2011 (National Report)*. Kathmandu.
[16]   Focused group discussion with Tharu farmers. GESI Diagnostic Study. 2 December 2018. Kailali, Nepal.

Figure 2.5: Women Ownership (Alone) of House and Land (%)

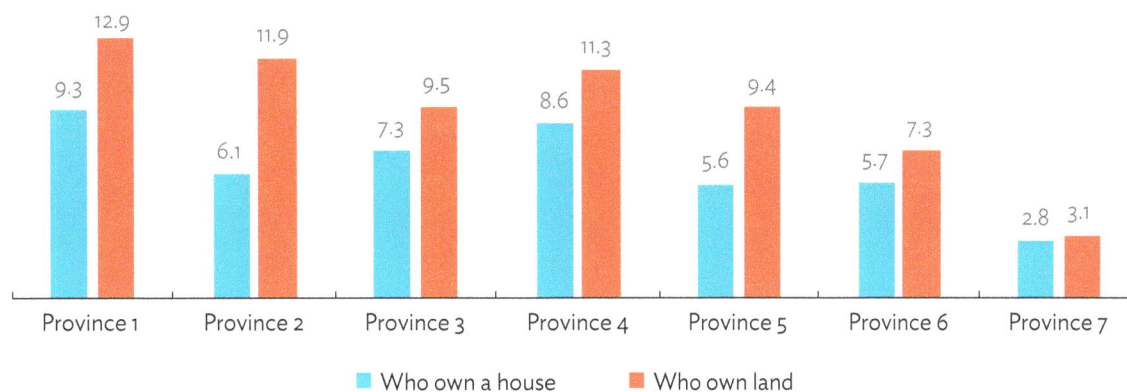

Note: Details are in Appendix Table A.16 of this document.

Source: Government of Nepal, Ministry of Health. 2016. *Demographic and Health Survey*. Kathmandu (Table 15.4.1, p. 315).

Reduced agricultural productivity due to limited irrigation facilities

In Nepal, 42% of the cultivated land is irrigated. Year-round irrigation facilities are, however, limited to less than 25% of the arable land, reducing productivity and commercialization of the agriculture sector. The 2011 NLSS report shows that 55% of the households have access to irrigation facilities, which means that nearly half of the households are dependent on rainfall, which exposes them to climate-related risks. The majority of the large, state-financed irrigation projects have benefited larger-scale farmers. Community-managed irrigation systems cater to the needs of smallholders. Nonconventional irrigation systems, being increasingly used, can help rural women, the poor, and excluded groups meet their practical needs and provide extra income.[17] Multiple factors, such as lack of land ownership and lack of access to information, constrain women's use of nonconventional irrigation technologies.

Women are unable to use and benefit from irrigation technologies when these are not designed based on their needs. For instance, specific design features can significantly help women in irrigating the land they work on. Given that it is typically the women's responsibility to collect domestic water, their involvement in the design of irrigation systems and their access to small-scale irrigation technologies can both reduce their time spent for collecting water, and make more water available for good hygiene practices.[18] For the very poor, access to credit for the installation of irrigation systems can be very difficult unless collateral-free loans are available.[19]

---

[17] An irrigation system that includes one or more than one of the following components is nonconventional: drip, sprinkler, treadle pump (manually [by feet] operated ground water extracting machine), low-cost water storage (Thai jars, soil-cement or plastic lined) tanks, rainwater harvesting. See K. Bhattarai. 2010. Nonconventional Irrigation Technology Project: An Introduction. *Irrigation Newsletter*. 58. pp. 4–5.

[18] E. Bryan and H. El Didi. 2019. *Considering Gender in Irrigation: Technology Adoption for Women Farmers*. http://a4nh.cgiar.org/2019/03/18/considering-gender-in-irrigation-technology-adoption-for-women-farmers/.

[19] In line with the Government of Nepal's initiative to provide subsidized loan, banks in Nepal have announced the launch of loan products which are "collateral free" (e.g., Nepal Merchant Bank [NMB] in its microfinance portfolio under the umbrella of "NMB Interest Subsidy Loans" has offered eight loan types, seven of the loans are collateral free. See Share Sansar. https://www.sharesansar.com/newsdetail/nmb-bank-to-offer-upto-rs-15-lakh-in-credit-without-collateral-and-6-interest-subsidy-check-out-raft-of-other-loan-packages-for-7-other-categories.

High costs of agriculture mechanization and inputs to production

The poor and excluded group farmers experience difficult access to production inputs such as seeds, fertilizer, high quality livestock, and forage seeds. Many times, they lose their profits due to the nonavailability of quality and affordable production inputs. According to a farmer, "We used seeds which just did not give any produce—we had no income that year. We go across the border and purchase fertilizers, even though it is very expensive, as it is not available here. We cannot compete with the Indian market prices since our produce becomes expensive with high prices of, among others, seeds, electricity, fertilizers."[20] Access to credit is challenging too.

Mechanization is being promoted as a key tool to shift from subsistence-level operations to commercial production. The use of mechanized tools aims to increase production quantity and quality. However, most of the designs are not women- or disabled-friendly. Also, excluded group farmers cannot afford the high costs of the equipment and maintenance. High operational costs and/or weak supporting infrastructure makes it more difficult for them to avail of the equipment. Without appropriate mechanization, it may be challenging for the agriculture sector to shift from subsistence-level operations to commercial ventures.

Inadequate extension services for women and excluded group farmers

Extension services allow farmers to improve their capacity to adopt new seed varieties and technologies and raise more productive livestock. However, as farmers are often perceived to be male, extension agents are more likely to contact men than women. The lack of legal ownership of land by most women, and the official listing of men as heads of households further put women in a disadvantaged position. As a result, agricultural extension is not directed for women even in areas where they are traditionally responsible, such as in vegetable growing. Additionally, there are not enough junior technical assistants to provide effective extension services due to limited human resources, coupled by inadequate capacity building and relatively low incentives to extension agents to reach excluded groups.

Before federal restructuring, a district agriculture development officer used to provide agriculture extension services, and there was just one junior technical assistant in a village development committee covering all wards. After restructuring, within municipalities or rural municipalities, the Economy Development Section (with agriculture, livestock and cooperative office) was established, but with limited human resources. At the provincial level, there is the Agriculture Knowledge Centre with technical staff members as specialists and agriculture extension officers under the Specialist Service Section and the Training and Extension Service Section. Low availability of agricultural workers has resulted in reduced farming and rapid urbanization of cities, which in turn, has created more job opportunities in the urban areas. High migration of men to the urban areas resulted in a decrease of agricultural workers in rural communities. Many households are farming less land. With such labor shortages, subsistence farmers are unable to move toward commercialization. Women receiving remittance funds choose to move to urban areas where they can find good schools for the education of their children, leaving the land fallow.

---

20   Meeting with Tharu farmers. GESI Diagnostic Study. December 2019.

Many farmers with disability make important contributions to the day-to-day survival of their households and communities. Despite this, disability remains an underrepresented agenda within the sector. Conventional agricultural policies and programs insufficiently involve PWDs, thus failing to capitalize on the potential contributions of this group as part of the labor force.[21]

Limited capacity of women and excluded groups to take part in leadership roles

There is a mandate for 33% representation of women in different users' and self-help groups. However, an environment that enables women and excluded groups to perform their leadership responsibilities is lacking. Lack of respect for women and the marginalized who are in executive positions is common. Caste-based marginalization and gender-based violence, including psychological violence, spousal violence, and harmful traditional practices, are key leadership barriers which are also applicable to the agriculture sector. Out-migration of men and youth for employment is resulting in increased responsibility for women left in the villages, leading to an even more demanding workload for them.[22] Government and partner agencies need to create enabling environments for the farmers, particularly women and excluded group farmers, to participate in decision-making.

Leaseholders and those who are renting land or working as sharecroppers do not always have the right to make decisions in water users' associations (WUAs) in the irrigation sector, as membership of WUA requires land titles.[23] An effort to provide temporary membership of sharecroppers and leaseholders to enable them to influence water management has been attempted (through an ADB-financed Community-Managed Irrigated Agriculture Sector Project—Additional Financing).[24] The WUA constitution includes a provision for meaningful participation of women, and farmers with small and marginal landholdings. However, implementation is still a challenge as this requires landlords to understand and agree on the provision of temporary membership.

[21] International Disability Alliance, Food and Agriculture Organization. 2018. *Disability and Food Security: An Unfinished Policy Agenda.* http://www.internationaldisabilityalliance.org/fao-food-insecurity.

[22] Women are managing agriculture related tasks that were earlier managed by their husbands along with their care work, which has increased stress and work burden. See Multidisciplinary Digital Publishing Institute. 2019. *Labour Migration in the Middle Hills of Nepal: Consequences on Land Management Strategies.* Geneva. https://www.mdpi.com/2071-1050/11/5/1349/pdf.

[23] Disaggregated data about women as sharecroppers, leaseholders or renting land is not available. Women landowners are 19% in Nepal according to Census 2011. Ethnic- and caste-discriminated minorities are high among the landless or marginal land holders. See Jagannath Adhikari. 2008. *Land Reform in Nepal. Problems and Prospects.* https://nepal.actionaid.org/sites/nepal/files/land_reform_complete_-_done.pdf.

[24] The Community-Managed Irrigated Agriculture Sector Project—Additional Financing (CMIASP-AF) focused on the rehabilitation and improvement of farmer-managed irrigation systems (FMIS) in 35 districts of Provinces 1, 2, and 3, and of five agency managed irrigation systems (AMIS) in Provinces 4, 6, and 7. The project empowered the WUAs to manage the rehabilitation of infrastructure, operate and maintain their systems without government support, and distribute irrigation water equitably and adequately throughout the command area. See CMIASP-AF. 2020. *Environmental Monitoring Report.* Kathmandu. https://www.adb.org/sites/default/files/project-documents/33209/33209-013-emr-en_4.pdf.

Limited recognition of gender and social differences across the agriculture value chains

There are few, if any, fully functioning value chain systems in the agriculture sector in Nepal. Even those which operate effectively (e.g., tea, fruit and vegetable, milk) suffer from constraints that reduce potential efficiency and weak linkages between component value chains, especially in relation to market information and lack of overall coordination.[25] In this context, the government and development partners need to explicitly examine GESI issues and proactively integrate components and development strategies which will address constraints of women and excluded groups at each step of the value chain (from production to marketing, covering various aspects of post-harvest operations and processing). The impact of value chain interventions on the target group should also be identified. For example, value chain analysis of products by a project in Nepal did not specify explicitly the issues and measures for women and the marginalized or include elements to help them achieve a better position in the value chain.[26] Attitudinal changes (changes at the household and community levels) require linkages between the production and organization level (addressed via certification) and the household or community levels, which agriculture value chain processes rarely include. No automatic correlation can be assumed between simple participation in value chain interventions and positive changes in household decision-making or shifts in discriminatory social practices without specific interventions.[27] Women spend a significant amount of time in irrigation activities, however, their work remains invisible.[28] There is a need for integrating irrigation investment with agriculture-related inputs for women and excluded groups to benefit fully from such investment, recognizing that irrigation is a factor of production, not a product itself.

More adverse impact of climate change on women and excluded groups

Agriculture has already been adversely impacted by climate change across all regions, ethnic, and income groups. Women and excluded groups are worst affected. Loss of productivity; crop failure; increase in pest infestation; depletion of water sources; change in rainfall pattern; excessive, deficient, and/or unusual rainfall; river and flash floods; risk of epidemics; and risk of glacial lake outburst, floods, landslides, and hailstorms are some of the negative effects of climate change.[29] Current climate-related programs have failed to target the ultra-poor and the landless or the poor with very little land, who live in remote areas far from service institutions.

---

[25] ADB. Agricultural Value Chain Analysis for the High Mountain Agribusiness and Livelihood Improvement Project of the Government of Nepal. Unpublished.

[26] See footnote 13, pp. 20–28. The leverage points identified for the reviewed products did not include specific steps to address constraints of women and the excluded.

[27] The Danish Institute for International Studies. 2010. *Evaluation Study: Gender and Value Chain Development*. Copenhagen. p. 18.

[28] ADB. 2012. Irrigation: Sectoral Perspectives on Gender and Social Inclusion. *Gender and Social Exclusion Assessment 2011*. Sectoral Series: Monograph 5. p. 38.

[29] Government of Nepal, Ministry of Agricultural, Land Management and Cooperatives; UNDP. 2018. *Impact of Climate Change Finance in Agriculture on the Poor*. Kathmandu. p. 24.

Existence of home- and community-based barriers and social norms that constrain women and excluded groups from accessing sector benefits

Women and excluded groups experience barriers at home and in the community, which constrain them from fully enjoying the benefits of their labor. Social and cultural beliefs affect access to resources and services. Gender-based discriminatory practices restrict the ability of women to be informed about available resources, access, and usage, including making responsible decisions relating to the income they make from their particular enterprises. Gendered decision-making within households, norms for women to seek permission from family gatekeepers, mobility restrictions, time poverty due to gendered division of labor, economic dependence on men, non-affordability of agriculture inputs, and distance to agriculture centers are some of the constraints women experience.

Structural issues such as beliefs about women's abilities and norms about women's work, historical neglect of Dalits, and language- and caste-based bias result in wage differences by Dalits, and adversely impact the effective participation and inclusion of women in the sector. The inability of the income-poor and small-scale producers to compete with larger producers and low labor availability due to high migration have also been impacting the access of the marginalized to sector benefits.

Good Practices and Lessons

Policy directives are important for inclusion of target groups in agriculture related forums and services and should be accompanied with social mobilization

Under the High Mountain Agribusiness and Livelihood Improvement Project, an ADB-supported project, there were directives on women's representation in skills development and committees. These directives enabled women to attend training in agribusiness development. Of the people trained, 35% were women (from diverse social backgrounds).

Policy reforms mandating 33% women's representation in groups provide the opportunity for women to participate in such groups. This must be coupled with specific measures for efficient planning, budgeting, implementation, and monitoring to ensure women's meaningful participation in agriculture and irrigation sector projects. Effective and targeted social mobilization, consultation, and capacity development can foster meaningful participation of women in decision-making. To get involved in sector activities and decision-making processes effectively, women and excluded groups need confidence building and incentives through training and leadership opportunities (Box 2.1).[30]

---

[30]   ADB. 2010. *Gender Equality Results Case Studies: Nepal.* Manila.

Box 2.1: Organizing and Mobilizing Women and Excluded Groups

Village-level cooperatives empower women by encouraging them to form women's groups and receive training in small-scale production—making tomato paste, pickles, chips, and bamboo handicrafts. "My heart used to pound whenever anyone from outside came to talk to me, but I am confident now," says cooperative member Radhika Ghimire. She said she learned more about seasonal farming after joining the cooperative. "I plant two to three cycles of crops and this gives me a good income. I am no longer dependent on my husband. In fact, I give him money sometimes when he needs it, and I am happy to be paying my children's school fees." The group practices savings techniques for their new incomes. "We have individual savings and group savings. We have [each] started saving NRs100 ($1.16) a month," says Deuka Uprety, member of the cooperative. "We plan to engage in productive activities by involving more women with the money collected." Uprety, who is single, says, "I have a home now and savings for rainy days. With the good income I make from farming, I can afford a better living and food. My health has improved, and I can work more." She adds that now, women earn more; they are also more confident to participate in other activities such as village cultural festivals. "We recently built a community hall for our (women's group) meetings and events," she says. "We organize prayers and singing on special festival days, which is very healing."

Source: ADB. 2013. *Nepal Farming and Agriculture.* https://www.adb.org/results/nepal-farming-and-agriculture.

In-depth poverty and social analysis enable a project to identify appropriate strategies for different social groups

Hariyo Ban II (funded by USAID and implemented by a consortium including CARE) conducted the study *Underlying Causes of Poverty Analysis* (UCPA) as a main approach for generating data.[31] The study used participatory tools such as (i) social and resource mapping; (ii) power mapping; (iii) dependency analysis; (iv) gender roles, socialization/women mobility analysis; (v) actors and institution analysis; and (vi) upstream and downstream relationship analysis. It identified poverty pockets, settlements with high concentration of Dalits, and indigenous ethnic groups and other excluded groups. Community Learning and Action Centers (CLACs) were identified as a good practice for organizing and empowering women and excluded groups; building women's knowledge, confidence, and skills to participate in groups; developing more sustainable livelihood opportunities for poor women; improving governance of community groups; and facilitating collective action against gender violence.[32]

---

[31]   UCPA consists of different participatory tools and methods to identify locally specific causes of poverty and pathways to address these. The process not only generates data but more importantly explores social structures and forms of discrimination (around economic class, caste, and gender); access to public resources; power relations; forms of exploitation between different economic and social groups within the location; and larger issues around political processes, governance, and culture of violence at different levels. See B. Bode. 2009. *Underlying Causes of Poverty Analysis and Contributions Towards a Program Approach.* Kathmandu: Care Nepal.

[32]   CLACs are like a Regenerated Freirean Literacy through Empowering Community Technique (REFLECT) circle, a forum where the excluded groups are brought together to identify, analyze, and take actions on issues that directly affect them. REFLECT/CLACs are found successful in organizing and empowering women and excluded groups for collective action against different forms of discrimination. See CARE Nepal. 2017. *Study Report, Social Analysis Identification of Marginalized Segments of the Society and Underlying Causes of Marginalization in Hariyo Ban II Working Areas.* Kathmandu.

Specific measures to address the barriers of women and excluded groups enhance their access to benefits

Various projects have adopted targeted measures to ensure access of women and excluded groups to project benefits. This has enabled the target group to deal with their barriers and access resources and services (Box 2.2).

The Raising Income of Small and Medium Farmers Project (RISMFP, 2011–2019), an ADB project extended assistance to existing and new farmer groups. These were predominantly women members and members from excluded groups in districts with very low human development indices. Excluded groups, women, and farmers with disability were given technical support on seeds storing, honey production, and lentils production. RISMFP provided post-harvest enterprises with high value crops and agribusiness training programs, supplier agreements, and support for preparing business plans and subproject proposals. The RISMFP helped develop and disseminate agriculture market information and build market chains which link buyers to farmer cooperatives, and cooperatives to existing farmer groups with supporting production plans. Community Agricultural Service Centers and Agricultural Resource Centers were strengthened to respond to the differing needs and constraints experienced by excluded groups and women and help widen the available opportunities for them.

Box 2.2: Targeted Support for Improved Livelihood Security through Agriculture

The Agriculture Food Security Support Program (AFSP) is an example of effective integration of agricultural development with public health, food security, and nutrition. It has been very successful in reaching out to the most excluded households and in focusing on women. Its key focus on supporting farmer field school groups proved to be an effective approach in mobilizing community participation. It has brought about positive change in terms of crop and livestock development and promoting nutrition and supporting livelihoods security through agriculture.

The AFSP successfully targeted and reached women as a priority throughout most activities and contributed to their empowerment. Women farmers benefited directly from nutrition and health education; they received support and equipment to reduce their workload, and new technologies and technical assistance to grow vegetables and develop livestock livelihoods (poultry, eggs, goats). Women's workload was substantially reduced because of equipment such as corn sellers, seed grading machines, processing mills, and improved cooking stoves. Before the project, it took women several hours to travel to a mill to get their grains processed and a greater amount of time to collect fuel/wood. The mother and child nutrition and health education entry point through Female Community Health Volunteers, together with the support to agriculture and livestock activities, has proven very effective in mobilizing women.

Aside from providing benefits through AFSP activities, the project has also brought about positive economic, social, and political changes in the communities. For example, women started group saving and organized themselves to apply for AFSP grants. With the project help, women were able to open bank accounts in their names. In all-women groups and mixed farmer field school groups, women have held leadership positions.

Source: World Bank. 2018. *Nepal Agriculture and Food Security Project: Implementation Completion and Results Report*. Kathmandu.

Climate change investment has positive socioeconomic impacts on the poor and vulnerable

Climate-related investments in agriculture have increased productivity of cereal crops. They have developed farmers' resilience by supporting multiple cropping and use of drought- and flood-resilient crop varieties. The investments have also helped improve irrigation facilities and promoted the use of organic fertilizer and tunnel farming.[33] Furthermore, it is important to create a platform that will bring together technical consultants, researchers, nongovernment organizations (NGOs), and practitioners to share innovative agricultural practices. The platform is also an opportunity for such stakeholders to identify key areas for collaboration around specific themes such as improved climate services, meteorological and extension services, enhanced adaptive capacity, and vulnerable people's resilience to external shocks (Box 2.3).[34]

Box 2.3: Gender and Climate Smart Agricultural Practices

Below are examples of innovative approaches for climate smart agricultural practices. New information and communication technologies involving communication-based partners and approaches for achieving scale include:

- farm reality TV-show targeting and informing millions of women, men, and youths on climate smart agricultural technologies;

- testing mobile-phone-based equitable agriculture advisory services;

- improved climate and agriculture information services targeted at women; and

- participatory farmer-led videos giving farmers a chance to share their perceptions, knowledge, and adaptation strategies for a changing climate.

Source: P. Kristjanson. 2014. *Gender Sensitive Climate-Smart Agricultural Practices*. FAO/MICCA Online Learning Event. http://www.slideshare.net/cgiarclimate/ccafs-the-gender-outcome-challenge-patti-kris.

Looking Forward: Issues and Opportunities to Consider

This section highlights lessons that merit consideration by ADB in sector and project analyses and in discussions with government counterparts.

Increase access of women and excluded groups to production inputs

To increase productivity and graduate the excluded groups, particularly women, from subsistence farming, give them more inputs such as access to credit, machinery, and technology; new crop varieties; improved techniques, approaches, and methods of protecting crops; and greater access to irrigation and agricultural lands (Table 2.1).

---

[33]   Government of Nepal, Ministry of Agricultural, Land Management and Cooperatives; UNDP. 2018. *Impact of Climate Change Finance in Agriculture on the Poor: An Executive Summary*. Kathmandu.

[34]   P. Kristjanson. 2014. *Gender Sensitive Climate-Smart Agricultural Practices*. FAO/MICCA Online Learning Event. http://www.slideshare.net/cgiarclimate/ccafs-the-gender-outcome-challenge-patti-kris.

Table 2.1: Selected Measures to Address Production Input Constraints of Women and Excluded Groups

Access to land	Federal, provincial, and local governments should formulate land-use policy with specific provisions for women and excluded group farmers to improve their access to land. A policy to encourage entitlement of land in women's names should be promoted to improve the status of women. A system of long-term tenancy of government land to women and farmers with marginal landholdings for cultivation purposes would also support their regular access to land.
Seeds	A regular supply of seeds to excluded group farmers, including women farmers, through certified seed suppliers is required so that there is timely availability of good quality seeds for them. Dissemination of localized information about improved seed varieties, suppliers, and price will make them better informed and seek better quality seeds. Women's traditional knowledge of seeds and community seed banks must be promoted for potential replication.
Fertilizer	For regular supply of good quality chemical fertilizers, targeted supply with subsidies for income poor and excluded group farmers, including women, is required. Adequate supply and use of organic fertilizers should be promoted. Training and information regarding soil testing and appropriate mix of chemical fertilizers would enhance the skills and knowledge of the target group. There must be increased access to information on fertilizers and fertilizer outlets among excluded group farmers, including women.
Extension services	Alternative methods need to be adopted for extension services to farmers, particularly women, and remote communities. Information should be disseminated in local languages and at appropriate times of the day. A diverse group of leader farmers and agro-vet workers need to be trained and authorized to work as extension agents.
Irrigation facilities	Women and farmers with marginal holdings should be encouraged to use small holder irrigation technologies, such as sprinkler, treadle pump, rainwater harvesting, and drip. Subsidized electricity for use of pumps for irrigation would be helpful in addressing gender and income-based barriers.
Access to credit or finance	A system to provide collateral free loans to excluded group farmers, particularly women, and expansion of formal financial institutions (cooperatives, banks) in rural locations would increase their access to finance. Loan processing systems need to be simple and understood by the semi-literate or illiterate. Women and excluded group farmers need to be informed about loans and provided with technical assistance for preparing business proposals and loan applications.
Access to market	Invest in strengthening the bargaining power of women and excluded group farmers to deal with market actors. Promote and subsidize establishment and functioning of collection and market centers. Work with families and/or communities to improve mobility of women and enable Dalits to use such centers. Provide improved market information to them.
Livestock	Give women and excluded group farmers better access to quality livestock through targeted distribution of improved animal breed, expansion of animal exchange programs, loan fund and targeted loan schemes, training for better livestock management practices, and increased coverage of agro-vet services. To address barriers in marketing livestock products—especially by gender- and caste-based ones—group selling to private and public institutional buyers should be promoted along with advocacy campaigns with family and community gate keepers.

Source: Human Resource Development Centre. 2014. *Draft Framework to Identify Gender Equality and Social Inclusion Indicators for Agriculture Programming.* Paper submitted to South Asia Social Development Unit, World Bank. Kathmandu.

Enable meaningful participation of women and excluded group farmers

The ability of women, Dalit, farmers with disability, and farmers with marginal landholdings to influence decisions in groups, cooperatives, and marketing networks must be strengthened. Social mobilization for empowerment and shifts in discriminatory practices are necessary, otherwise the excluded will not be able to access and use the production inputs equitably. The income poor are very rarely organized. This results in their low voice to claim rights, and the potential socioeconomic impacts of different schemes are very limited for them. Mobilization combined with information dissemination and community education can be extremely effective in building the voice of women and excluded groups and strengthen their capacity to influence decisions. Policy frameworks are necessary to ensure participation of target groups in marketing networks and channels. The local and indigenous knowledge and practices of different communities, their cultural practices, beliefs, and ideologies need to be understood to avoid reinforcing inequities. A space for the excluded groups to share their experiences and influence decisions should be created.

Integrate gender equality and social inclusion across the agriculture value chain

The primary mechanisms for enhancing value chain performances are by reducing costs, making products uniquely valuable for consumers, using appropriate technology, and enhancing collaboration between stakeholder organizations. In each step, GESI aspects need to be analyzed, identified, and addressed.[35] The following may be considered:

- Gain an accurate understanding of existing gender and social-based power relations for specific crops. Labor allocation, returns, and ownership along the chain can be determined using the following information: (i) gender and caste or ethnicity differentiated participation and benefits, and (ii) disaggregated data for different stages of the value chain regarding who has access to different resources, who puts in the labor, and who has the authority to decide. Qualitative and quantitative information should be collected and analyzed to understand the various stages of the value chain.

- Assess structural and institutional barriers based on gender and social roles and norms that limit access to resources and opportunities along the value chain. Both structural barriers (e.g., mobility restriction, gender biased work division, and gender- and caste-based violence) and technical barriers (e.g., limited awareness and skills regarding better quality cropping, use of fertilizers, and storage of produce) need to be addressed through planned interventions, differentiating between the issues experienced by different groups of people (e.g., women, Dalits, and PWDs).

- Provide interventions that can strengthen livelihood and voice empowerment of women and excluded groups and contribute in the reduction of discriminatory practices. Strategic and market-driven solutions with transformative potential should be budgeted and implemented. Monitoring and evaluation systems to measure outcomes, such as proportion of increased sales and yields of women and excluded group farmers, should be used to identify successes and areas of improvement (Table 2.2) (footnote 34).

35   USAID. 2010. *A Guide to Integrating Gender into Agricultural Value Chains.* Washington DC. p. 4. https://www.fsnnetwork.org/sites/default/files/gender_agriculture_value_chain_guide.pdf.

Table 2.2: Tip Sheet on Integrating Gender Equality and Social Inclusion Perspectives in the Agriculture Sector

Barriers	Actions to Address the Barriers
Limited access to production inputs (seeds, fertilizers)	Increase seed and fertilizer quality awareness interventions for women and excluded group farmers. Strengthen capacity of women and excluded group farmers to collect, grow, and store seeds. Manage supply of seeds and fertilizers. Increase awareness about soil tests to determine the quality of soil and type of seeds farmers need to buy and plant to ensure optimal and efficient use of agricultural land.
Limited availability of irrigated land	Review existing land policies and push for reforms that will allow long-term tenancy systems on government land for women and excluded group farmers. Mobilize community-based irrigation systems toward improved access and efficient use of irrigated facilities.
Access to employment, finance, and credit	Support the creation of inclusive employment and income generation opportunities in agro-food value chains. Mobilize women farmers' savings groups. Expand formal financial institutions (cooperatives, banks) in rural locations; disseminate information about the availability of credits and loans.
Inadequate extension services	Provide incentives for extension agents to serve target communities. Enhance agricultural extension services to address the training needs of farmers with disabilities. Conduct training of trainers with women's groups so they can roll-out the services to other self-help groups in their community.
Low agency to make service providers accountable for good quality services	Establish guidelines or procedures for information, consultation, and grievance resolution to allow excluded groups to make their voices heard and ensure adequate attention and support for their needs, such as regular supply of seeds and fertilizers. Strengthen the capacities of self-help groups to voice their rights and access resources. Promote the full participation of person with disabilities in decision-making processes around agriculture and irrigation.
Inadequate gender equality and social inclusion (GESI) mainstreaming across value chains	Conduct a GESI analysis of division of labor, access to resources, and decision-making authority along the value chain. Provide women, farmers with marginal landholdings, and farmers with disability with agro-technical, entrepreneurial, and business management skills to expand their livelihoods. Upgrade agricultural technologies to meet the specific requirements of workers with disability.
Adverse impact of climate change	Assess impacts, coping strategies, and capacities; and develop creative interventions using information and communication technologies.
Discriminatory gender and social norms constraining women and excluded groups from accessing sector resources and opportunities	Promote social marketing and gender equality; women's empowerment; and social inclusion awareness raising for women, their families, and communities to reduce gender-related discriminatory practices. Conduct exposure visits, interactive discussions, and demonstration.
Limited transformative elements in project design, design and monitoring framework, and GESI action plans	Formulate results in project plans and log frames with the aim to improve assets, capabilities, and voice of women and excluded groups. They must address formal and informal practices that are inequitable and discriminatory and aim to transform existing structural frameworks that disadvantage women and/or excluded groups.

Source: Table prepared for this study, 2019.

3

ENERGY

Area of collaboration

ADB has been a leading partner in Nepal's power sector and its support is focused on on-grid and off-grid projects, including generation, transmission, and distribution projects. ADB also works on increasing energy access, rehabilitating small hydropower plants, and supporting other clean energy interventions.

ADB has provided loans, grants, and technical assistance through 69 projects in the energy sector amounting to 19% of its investments in Nepal from 1966 to 2018.

Sector context

Scattered settlements and complex topography make the provision of electricity through the national grid challenging.

The main sources of energy are biomass fuels, oil products, coal, and hydropower. Majority of Nepal's population live in rural areas, where access to energy facilities is minimal and energy consumption pattern is dominated by traditional biomass fuels. Indoor air pollution thus exists.

Hydropower has the largest development potential but less than 2% of the total commercially exploitable generation potential has been exploited.

Commercial use of electricity is not commonly practiced since energy supply has been insufficient even for household consumption.

Gender equality and social inclusion (GESI) considerations relevant to sector planning and outcomes

Limited access to finance, appliances, information, training, and education constrain women and excluded groups from accessing energy sources.

Decision-making regarding energy products and services is usually with men and advantaged groups and dictated by social norms.

Lack of access to modern energy sources increases work burden and susceptibility to illnesses of women and excluded groups, especially lower income people. Challenges constrain women and excluded group entrepreneurs from productive end use of energy.

There is limited integration of GESI dimensions in all elements of energy planning and policymaking.

Institutional capacity of the sector has to be strengthened to work on GESI issues.

Good practices and lessons	Specific approaches to increase access of local people, especially women and excluded groups are necessary.
	Technologies, which benefit women and excluded groups, can have multiple benefits.
	It is important to engender utilities as women and excluded groups face structural barriers to participation in the power sector, including underrepresentation in employment, especially in technical, higher-paying positions and leadership roles.
Looking forward: Issues and opportunities to consider	Increase access to modern forms of energy for women and excluded groups.
	Mainstream GESI in energy projects and in different phases of electricity generation, transmission, and distribution.
	Ensure participation of women and excluded groups in energy plans, programs, and decision-making.
	Promote productive end use of energy by women and excluded groups.
Further resources	ADB tip sheet on addressing barriers experienced by women and excluded groups and on integrating GESI in the energy sector (Table 3.2).

GESI = gender equality and social inclusion.

Area of Collaboration

ADB has provided assistance to Nepal's energy sector through 69 projects amounting to $1,213.98 million which is 19.19% of its lending, grant, and technical assistance commitments to Nepal (as of 31 December 2018).[1] ADB has been the leading partner[2] in Nepal's power sector, focusing particularly on on-grid support which has amounted to $521 million.[3] On-grid and off-grid ADB funded projects, including generation, transmission, and distribution, such as in Kaligandaki have contributed immensely to the energy sector in Nepal. The projects have helped increase energy access and rehabilitate small hydropower plants; supported clean-energy interventions, such as solar street lighting and energy-efficient lighting; strengthened energy sector institutions; and assisted rural electrification projects with the participation of local communities.

[1]   ADB. 2018. Cumulative Lending, Grant, and Technical Assistance Commitments. *ADB Data Library*.
      https://data.adb.org/dataset/cumulative-lending-grant-and-technical-assistance-commitments.
[2]   World Bank is also supporting five big projects worth $341.9 million. See World Bank. 2018. *Country Overview*.
      http://www.worldbank.org/en/country/nepal/overview#2.
[3]   ADB. 2017. *Nepal Energy Sector Assessment, Strategy and Road Map*. Manila.

Sector Context

In Nepal, the scattered settlement and complex topography make it challenging to provide electricity through the national grid alone. According to 2011 census, 81% of Nepal's total population of 26,494,504 lived in rural areas, where access to energy facilities is minimal and energy consumption pattern is dominated by traditional biomass fuels such as fuelwood, agricultural residues, and animal waste. The main sources of energy in Nepal are biomass fuels, oil products, coal, and hydropower. Among these, hydropower has the largest development potential of 83,000 megawatts (MW) and commercially exploitable hydropower generating potential of about 42,000 MW (footnote 3). However, by the end of fiscal year (FY) 2016, existing hydropower stations had a total installed capacity of only 802.4 MW, or less than 2% of the total commercially exploitable generation potential (Figure 3.1) (footnote 3).

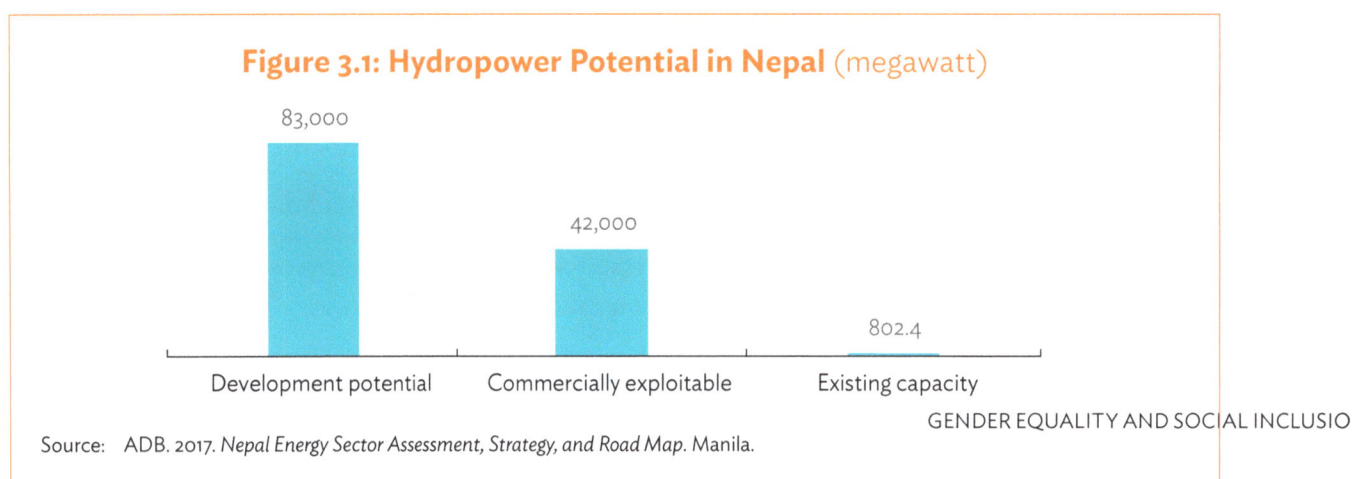

Figure 3.1: Hydropower Potential in Nepal (megawatt)

Source: ADB. 2017. *Nepal Energy Sector Assessment, Strategy, and Road Map*. Manila.

The Annual Household Survey 2016 reports that electricity has become the primary source of lighting for Nepal's households—as 76.3% of the households are using electricity, 93.1% in urban areas and 64.9% in rural areas. For the country as a whole, fuelwood is the predominant energy carrier, accounting for more than 75% of consumption. In rural Nepal, more than 92% of total cooking energy consumed is traditional biomass, of which fuelwood constitutes 75%. In 2016, in urban areas, 53.3% households were using liquefied petroleum gas (LPG) and 37.9% were using fuelwood for cooking.[4] Renewable energy is being promoted by the government, and 12% of the population have access to electricity through renewable energy sources.[5] Use of solar energy, mostly by rural households, has also increased in 2014–2015 from 10.3% to 13.4% households. Solar energy is used by 20.8% rural and 2.5% urban households, and by 20.7% of the poorest quintile (footnote 4).

4 Central Bureau of Statistics. 2016. *Annual Household Survey (Major Findings), 2015/16*. Kathmandu.
5 ADB. 2015. *Gender Review of National Energy Policies and Programs in Nepal*. Manila. https://www.energia.org/cm2/wp-content/uploads/2016/05/Gender-Review-NEPAL.pdf.

The government and its development partners have been providing financial and technical support to increase energy access in rural areas both for household consumption and commercial use. Around 30 MW of electricity has been generated from mini- and micro-hydro schemes. More than 1.5 million households have benefited from different renewable energy sources for cooking, lighting, and productive use but still Nepal's average annual per capita electricity consumption is about 163 kilowatt-hours (kWh), one of the lowest consumptions in South Asia.[6] Despite its vast energy potential, Nepal suffers from a severe energy supply crisis, especially in the rural areas. Commercial use of electricity is not commonly practiced since energy supply has been insufficient even for household consumption.

Policy Framework

SDG 7 aims to ensure access to affordable, reliable, sustainable, and modern energy for all. The Constitution of Nepal directs the government to "ensure reliable supply of energy in an affordable and easy manner, and make proper use of energy, for the fulfillment of the basic needs of citizens, by generating and developing renewable energy." The Government of Nepal through its five- and three-year plans has been attempting to promote both on-grid and renewable energy, and has formulated several policy instruments for the energy sector.[7] While GESI has not been adequately integrated in all policies, the policies after 2006 have been more sensitive to GESI issues (Table 3.1).

---

[6]   Eglitis-media. 2018. *World-data.info.* https://www.worlddata.info/asia/nepal/energy-consumption.php.

[7]   Some key policies impacting the sector include The Hydropower Development Policy 2001; Hydropower Studies Guidelines, Department of Electricity Development, December 2003; Electricity Act 1992; Electricity Regulations 1993; Water Resource Act 1992; Water Resources Rules 1993; Renewable (Rural) Energy Policy 2006; Subsidy Policy for Renewal Energy 2009; Rural Energy Subsidy Delivery Mechanism 2009 and 2013; Land Reforms Act (Sixth Amendment Bill), (2071) 2014–2015; Land Acquisition Act 1977; National Water Plan 2005; Environment Protection Act 1997; and Environment Protection Rules 1997.

Table 3.1: Potential for Addressing Gender Equality and Social Inclusion Issues in Selected Energy-Related Policies and/or Legislations Recognition of Existing Conditions

	Recognition of Existing Conditions			Procedural/Implementation Considerations				Enhancement of Impacts/Benefits		
	Differential needs, capacities, and usage	Existing societal inequities	Barriers to participation and decision-making	Improve access and choices	Ensure affordability	Enhance participation	Enhance voice and agency	Welfare	Efficiency	Empowerment
Water Resource Act 1992/Rules 1993	◑	◑	○	○	○	◑	◑	●	○	◑
Electricity Act 1992/Regulations 1993	○	◑	○	○	◑	○	○	◑	○	○
National Environment Impact Assessment Guidelines, 1993	◑	●	◑	○	○	○	◑	○	○	○
Environment Protection Act 1997/Rules 1997	◑	◑	○	○	○	○	●	●	○	○
Local Self Governance Act, 1999	◑	●	◑	●	○	●	○	●	◑	●
Hydropower Development Policy, 2001	◑	○	○	●	●	◑	○	●	●	○
Community Electricity Distribution By-Laws 2003	◑	◑	○	●	●	◑	○	●	○	◑
Rural Energy Policy, 2006	◑	◑	○	◑	●	●	●	●	●	●
Renewable Energy Subsidy Delivery Mechanism, 2016	○	◑	◑	●	●	◑	●	◑	◑	○
Renewable Energy Subsidy Policy, 2016	◑	●	◑	●	●	◑	●	●	●	◑
Land Acquisition, Rehabilitation, and Resettlement Policy for Development Projects, 2015	◑	●	◑	●	○	●	●	●	○	●
GESI Policy of AEPC	●	◑	●	●	◑	●	◑	◑	●	●

● = Present to a large extent, ◑ = Present partially but not substantial enough, ○ = Almost or fully absent

AEPC = Alternative Energy Promotion Centre; GESI = gender equality and social inclusion.

Source: ADB. 2017. *Gender Equality and Social Inclusion Assessment of the Energy Sector: Enhancing Social Sustainability of Energy Development in Nepal.* Manila.

The Renewable Energy Subsidy Policy 2016 (an updated version of 2013) provides subsidies for micro-hydropower, improved water mill, solar energy (home systems, mini-grids, grid connections), biogas, biomass energy, wind energy, and wind–solar hybrids to encourage households of the poor, Dalits, and other excluded groups to use renewable energy. The subsidy amount differs according to technology and the region, with higher subsidy being offered for remote areas. The subsidy covers 40% of the total cost: 30% comes from credit and around 30% from private sector investment and/or community or households' contribution (cash or in kind). It may vary and covers up to 80% depending on the technology.

An important policy that impacts the sector is the Land Acquisition, Resettlement and Rehabilitation Policy 2015. It lays out consultations, programs, and preferential employment procedures for project-affected families belonging to groups such as Dalits, Adivasi Janajatis, and single women. Rural electrification became a priority subsector from the Tenth Plan (2002 2007) onwards, which sets concrete goals for rural electrification: 55% of all households were to have electricity by the end of plan period (though this was not achieved). Rural electrification requires land acquisitions to be handled sensitively, to address gender issues, and ensure that compensation funds can be accessed by both women and men.

Institutional Arrangements

The Ministry of Energy, Water Resources and Irrigation governs the development and implementation of energy, including its conservation, regulation, and utilization. It develops and operates electricity projects including hydropower projects. In 2018, the portfolio of the ministry was enlarged with the addition of water resources and irrigation. The Department of Electricity Development is responsible in developing and promoting the electricity sector. The Nepal Electricity Authority (NEA) is responsible for the generation, transmission, and distribution of electric power. The Environment and Social Studies Department of NEA is responsible for social and environmental issues but not specifically for GESI. The Water and Energy Commission formulates policies and strategies for the water resources and energy sector and has a secretariat. The Alternative Energy Promotion Centre aims to promote the use of alternative and/or renewable energy technology and has a GESI mainstreaming policy and a functional GESI team. Since the federal restructuring, the Ministry of Physical Infrastructure and Transport (MOPIT) has assumed the responsibility for energy issues at both provincial and municipal levels. The responsibility for GESI issues lies with the Ministry of Social Development at the provincial level, and the social development section at the municipal and rural municipal levels.

Gender Equality and Social Inclusion Considerations Relevant to Sector Planning and Outcomes

Limited access to appliances, information, training, and education constrain women and excluded groups in accessing energy sources

Women and excluded groups are often hindered from using energy even when the physical infrastructure is available. The lack of finance; limited availability of affordable appliances; and inadequate information, training or education inhibit their access to electricity.[8] For example, obtaining subsidized electricity connection or LPG registration may require a bank account and extensive paperwork, which places women and excluded groups at a disadvantage. The ability to pay for energy technologies or make cash contributions and payments affects those with limited assets and access to credit. The poor require wage labor employment for their daily survival and hence it is challenging for them to provide voluntary labor. Additionally, if the households are at a distance, installation costs increase, which income-poor families are unable to afford. For women, dependence on male family members or technicians, for even small repairs of energy technologies, restricts their control over such technologies.[9] Information is often accessible only to local leaders. When communities are informed,

---

8   S. Dutta et al. 2017. *Energy Access and Gender Getting the Right Balance*. Washington DC. p. 3. http://documents.worldbank.org/curated/en/463071494925985630/pdf/115066-BRI-P148200-PUBLIC-FINALSEARSFGenderweb.pdf. World Bank/ENERGIA/International Network on Gender and Sustainable Energy.
9   I. Mahat. 2006. Gender and Rural Energy Technologies: Empowerment Perspective—A Case Study of Nepal. *Canadian Journal of Development Studies*. Ottawa: University of Ottawa. p. 540.

various processes need to be followed, and the necessary funds need to be raised for the project. Lack of complete information and inability to access processes to make service providers accountable render the target group vulnerable. Attesting to this issue, community people say, "We paid the earlier team of the cooperative five years ago, but electricity did not come. We did not know how to bring the contractor back. A new committee is now in place and trying to bring electricity to the area."[10]

Decision-making regarding energy products and services is usually with men and advantaged groups and dictated by social norms

Household heads (usually men in Nepal except in women headed households) and prevailing gender norms generally determine what energy sources will be used, when and by whom, and within what budget.[11] Energy products and services are typically not designed in collaboration with the end user; hence the experiences of women and the excluded groups do not influence the design of the products, decreasing the likelihood of their being accepted and used by the target group. Women and excluded groups are particularly disadvantaged in situations of shortages and unavailability of electricity for social uses such as drinking water, lighting for education, media for information, and refrigeration for health clinics, as well as for productive uses such as water pumping for irrigation, agro-processing, and income-generating applications. The ownership of renewable energy technologies is usually with advantaged men, as women and excluded groups lack financial resources, information, and training, and they are mostly not well represented in decision making at all levels.

In households that can afford rice cookers and mixer and/or grinders, women do have a say in their purchase as these appliances support their traditional responsibility of cooking. The funds required to purchase such appliances has to be agreed to by the primary breadwinner of the household.[12] Within households, decisions dictated by gender and social norms determine what form of lighting or fuel will be used. Despite provision of improved cooking stoves, fuelwood is still preferred due to cultural and preferred cooking habits. A village woman from an ethnic group relates "I need to use large utensils in my household, so I have to use my mud-stove even though the improved cooking stove is there" (footnote 10). Rice cookers are not permitted as the power supply of the project is insufficient. The barriers faced by women and excluded groups in influencing decisions made by government agencies, users' committees, and construction companies have not been well addressed.

Lack of access to modern energy sources increases work burden and illnesses of women and persons with disabilities

In rural Nepal, women play a significant role in the biomass energy systems, fetching fuel for household use and microenterprises. Women and girls, especially of low-income and rural households, are often forced to walk long distances in search of fuelwood where other energy sources are unavailable. Cooking and processing food without improved energy can also take several hours. Fetching fuel, fodder, and water for homes, and manual grinding or pounding of grains or tubers to prepare food

10 Focused group discussion with women. GESI Diagnostic Study. 4 December 2018. Ghodaghodi, Kailali, Nepal.
11 In 2011 census, 25.73% households are headed by women. See CBS. 2011. *Nepal Population and Housing Census, 2011.* Kathmandu.
12 Frontiers in Energy Research. 2019. *Rice Cookers, Social Media, and Unruly Women: Disentangling Electricity's Gendered Implications in Rural Nepal.* https://www.frontiersin.org/articles/10.3389/fenrg.2018.00140/full

are heavy tasks that demand an inordinate amount of time and effort, usually for women, since these responsibilities fall on them (footnote 10). The lack of social awareness on alternative or potential energy sources and the need to purchase these constrain the use of energy by rural women, whose labor is considered cheaply available.

The substantial amount of time and effort spent in fuel collection leads to missed opportunities for employment, education, and self-improvement. Women's health also suffers from the smoke from burning biomass as a cooking fuel. Some evidence indicates that women and girls are at risk of sexual violence when they collect fuel and water or when they are outside after dark, especially in the absence of community lighting.[13] Women face long-term health problems, such as respiratory and eye diseases due to the traditional fuel cycle causing indoor air pollution, and backaches and prolapsed uterus from carrying heavy loads.[14] Biofuel smoke increases the risks of breathing-related ailments such as acute lower respiratory infections, as well as having adverse effects on birth weight. A study reveals that stunting prevalence among children with exposure to biofuel smoke was about twice as high as those without exposure.[15]

A global research states that the annual energy bills of families living with persons with disability (PWDs) is 50% more than those without PWDs.[16] In developing countries where 80% of PWDs live, many of them use traditional forms of energy inside their houses, negatively impacting their health. This health issue points to the importance of their access to modern forms of energy.[17]

Challenges constrain women and excluded group entrepreneurs from productive end use of energy

Studies find that once homes are electrified, women in Nepal can spend evenings on handicraft work which can provide them additional income. Also, research reveals that families are more likely to adopt modern technologies if they have benefits for income generating efforts;[18] but for productive end use of energy, women and excluded groups experience various constraints. They find it challenging to access funds to meet both investment and recurring costs of enterprises. Microfinance institutes are wary of funding this target group and have limited reach in remote areas. Women are forced to locate their enterprises at home due to gender-based norms restricting their mobility, reproductive responsibilities, and permission to interact with the public domain. While this helps them to combine household chores and income generation, they are often at a distance from energy sources. The market linkages, the network needed to market products, and the energy requirements for using different media to advertise products are not easily accessible to women and excluded group entrepreneurs.

[13] R. Rewald. 2017. Energy and Women and Girls: Analyzing the Needs, Uses, and Impacts of Energy on Women and Girls in the Developing World. *Oxfam Research Backgrounder Series*. https://www.oxfamamerica.org/explore/researchpublications/energy-women-girls.
[14] UN Women Report on SDGs. 2018. *Turning Promises into Action*. New York. p. 14.
[15] thethirdpole.net. 2018. *Stunting in Nepal: Kitchen Smoke Adding Fuel to the Fire*. https://www.thethirdpole.net/en/2018/03/30/stunting-in-nepal-kitchen-smoke-adding-fuel-to-the-fire/.
[16] M. George et al. 2013. *The Energy Penalty: Disabled People and Fuel Poverty*. Leicester: University of Leicester. pp. 27–34.
[17] S. Kajima. 2017. *Energy and Disability*. Paper prepared for the 5th Expert Group Meeting on Monitoring and Evaluation for Disability-Inclusive Development. United Nations Department of Economic and Social Affairs.
[18] I. Mahat. 2004. *Implementation of Alternative Energy Technologies in Nepal: Towards the Achievement of Sustainable Livelihoods*. Ottawa: University of Ottawa. https://www.researchgate.net/publication/241595980_ Implementation_of_alternative_energy_technologies_in_Nepal_towards_the_achievement_of_sustainable_livelihoods.

GESI dimensions are not fully integrated in energy planning and policymaking

The active participation of women and excluded groups in planning and decision-making processes is limited in most on-grid projects. This restricts the potential project benefits and the advancement of the GESI agenda. While ADB-financed projects categorized as gender equity (GEN) or effective gender mainstreaming (EGM) include GESI action plans, these plans do not fully address structural issues of inequity, thus, restricting women and excluded groups from fully benefiting from the projects.[19] Projects of NEA and the government usually do not have such plans, and hence, integration of GESI issues in planning and policymaking has been limited.[20]

In off-grid energy projects supported by donors, participation of locals is better, as these projects follow a more inclusive process; but generally, the influence of women and excluded groups on the projects' agenda is inadequate. The level of participation is at the most physical labor, limited to a few days. Every house in the village usually gives free labor for the required number of days that the managing committee decides. Most of the ideas and knowledge needed for an effective participatory exercise remains with selected groups of people.[21]

Institutions in the energy sector have limited capacities to work on GESI issues

A review of the functions and responsibilities of NEA, Nepal's public entity responsible for generation, transmission, and distribution, indicates requirement of institutional strengthening to implement projects that are sensitive to GESI. Further, GESI has to be adequately integrated to those projects which require environmental and social impact assessments.[22] AEPC has a GESI mainstreaming strategy and has instructions in job descriptions of officers to ensure that GESI is integrated in the preparation of the annual budget and programs; monthly, trimestral, and yearly progress reports; and monitoring and evaluation reports. However, staff diversity and skills have to be enhanced to ensure GESI mainstreaming in all aspects of the project.[23]

Good Practices and Lessons

Various initiatives have been implemented in the sector which have enhanced benefits for women and excluded groups and generated lessons.

Specific approaches to increase access of local people to energy

The Community Rural Electrification Program of Nepal is an effort to reach the local population (Box 3.1). While it has supported local people to access electricity, the mechanisms have limited space for the beneficiaries to voice their requirements or concerns. Some of the constraints discussed earlier are not adequately addressed in the program.

[19] Nepal Energy Funds, AEPC. 2018. Meeting notes with National Association of Community Electricity Users-Nepal. Kathmandu.
[20] Nepal Electricity Authority. 2018. Meeting notes with Nepal Electricity Authority staff. Kathmandu.
[21] Intermediate Technology Consultants. 1999. *Participative Planning of Off-Grid Electricity Supplies*. London. https://assets.publishing.service.gov.uk/media/57a08d98ed915d3cfd001b00/R6249.pdf
[22] World Bank. 2018. Getting to Gender Equality in Energy Infrastructure: Lessons from Electricity Generation, Transmission, and Distribution Projects. *Energy Sector Management Assistance Program (ESMAP) Technical Report 012/18*. Washington, DC.
[23] ADB. 2018. *Gender Equality and Social Inclusion Assessment of the Energy Sector: Enhancing Social Sustainability of Energy Development in Nepal*. Manila. p. 25.

Box 3.1: Community Rural Electrification

The Government of Nepal has supported the Community Rural Electrification Program (CREP) since 2003, revived it in 2013 and executed it through the Community Rural Electrification Department (CRED), Nepal Electricity Authority (NEA). The program aims to facilitate access to electricity by the rural population through national grid extension or densification. NEA is leading the program as the main implementing partner and supervisor of the fund. The program allows community-based organizations, represented by the local communities, to buy electricity in bulk from NEA and sell it within the catchment area by utilizing the existing or newly constructed distribution networks. The regulation provides for any type of community rural electrification entity (CREE)—company, electricity cooperative, nongovernment organizations, user's association—to enter into agreement with CRED, NEA.

These CREEs are required to contribute 10% of the project cost to get connected to the grid and the remaining 90% (previously 80%) is provided by the government via NEA. After electrification, NEA supplies the electricity and the CREEs are responsible for the operation and management of the distribution network, collection of revenues from villagers, and payment for bulk power purchased from NEA. The CREE has the flexibility to set up the tariff, but they are not allowed to take higher than the normal charge. Consumers have a sense of ownership of such projects because the project cost is financed together by the government and the community. By December 2017, 55 CREEs received loans and 47 were connected to the grid providing electricity services to 535,000 households. With the support of Energising Development, Deutsche Gesellschaft für Internationale Zusammenarbeit GmbH, 525 small infrastructures and 3,042 micro, small, and medium enterprises were established.

The CREEs also have assisted women entrepreneurs. For example, in response to the request of the Women Economic Empowerment–Nepal Project of ENERGIA and Hivos, CREEs recommended or linked women entrepreneurs to local financial institutions. CREEs negotiated concessions for women entrepreneurs, such as discount on service charges and lower interest rates. Through the project, 227 women entrepreneurs obtained loans worth €223.056 from 35 different local financial institutions. Similarly, ADB has assisted CREEs through technical assistance projects linked to the energy loan projects. ADB's ongoing support to Power Transmission and Distribution Efficiency Enhancement Project is working with 15 CREEs to promote gender equality and social inclusion in accessing and supporting productive end use of clean energy technologies and services by 500 women.

€ = euros.

Sources: NEA. 2019. *Annual Report*. Kathmandu. p. 81; EnDev Nepal. 2018. *Community Rural Electrification*. http://endev-nepal. org/sites/default/files/publications/2018-02/EnDev_Nepal_On-grid_factsheet.pdf; S. Dutta. 2018. *Supporting Last-Mile Women Energy Entrepreneurs: What Works and What Does Not*. ENERGIA, The International Network on Gender and Sustainable Energy.https://sun-connect-news.org/fileadmin/DATEIEN/Dateien/New/Supporting-Last-Mile-Women-Entrepreneurs.pdf; and ADB. 2017. *Report and Recommendations to the President: Power Transmission and Distribution Efficiency Enhancement Project*. Manila. https://www.adb.org/projects/documents/nep-50059-002-rrp.

Multiple benefits of technologies for women and excluded groups

The Biogas Support Program has reduced the workload of women and girls and enabled them to engage in more productive activities (Box 3.2).

Box 3.2: Biogas Support Program

In 1975, the government launched a biogas program providing interest-free loans. The sector developed with further funding and technical support of the principal stakeholders, such as AEPC (responsible for policy formulation), Biogas Sector Partnership Nepal (BSP-N) (responsible for management and monitoring), and Nepal Biogas Promotion Association (responsible for installation).

BSP-N has played a role in changing the lives of women and excluded groups in rural areas. These changes have been brought about by deliberate actions such as encouraging women's participation in training for supervisors and masons, and management of installation companies, through women-friendly event management; provision of additional installation subsidies to single women, the poor, and remote areas; enhancing income through sensitization on use of bio-slurry in vegetable farming, fish and pig raising; and financial education and access to finance through cooperatives.

BSP-N calculated in 2017 that due to reductions in the use of fuelwood and kerosene, as well as in chemical fertilizers, the annual financial savings totaled NRs345,700 per household per year ($3,457). Additionally, six companies were now being managed by women, employing women as managers, supervisors, and masons.

A dedicated program, Biogas Support Program (BSP) Nepal, was launched in 1992. The BSP disseminated more than 250,000 biogas plants which are mostly used for cooking and lighting (in selected areas). The technology has benefited more than 260,889 households and is said to have reduced the workload of women and girls by about three hours per day. This saved time is used for education, income generation activities, and leisure. BSP has increased women's ownership of biogas plants by 23% and their ownership of assets through establishment of women-owned construction companies. This has increased savings and credit transactions, which in turn, expanded women's access to capital. The success of the program is credited to its targeting the income poor section of the population and the various measures it applied to mainstream GESI. These measures include engaging microfinance organizations to provide seed money to enterprises led by women and excluded groups; focused trainings for women as users of technology, enabling them to undertake repair and maintenance activities and become supervisors/owners of construction companies; and capacity development of staff and partners on GESI, code of conduct against any form of discrimination, and poverty sensitive project monitoring.

BSP=Biogas Support Program, BSP-N=Biogas Sector Partnership Nepal, GESI=gender equality and social inclusion.

Sources: I. Shakya. 2017. Gender Analysis of the Nepal Biogas Programme. *Urban Agriculture Magazine 32. Urban Food-Waste-Energy Nexus and the Private Sector.* pp. 33–35; and UNDP. 2013. *Annual Progress Report, Renewable Energy for Rural Livelihood Program.* Kathmandu.

Engendering utilities

Women and excluded groups face structural barriers to participation in the power sector, including under representation in employment, especially in technical, higher-paying positions and leadership roles. The utilities in Nepal also lack diversity in their personnel. *Increasing Women's Participation in the Power*

Sector through Human Resources Interventions: A Best Practices Framework identifies good practices in addressing gender across human resource dimensions, such as attracting and/or hiring employees, compliance and reporting compliance, human resource policies, payroll and administration, employee development system, financial benefits, risk management, and separation and/or retirement (Box 3.3).[24]

Box 3.3: Best Practices for Engendering Utilities

Corporate-level commitment to gender equity. The Women-Owned Small Business Federal Contracting Program was implemented in Pakistan. The goal of the Government of Pakistan is to award at least 5% of all federal contracting dollars to women-owned small businesses each year.

Internship program. The Energy Sector Internship Program of USAID in Pakistan received a huge response with many of the applicants being young women. Ultimately, 20 women from varying disciplines and income levels were selected. The internship program provided these women with an opportunity to gain on-the-job training in a male-dominated profession in Pakistan, and gain access to a network of young graduates in the energy sector.

Source: RTI International. 2018. Produced by RTI International for USAID's Office of Energy and Infrastructure, Energy Division within the Bureau of Economic Growth, Education and Environment. Washington DC. https://pdf.usaid.gov/pdf_docs/PA00KWT8.pdf.

How Mindtree supports employees with childcare needs. To encourage and enable parents to stay employed, Mindtree in India offers an extensive set of child-related benefits, including subsidized workplace childcare; a "Baby's Day Out" facility to allow parents to bring their children to work in emergency situations; enhanced maternity leave; paternity leave; a program to help women navigate pregnancy, maternity leave, and their return to work; and flexible work options for returning mothers. As Mindtree's chief financial officer Jagannathan Chakravarthi explains, "If we want gender diversity, we have to offer childcare; if women are forced to choose between work and childcare, they will choose their kids."

Source: RTI International. 2018. Produced by RTI International for USAID's Office of Energy and Infrastructure, Energy Division within the Bureau of Economic Growth, Education and Environment. Washington DC. https://www.ifc.org/wps/wcm/connect/87df44f4-c322-484e-87a0-4e4bbfdc1a04/Mindtree_Layout+1.pdf?MOD=AJPERES&CVID=IXu8DEX.

Gender equity in utilities. USAID's Engendering Utilities program has strengthened energy utility operations by:

- identifying and implementing gender equity best practices that helped them meet their core business goals while providing tangible economic opportunities for women; and

- partnering with seven electric distribution companies in five countries—Georgia, Jordan, Kenya, Macedonia, and Nigeria—to collaboratively design tailored interventions to improve gender

continued on next page

---

[24]   RTI International. 2018. Produced by RTI International for USAID's Office of Energy and Infrastructure, Energy Division within the Bureau of Economic Growth, Education and Environment. Washington DC. https://web.archive.org/web/20190208155415/https://www.usaid.gov/sites/default/files/documents/1865/gender-equity-energy-sector-best-practices.pdf.

Box 3.3 continued

outcomes within their organizations and develop action plans to incorporate gender equity in their business practices. At the end of the project, all seven partner utilities drafted, adopted, or implemented policies on:

» addressing gender equity and equal employment opportunities;

» conducting equal pay salary gap analyses;

» setting up systems to collect sex-disaggregated employment and employee satisfaction data, to inform corporate decision-making;

» adopting behavior-based interviewing techniques to reduce bias in hiring processes, and engaging educational institutions in outreach activities;

» investing their own time and $500,000 in aggregate and in-kind contributions to implement interventions; and

» expanding their efforts through outreach to local communities, with three utilities extending outreach to national leaders.

Most utilities saw increases in women training participants, interns, job applicants, and trainee hires. Utilities also saw more women promoted and identified as high potential for succession planning, increasing the number of women in succession plans from 83 in 2015 to 387 in 2017. Outreach activities motivating both women and men students to attend training increased from 66 educational institutions in 2015 to 77 in 2017.

Source: USAID. 2017. Engendering Utilities: Strengthening Utilities through Gender Equality Initiatives. California. https://www.usaid.gov/energy/engendering-utilities.

Looking Forward: Issues and Opportunities to Consider

This section highlights the key issues and opportunities that merit consideration by ADB in sector and project analyses, and potential collaborations with government counterparts and other key stakeholders.

Increase access to modern energy services for excluded groups, particularly women

It is important to increase the access to modern energy services (e.g., smart meters, smart appliances, renewable energy resources, and energy efficient resources) for excluded groups, particularly vulnerable women, to improve their life quality, reduce illnesses caused by pollution, and address time poverty issues arising from lack of energy. For instance, the use of induction stoves is smoke-free, promotes clean cooking, and saves the time that women can use for other activities. Also, the induction stove is easy to use and can be operated by any member of the household.

As their mobility is constrained, PWDs have different energy needs and usage time. To optimize their mobility around the household, they require essential energy assistive technologies (e.g., Braille displays [note takers], screen readers, simplified mobile phones, digital hearing aids, and electrical wheelchair) for independent living.

Mainstream GESI in energy projects and across phases of electricity generation, transmission, and distribution

Mainstreaming GESI in all aspects of a project cycle is required for projects and programs to be beneficial for excluded groups, particularly women. There is a need to integrate GESI dimensions in different phases of electricity generation (pre-construction, construction, post-construction), transmission, and distribution. This needs to be done from the very first step of a project so that even in the initial surveys and mapping, GESI-related issues are identified and included in the succeeding tasks of project description and/or design, assessments, costing, construction planning and schedule, and environment impact assessment. Some aspects for GESI integration in the different phases are discussed below.[25]

At pre-construction stage, it is important that the GESI analysis determines who has access to what resources and opportunities, and what are the requirements to increase access to assets and benefits of women and excluded groups. Identify excluded groups, including women, for the purpose of skills training and development in view of potential access to employment opportunities during construction stage. Project teams must conduct timely consultation with community women and men across socioeconomic groups in all steps—from inception to project design and implementation— and ensure dissemination of key project information (i.e., specifics, cost estimates, and schedule) to all so they are properly informed. These activities can boost support for the project. Gender and power relations analyses to identify the social practices constraining and/or supporting women and the gender differentials in decision-making power will also help the project team identify strategic interventions toward increasing women's level of participation and strengthening their decision-making power.

At construction stage (covering agreement with civil contractor for civil works and monitoring), the conditions of contract with the civil contractor must include provisions for employment opportunities for the excluded groups, particularly eligible women to work as laborers, sub-contractors, suppliers, and skilled workers. The provisions for childcare facilities and breastfeeding time, among many other women-friendly facilities, encourage women workers to be more productive. Company policies for protection against violence/sexual abuse, including equal pay for labor, can create a safer and secure working environment for women workers. The civil construction contractors must take steps to fully inform the community of the potential employment opportunities available for excluded groups, particularly women community members. Additional community consultations on income generating activities that the project can bring, and better use of potential savings from there can be organized.

At post-construction phase, sustainability of the interventions is crucial to ensure continuity of project benefits. Employment of local people as project staff and creating platforms to increase their representation in different forums and/or committees reflect the project's intention to ensure

---

[25]   Human Resource Development Centre (HURDEC) Pvt. Ltd. 2014. *Background Report on GESI Impacts of Kaligandaki Hydropower Project.* Kathmandu.

ownership of development benefits to the community. The community women and men must be duly and timely informed about the project office, its functions, and accountabilities. Gender inclusive dimensions must be integrated in human resource policies and systems.

For transmission (covering route map, estimated cost and time), identify what are the community and individual assets (e.g., land, equipment, and facilities) that will be impacted by the transmission line route and its right of way. Identify possible community development activities and conduct strategic consultations with the community, including women, PWDs, and excluded groups, regarding the route-map, project impacts, and due compensation where applicable. Disaggregated information about who is affected by the proposed route and affirmative actions for women and excluded groups are required.

For distribution (covering customer mapping, tariffs), determine subsidy for the extremely poor women and men of all social groups; consult the community on who are not receiving electricity; and disaggregate index of consumers to identify who are getting electricity and who are not and why not. Existing policy instruments—such as affordable tariffs, subsidies, schemes, and revolving funds that provide cheap credit for connection—should be adopted to target women and excluded groups of consumers in the lower consumption band.[26]

With support from ADB, the NEA's Board endorsed its GESI strategy and operational guidelines. These guidelines aim to mainstream GESI in all aspects of NEA's policies, project design and implementation process, and institutional structure.

Ensure participation of women and excluded groups in energy plans, programs, and decision-making

It is important to ensure that women and excluded groups can participate meaningfully to influence sector policies and programs. Social mobilization combined with information dissemination and community education has been proven effective in raising the voice of women and excluded groups and their capacity to influence decisions. Where communities have been mobilized to reflect on the social norms that perpetuate untouchability, gender bias or violence against women, there has been an increase in access to services and greater involvement in community-level planning for these groups. Setting quotas for women and excluded groups in user groups and committees, along with creating training opportunities, has ensured their representation and participation in development activities, and strengthened their access to resources and benefits. Still, further efforts are needed to reach excluded groups, in particular women members, and promote their representation in key decision-making positions in executive bodies and their ability to influence decisions in the energy sector (Footnote 5). PWDs should be included in national governing bodies working on energy access. Awareness within ministries needs to be raised and interministerial coordination promoted to address fuel and energy poverty among PWDs.[27]

---

[26] R. Mohideen. 2018. Energy Technology Innovation in South Asia: Implications for Gender Equality and Social Inclusion. *ADB South Asia Working Paper Series No. 61*. Manila.

[27] UN. 2018. *Disability and Development Report Realizing the Sustainable Development Goals By, For and With Persons with Disabilities.* New York.

Promote productive end use of energy by women and excluded groups

A range of advisory services (covering strategic planning, investments, operations and logistics, financial planning and analysis, marketing and sales and project development, and training) should be provided to energy-based enterprises led by women and excluded groups. Consistent support and mentoring can address the different barriers women and the excluded experience. Working with this target group requires a process-oriented approach to be available at their doorstep since they have mobility restrictions and high time poverty. Women and excluded groups typically start with small energy businesses, as they have limited access to credit and have low risk-taking abilities in addition to the gender and caste- or ethnicity-based disadvantage they experience (Box 3.4 and Table 3.2).

Box 3.4: Ramite Khola Solar Mini-Grid Experience

The Ramite Khola Solar Mini-Grid subproject of South Asia Sub-Regional Economic Cooperation Power System Expansion Project (Off-Grid Component, AEPC) has provided all households (which were previously without any electricity) in the area (which has Rai and Dalit population) with electricity through a solar mini grid. Eight households (soon two more will also join) have received 40% subsidy (for Dalits and single women it is 50% subsidy) to start enterprises. Three women benefited, one is running a tailoring shop, another a beauty parlor, and one a grinding mill. The chair of the solar mini-grid committee, an Adivasi Janajati, started a photo studio which has helped the local public a lot as they do not need to go down to town for such services. The vice chair, a Dalit, has started a gold and silver jewelry shop. Most of the enterprises are growing and earning a respectable income for the entrepreneurs using solar energy.

Source: GESI Diagnostic Study. 2018. Field visit. Ramite Khola, Morang. Nepal.

Table 3.2: Tip Sheet on Integrating Gender Equality and Social Inclusion Perspectives into Analysis and Planning in the Energy Sector

Barriers	Actions to Address the Barriers
Lack of finance, appliances, information, training, and education constrain women and excluded groups from accessing energy sources	Adopt focused interventions to increase access of women and excluded groups to resources.
Lack of access to modern energy sources increases work burden and illnesses of women and excluded groups	Increase access to energy sources. Raise awareness about the harm caused by traditional energy sources and ways to reduce their use. Consider the extra energy costs and other needs that PWDs are facing.
Challenges constrain women and excluded groups of entrepreneurs from productive end use of energy	Address barriers, such as finance market, time, knowledge, and technical skills, to enable income generation from energy use.
Decision-making regarding energy products and services is usually with men and the non-excluded groups, and dictated by social norms	Strengthen capacity of women and excluded groups for them to be better informed about sector issues and participate in discussions and decision-making forums. Advocate with the advantaged to be open and listen to others.
There is limited integration of GESI dimensions in all elements of energy planning and policymaking	Adopt GESI mainstreaming as an approach and address GESI issues in each step from situation assessment to evaluation. Engage PWDs in the energy planning process. Raise awareness of policymakers on differing forms of disability and PWDs' energy needs. Policymakers must proactively reach out to PWDs to identify their needs.
Institutions in the sector have limited capacities to work on GESI issues	Promote institutional arrangements on specific location of GESI responsibility, integration of GESI in job descriptions and/or terms of references, staff diversity, analytical and responsive GESI skills of staff, GESI criteria in staff performance evaluation, and a positive work environment.
Discriminatory gender and social norms constrain women and excluded groups from accessing sector resources and opportunities	Conduct social marketing and raise awareness of women, families, and communities on the benefits of accessing energy. Organize exposure visits and interactive discussions and support learnings on how traditional inequitable practices are changed. Provide access to electricity in schools to increase the use of assistive technology in education and enhance opportunities for students with disability to participate equally in educational systems.

GESI = gender equality and social inclusion, PWDs = persons with disabilities.

Source: Table prepared for this study.

4

SKILLS DEVELOPMENT

Area of collaboration

Initial support of ADB focused on reforms in primary and secondary education. Since 2002, ADB has been supporting the technical education and vocational training (TEVT) sector.

ADB assisted the education sector through 54 projects, which is 14.4% of its cumulative lending, grant, and technical assistance commitments to Nepal from 1966 to 2018.

Sector context

The Constitution has identified TEVT as a means for preparing skilled human resource which is essential for Nepal's economic growth. It has directed that special provisions be made for excluded groups in TEVT.

The Council for Technical Education and Vocational Training provides certified Technical School Leaving Certificate programs of 18 months, 3-year diploma programs, and a variety of short-term training courses. Vocational trainings are also offered by 12 other ministries.

Wide educational disparities exist, and poor literacy rates challenge the ability of women and excluded groups to enhance their technical and vocational skills.

Gender equality and social inclusion (GESI) considerations relevant to sector planning and outcomes

Strong social and gender norms and heavy burden of unpaid care work limit skills building and employment options of women and excluded groups.

Social acceptance and employers' acceptance of women and excluded groups in nontraditional sectors can be a challenge.

Labor force participation of women and excluded groups is high primarily as unskilled and low paid workers.

Trainees and employers have negative perception about vocational education or training.

Service providers show less interest in and low priority for training women and excluded groups.

Good practices and lessons	Special measures to promote skills training and employment of women and excluded groups are needed, such as setting of enrollment targets for equitable access to training, enhancing support for both pre- and post-training to facilitate transition into waged employment or self-employment, and opening up opportunities for women in nontraditional industries/skills.
	Various strategies to encourage and prepare women and excluded groups for skills training and employment are required.
	Structural gender-based constraints need to be addressed with orientation of families and decision makers as they limit options of women in selection of training and employment.
	Caste-based bias restricts employment opportunities; hence, employers' orientation is important.
Looking forward: Issues and opportunities to consider	Market feasibility studies and alignment of demand and supply are essential for better employment of trained women and the excluded.
	Targeted courses can facilitate access of women and excluded groups to different sectors, including nontraditional sector.
	Setting targets in training courses and ensuring quality should be balanced.
	Preparation and sensitization of service providers on GESI is needed for effective training and employment of women and excluded groups.
	TEVT service providers require policy directives, incentives, and systematic follow up and monitoring to ensure GESI aspects are integrated in their services.
	Along with technical focus, it is important to do parental education and work with society toward elimination of discriminatory norms.
Further resources	ADB tip sheet on addressing barriers experienced by women and excluded group and integrating GESI in the skills development sector (Table 4.1).

GESI = gender equality and social inclusion, TEVT = technical education and vocational training.

Area of Collaboration

From 1996 to 2018, the Asian Development Bank (ADB) supported Nepal's education sector covering primary and secondary education and vocational education and training. The intervention included 54 projects amounting to $912.70 million,[1] which is 14.4% of its cumulative lending, grant, and technical assistance commitments.[2] Initial support focused on reforms in primary and secondary education. Also, ADB has been supporting the country's technical education and vocational training (TEVT) sector. The high unemployment rate and lack of opportunities for economic and social mobility were recognized as primary causes of conflict and poverty. To reduce poverty rate and income inequality, it was vital to increase the employment rate and income level of workers, especially those belonging to excluded groups. In 2002, the Government of Nepal requested ADB to prepare a project to enhance TEVT to promote broad-based and inclusive social and economic development through sustainable human development. Improved TEVT access and quality would enable unskilled youth to avail themselves of income opportunities.

Sector Context

Policy Commitments

The policy and institutional framework for GESI in TEVT is positive in Nepal. The Constitution has identified TEVT as a means for preparing skilled human resource, which is essential for Nepal's economic growth.[3] It has directed that special provisions should be made for Dalits in TEVT.[4] To ensure inclusive and equitable access to quality technical education and vocational skills development, the 15th Five-Year Plan (FY2019–2020 to FY2020–2024) envisions increasing access and developing a master plan with the establishment of an integrated fund for TEVT.[5]

The 15th Five-Year Plan's objectives are to: (i) guarantee the right to work by gradually reducing semi-unemployment, underemployment, and unemployment; (ii) develop a competitive workforce by increasing opportunities for training and skills development; and (iii) make foreign employment more productive, safe, disciplined, and regulated. The Approach Paper to the 15th Plan emphasizes skills development of youth and people at risk of trafficking.[6] It targets 500,000 people to be vocationally and technically skilled annually. Under the Act Relating to Rights of Persons with Disabilities (2017), the government provided for the establishment of vocational trainings for and concessional loans to PWDs who wish to do business.[7]

---

[1]   ADB. 2018. *Asian Development Bank Member Fact Sheet, Nepal: 2018 Committed Loans, Grants, and Technical Assistance.* https://www.adb.org/sites/default/files/publication/27783/nep-2018.pdf. Data about projects and funds is cumulative from 19 December 1996 to 31 December 2018 and covers all assistance.

[2]   ADB. 2019. Cumulative Lending, Grant, and Technical Assistance Commitments. https://data.adb.org/dataset/cumulative-lending-grant-and-technical-assistance-commitments (accessed 27 December 2019).

[3]   Constitution of Nepal. 2015. Part-4 Directive Principles, Policies and Obligations of the State. Policies relating to basic needs of the citizens state "to prepare human resources that are competent, competitive, ethical, and devoted to national interests, while making education scientific, technical, vocational, empirical, employment and people-oriented."

[4]   Constitution of Nepal. 2015. Special provision shall be made by law for the Dalit in technical and vocational education (Part-3 Fundamental Rights and Duties, Clause 40. Rights of Dalit, point 2).

[5]   National Planning Commission, Government of Nepal. 2017. *15th Five-Year Plan Approach Paper* (Section 7.2 Education). Kathmandu. p. 182. https://www.npc.gov.np/images/category/15th_Plan_Approach_Paper2.pdf.

[6]   Government of Nepal, National Planning Commission. 2019. *Approach Paper to 15th Plan*. Kathmandu. https://www.npc.gov.np/images/category/15th_Plan_Approach_Paper2.pdf.

[7]   Government of Nepal. 2017. The Act Relating to Rights of Persons with Disabilities, 2074 (Chapter 6). *Skill Development and Employment.* http://www.lawcommission.gov.np/en/archives/20833.

The Technical Education and Vocational Training Policy (2012) identifies five key objectives, one of which is the inclusion of socially underprivileged, regionally backward, and economically poor classes of the society in TEVT programs. A central feature of the 2012 TEVT policy is the promotion of access and inclusion of excluded groups in skills enhancement by preparing appropriate training packages and offering incentives through scholarships, free quotas, minimum fee, and easy loans. The main aim of the CTEVT Strategic Plan (2014–2018) is to implement the provisions of the 2012 TEVT policy. One goal is to expand TEVT programs to ensure access and equity, as well as geographical balance of programs; enforce affirmative action for women and excluded groups;[8] and implement TEVT programs for special need populations.

The new Labor Act of 2017 mandates gender equality and non-discrimination at work, and provides for 98-day maternity leave (with up to 60 days fully paid) and 15 days fully paid paternity leave.[9] In case of sexual harassment, section 132 of the Labor Act states that services of the perpetrator may be terminated on the basis of the seriousness of offense. The National Employment Policy 2015 identifies inadequate skills development and diverse barriers for youth and other social groups as some of the major problems and challenges in national employment. This policy targeted women, youth, Adivasi Janajati, Dalits, Madhesis, and other excluded communities or regions to address existing inequalities; and incorporated their concerns into the policy formulation. Specific policies such as policies related to Objective 2 ("improve the quality of employment by gradually transforming informal employment into formal employment"), include various directives for the youth, women, Adivasi Janajatis, and other excluded communities, and for programs to gradually eliminate gender, geographical, and caste-based inequalities in employment.[10]

Various other acts have positive provisions such as the Education Act and Regulations (2002), which emphasizes women's representation in management, and has arranged scholarships for girls; and the Gender Equality Act 2006, which made amendments to discriminatory provision to further protect women's rights. One of the stated objectives of the Industrial Policy 2011 is to increase employment through promoting opportunities for self-employment and developing industrial skills and entrepreneurship. It also aims to improve youth employment under special strategies.

The Government of Nepal allocated more than NRs3 billion in FY2018–2019 for the Prime Minister Employment Program, which aims to provide jobs for 500,000 Nepalese.[11] However, there are no clear provisions for targeting excluded groups.[12]

---

8   Affirmative action is the practice or policy of favoring individuals belonging to groups known to have been discriminated against previously (in the context of allocation of resources or different opportunities). https://www.lexico.com/definition/affirmative_action.

9   Labour Act. 2017. Clause 6 of Article 2. Labour Act 2017 prohibits discrimination on grounds of sex, caste, religion, language, ideology, pregnancy and disability. Clause 7 has provisions for equal pay for equal value of work. Clause 33 of Article 7 directs employers to provide safe transport facilities for women during evening and night duty. Article 16 clause 108 specifies representation of women. Other supportive clauses for women include easier work for pregnant women and leave on International Women's Day. http://www.lawcommission.gov.np.

10 Ministry of Labour and Employment. *National Employment Policy*. 2015. Policies for Objective 2 are: 11.2 "Credit, information and business development services for the youth, women, indigenous nationalities and marginalized communities will be made more accessible to help them start cottage, small and medium industries;" 11.4 "a policy will be adopted through which the poor and marginalized communities can get involved in income-generation activities through these small financial institutions."

11 Government of Nepal, Ministry of Finance. 2018. *Budget Speech 2018–19*. Kathmandu.

12 Meeting with sector expert. GESI Diagnostic Study. 2018. Kathmandu.

Institutional Structure of TEVT

Formal TEVT in Nepal includes the Council for Technical Education and Vocational Training (CTEVT), which provides certified Technical School Leaving Certificate (TSLC) programs of 18 months, 3-year diploma programs, and a variety of short-term training courses accredited by the CTEVT and other agencies, under the Ministry of Education (Box 4.1).

Box 4.1: Institutions for Skills Development in Nepal

The Ministry of Education is the apex body for all educational organizations and is responsible for the development of education in the country. Within this purview, it has the responsibility to supervise the Council for Technical Education and Vocational Training (CTEVT). There are altogether 40 technical education and vocational training (TEVT) institutions under the Ministry's direct contract. CTEVT, formed under the Council for TEVT Act 1989, is responsible for managing and accrediting TEVT provision, determining TEVT policy, coordinating training providers, and testing and certification. It is also responsible for conducting TEVT.

The National Skills Testing Board (NSTB) under CTEVT provides testing and certification of skills. NSTB has developed National Occupational Skills Standards for 237 occupations based on International Labour Organization guidelines. It also manages the Nepal Vocational Qualifications Framework.

The Ministry of Labor and Employment is responsible for employment policy, legislation, and regulation, and prepares migrants before their departure for foreign jobs. It also conducts TEVT.

In addition to CTEVT, TEVT is delivered by private institutions, technical institutions of universities, secondary schools, and government agencies associated with various ministries and training programs supported by national and international nongovernment organizations.

CTEVT = Council for Technical Education and Vocational Training, NSTB = National Skills Testing Board, TEVT = technical education and vocational training.

Source: UNDP. 2015. *SKILLS Program Document*. Kathmandu.

Though public financing of TEVT has increased over time, it is largely subsumed under the education budget, and is small. For example, in FY2016–2017, the allocated budget for TEVT was 1.87% of the total MOE budget and other government departments have nominal expenditure on TEVT.[13]

The TEVT section in the MOE is responsible for coordinating the 12 ministries conducting vocational trainings and working with two key committees—the TEVT Policy Coordination Committee and the TEVT Technical Coordination Committee. The Technical Coordination Committee has an explicit responsibility to ensure that GESI aspects are addressed in the programs they coordinate.[14] CTEVT has a GESI unit under its Research and Information Section and has appointed a staff as GESI coordinator. The authority and resources required for GESI coordinator to substantively influence the work of the organization is inadequate. There is no mechanism by which the planning and budgeting processes can be informed of GESI issues; and the GESI coordinator is not invited to the meetings where such decisions are taken.[15]

---

[13]   World Bank. 2017. *Project Appraisal Document on Enhanced Vocational Education and Training Project II, Nepal*. Kathmandu. p. 5.
[14]   Ministry of Education. 2018. *Meeting with Undersecretary of TEVT Development Unit, personal communication*. Kathmandu.
[15]   Council for Technical Education and Vocational Training (CTEVT). 2018. *Meeting notes with CTEVT Coordinator, GESI Unit*. Kathmandu.

Gender Equality and Social Inclusion Considerations Relevant to Sector Planning and Outcomes

Situation of women and excluded groups in the education sector

Literacy and employment status of women and excluded groups is lower than of dominant groups

The literacy rate of population 15 years and older in Nepal is 56%, with men at 72% and women at 45%. Caste or ethnic disparities are high with literacy rate of Hill Brahmins at 76%, and Madhesi Dalits at 29%. Only 11% Madhesi Dalit women are literate. Within the Janajati group, Newars have the highest literacy rate at 72.2%, and Tarai Janajatis (excluding Tharus, a subgroup of Adivasi Janajatis who are 55% literate) have the lowest at 50%.[16] The literacy rate of Muslims is 43% with only 28% literate Muslim women. These wide educational disparities indicate the challenges that women and excluded groups experience in enhancing their technical and vocational skills (Figure 4.1).

Figure 4.1: Literacy Rate in Nepal (%)

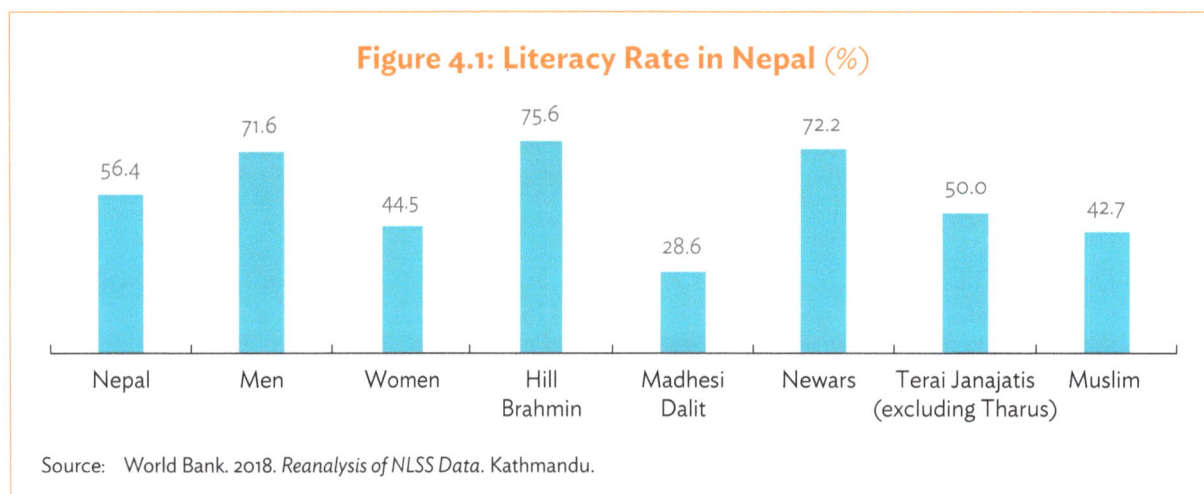

Nepal	Men	Women	Hill Brahmin	Madhesi Dalit	Newars	Terai Janajatis (excluding Tharus)	Muslim
56.4	71.6	44.5	75.6	28.6	72.2	50.0	42.7

Source: World Bank. 2018. *Reanalysis of NLSS Data.* Kathmandu.

Children are dropping out of school because boys either migrate or help with family farm work, and girls either help in the household or marry early. Nepal's early marriage rates are one of the highest in the region, with 18% of women aged 20 to 49 years having married before the age of 15, and 49% of women aged 20 to 49 years having married before the age of 18.[17] In Nepal, married girls are 11 times more likely to be out of school compared to their unmarried peers, and early marriage is cited as the second most common reason for school dropout for girls aged 15 to 17, and the most common reason for school dropout for women aged 20 to 24. Additionally, it is often difficult for low income students to pursue further studies as secondary schools charge monthly fees in grades 11 and 12.[18] These realities result in limited employability of students, particularly of women and excluded group students. For students who left school without a school-leaving certificate and marketable skills, and are unemployed, training is necessary to avail of income opportunities to help them move out of poverty.

---

[16] World Bank. 2018. *Country Level Gender Equality and Social Inclusion Assessment, Re-analysis of Nepal Living Standards Survey (NLSS) data.* Kathmandu (Annex 2, Table 6.1 Education and Literacy).

[17] Government of Nepal, Central Bureau of Statistics. 2014. *Population Monograph.* Kathmandu. http://cbs.gov.np

[18] Government of Nepal, Ministry of Education. 2016. *School Sector Development Plan 2016–2023.* 1.3 Key Issues and Challenges (subsection on Equity and Access). Kathmandu. p. 13.

According to the Nepal Demographic Health Survey (NDHS) 2016, 57% of women and 78% of men are currently employed. The employment rate in Nepal is around 68% (Figure 4.2). This means 32% of the country's working age population, aged 15 to 64, are either unemployed or voluntarily inactive.[19] The labor market sees entry of at least 512,000 youths per year, according to the Economic Survey of the Ministry of Finance.[20] In 2011, the male working age population was 58%, and the female working age population was 62%. A population growth projection conducted by the Central Bureau of Statistics (CBS) shows that by 2021, the working age population will increase from 58% in 2011 to 64% in 2021 for men and from 62% and 67% for women.[21] Nepal is going through a phase of demographic dividend as growth of the working age population is higher than the growth of the total population, and currently has a historically high young working age population which is an opportunity for the TEVT sector.[22]

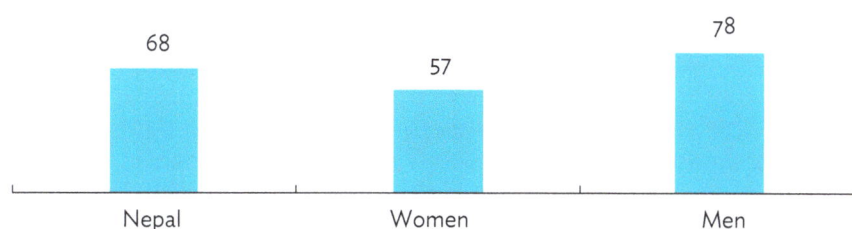

Figure 4.2: Employment Rate (%)

Source: World Bank. 2018. *South Asia Economic Focus, Spring 2018: Jobless Growth?* Washington, DC: World Bank. https://openknowledge.worldbank.org/handle/10986/29650. License: CC BY 3.0 IGO.

Although the share of women in the working age population is high, their employment in the formal sector is low. In the informal and private sectors, their employment is high, but the wages are lower for the same type of job compared to their male counterparts. Besides, young girls often start working at an early age for virtually no wage.[23] Women are less likely than men to be employed in professional, technical, and managerial occupations (6% versus 10%), clerical services (2% versus 6%), sales and services (13% versus 23%), skilled manual labor (6% versus 15%), and unskilled manual labor (3% versus 13%).[24]

[19] World Bank. 2018. Jobless Growth? *South Asia Economic Focus*. Spring 2018. https://openknowledge.worldbank.org/handle/10986/29650 License: CC BY 3.0 IGO. Washington DC.
[20] The Kathmandu Post. 2018. *Nepal's Employment Rate Highest in South Asia*. Kathmandu. http://kathmandupost.ekantipur.com/news/2018-04-17/nepals-employment-rate-highest-in-south-asia.html.
[21] UNFPA Nepal. 2017. *Population Situation Analysis of Nepal (with respect to sustainable development)*. p. 7. https://nepal.unfpa.org/sites/default/files/pub-pdf/Nepal Population Situation Analysis.pdf.
[22] UNFPA Nepal. 2017. *Nepal Population Situation Analysis: Executive Summary*. Kathmandu. p. 3.
[23] UNFPA Nepal. 2017. *Nepal Population Situation Analysis (with respect to sustainable development)*. Kathmandu. p. 15.
[24] Government of Nepal, Ministry of Health. 2016. *Demographic and Health Survey*. Kathmandu.

Situation of women and excluded groups in TEVT

CTEVT and/or NSTB have tested about 348,566 candidates and certified 269,573 individuals in different occupations at different levels up to 14 July 2017.[25] Between 2000 and 2010, the number of TEVT graduates increased from 15,000 to 80,000 per year and the number of technical schools offering TSLC or diploma programs increased from 150 to over 400. Short-term training programs offered increased from 45 to more than 225, and the average number of certifications by the NSTB increased multifold per year.[26]

From 2014 to 2017, a total of 54,423 individuals received diploma level training from CTEVT and 177,680 were trained for TSLC level. Special program for excluded groups (Janajati, Dalit, Muslims, and other excluded groups) had a total of 2,444 graduates from 2010 to 2014, and 2,100 were studying under the program. Out of the 2,444 students, 69% were Dalits, 18% were Muslim, and the remaining 12% were from other excluded groups. About 51% chose the nursing certificate course, 21% took an 18-month assistant nurse midwife (ANM) course, and 16% enrolled in the 29-month ANM course. The rest of the courses had minimal number of students.[27]

Due to a lack of comprehensive national program for vocational training for PWDs, there have been limited interventions for equipping them with skills. The PWDs have received vocational trainings with residential facilities from the Ministry of Women, Children and Senior Citizens (then Social Welfare) since 2001 but the coverage has been very small.

Gender stereotyping and perceptions about women-friendly occupations result in higher presence of women in traditional occupations like tailoring and their minimal presence in nontraditional sectors like electrician training. Caste and ethnic groups' participation in training and education programs is limited, and more individuals from the advantaged groups access these programs.[28]

There is low participation among excluded groups due to the lack of social preparation needed to train them. Most of the time, the types of trades selected for central level training are not attractive to excluded groups.[29] They continue to face economic hardship in traveling to and staying in training venues. Regional inequality in skills development opportunities is likely to become more visible in the federal structure.[30] There has been very little effort to work on existing skills sets (such as those of Dalits) and help them develop in their traditional occupations (e.g., shoe making and pottery crafts).[31]

---

[25] CTEVT/NVQS (Swiss Contact). 2018. *Tracer Study of Skill Test Graduates, Final Report*. Kathmandu. p. 1 (Disaggregated data is unavailable).

[26] World Bank. 2016. World Development Indicators. In *Enhanced Vocational Education and Training Project II, PAD*. Kathmandu.

[27] Of the students, 5% took certificate level normal physician course, 3% students completed Diploma in Civil Engineering, 2% Veterinary Junior Technical Assistants, 1% Civil Sub-Overseer, and 1% Diploma in Agriculture.

[28] K. Bhatta. 2016. Gender Equality and Social Inclusion in Vocational Education and Training. *Journal of Advanced Academic Research (JAAR)*. 3(2). July. Rajasthan, India: Department of Sociology, Mewar University.

[29] ADB. 2013. *Project Completion Report, Skills for Employment, Nepal* (Appendix 2). Manila. p. 24.

[30] World Bank. 2017. *Project Appraisal Document on Enhanced Vocational Education and Training Project II, Nepal*. Kathmandu. p. 4.

[31] TEVT. 2018. *Meeting with Hari Pradhan, TEVT expert*. Kathmandu.

Strong social and gender norms and heavy burden of unpaid care work limit skills building and employment options of women and excluded groups

Entrenched norms regarding work suitable for women and excluded groups restrict their employment opportunities. Employers may adhere to conventional beliefs that women are not suitable for nontraditional jobs and that Dalits will not be accepted in certain sectors. For instance, bias based on caste restricts Dalits from certain sectors as untouchability is still practiced.[32]

In Lamjung, the service providers convinced Dalit applicants that the training course for waiters was not for them.	For adolescent girls and women, access to technical schools in central locations is a challenge as parents are unwilling to permit their daughters to travel or stay away from home. Additionally, mobility of girls and women is challenged by the inadequate security system.

Spending on technical education is considered more appropriate for sons rather than for daughters as they are regarded as primary bread winners. Technical work is also considered a "hard skill" work and not suitable for women. The courses and curriculum reinforce these structural patriarchal values encouraging women students to choose subjects considered suitable for their gender roles, such as nurse, tailor, and beautician. In school year 2016/2017, though about 51% of the total students enrolled in CTEVT were girls, they were studying gender-stereotyped subjects. Girls' enrollment in health-related subjects was 71%; in engineering related subjects, 13%; agriculture and science, 38%; hospital management, 29%; and entrepreneurship development and social works, 100% (Figure 4.3).[33]

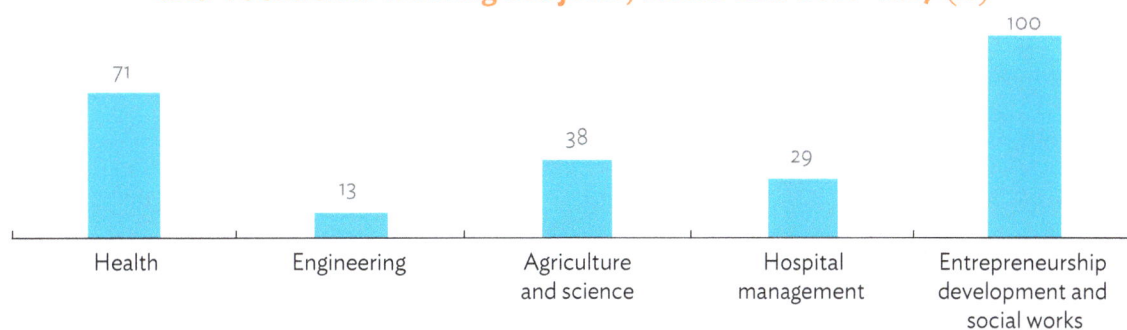

Figure 4.3: Women's Enrollment in Council for Technical Education and Vocational Training Subjects, Fiscal Year 2016–2017 (%)

Source: CTEVT. 2017. *Annual Report 2016/17*. Kathmandu.

---

[32]   Meeting with gender officers of different projects. GESI Diagnostic Study. 2018. Kathmandu.
[33]   CTEVT. 2017. *Annual Report 2016/17*. Kathmandu. p. 5.

There were women who had stopped work or changed from a nontraditional trade (e.g., as a mason or plumber) because of household obligations or family's disapproval of their current employment.[34] Unpaid care work, which is primarily women's responsibility in Nepal, reduces women's available time for employment and other income generating activities. This impacts their course and skills selection—related to paid work at home or not far from home (footnote 34). For Dalits, such caste-based discriminatory practices and norms similarly curtail their opportunities (footnote 32).

For Dalits, food and beverage related trades are traditionally not considered caste-friendly. For example, after vocational training, a participant who was working in a bakery in Kathmandu had to hide her caste identity.

In Accham, a milk collection center closed down because the community did not patronize the milk collected by Dalits.

Social acceptance and employers' acceptance of women and excluded groups in nontraditional sectors is a challenge

Poor literacy, lack of technical "hard" skills and poor "soft" skills,[35] combined with market and employers' bias, constrain opportunities of women and excluded groups in sectors and subsectors (Box 4.2).

Box 4.2: Challenges in Nontraditional Trades

Challenges encountered by women in nontraditional trades include the belief of their families and community members that women should not be doing "men's work" and the belief of the society that they cannot do the job. They must gain the trust and confidence of customers and employers that they can carry out the tasks effectively. Empowered women overcome this challenge by honing and proving their skills. However, there are many women who remain unemployed because they fail to get the permission of their families, usually their husband or in-laws; or they lack the confidence to take on a job or be self-employed in a nontraditional trade.

With regards to women's employment, differences exist between the community from the hills (called Pahadi in Nepal) and the Madhesi community in the Tarai. In Madhesi culture, numerous practices inhibit women from leaving their homes to go to work in the bazaar or out in the fields. The families totally prohibit women from interacting with men other than their family members. It was better to train Madhesi women in trades such as poultry and vegetable growing where they do not have to leave or travel far from their own homes to engage in nontraditional trades. For women of hills origin (i.e., Pahadi women), social rules are not so conservative but the gender realities of care work burden and inability to travel and leave home for long periods are real constraints.

Source: Employment Fund/Helvetas. 2015. *Note on Nontraditional Trades for Women.* Kathmandu. https://www.s4ye.org/agi/pdf/Project_Design/Factsheet%20T&E%20strategies.pdf.

---

34   Employment Fund. 2015. *Learning Series: T&E Observations and Strategies Regarding Women in Non-traditional Trades.* https://web.archive.org/web/20180907040928/http://www.employmentfund.org.np/wp-content/uploads/2015/05/TE-Observations-and-Strategies-of-Women-in-non-traditional-trades.pdf.
35   Soft skills are the necessary and basic personal and social skills people must have in order to do most jobs. https://ied.eu/importance-soft-skills-existing/.

Under the ADB Skills for Employment Project, a total of 59,129 (including 53.8% women) candidates completed short-term skills training, meeting the target of providing market-oriented short-term skills training to at least 60,000 trainees. The project completion report (PCR) of the Skills Development Project (SDP) indicated that of the 47,284 graduates, 76% (35,992) were gainfully employed and of which 40% were women and 72% were from excluded groups. Women were less gainfully employed as many jobs were not perceived to be suitable for them such as chef, driver, wall painter, and mason.[36] Programs which offer electrical wiring or mason training often saw minimal or no women applications. For instance, in a house wiring training, there were only two women out of 15 participants.[37]

Labor force participation of women and excluded groups is high but primarily as unskilled and low paid workers

Women were 51.8% of the total labor force in Nepal in 2017.[38] Women's participation in the labor force is high mainly because of their participation in agriculture sector as wage laborers. A larger proportion of women (84%), compared to men (62%), are engaged in agricultural work, household-based extended economic activities, and maintenance work.[39] Three quarters of the unpaid family labor force are women.

The number of women in the nonagricultural sector is very low due to lack of skills, education, and mobility; household responsibilities; and inadequate time to seek opportunities or to participate in skills and capacity development activities. They also lack financial resources and have low risk-taking ability due to their dependence on family members. Agriculture is the most dominant source of livelihood for many social groups. Around 75% of the households in groups like Hill Chhetri and Tarai Janajati mainly rely on agriculture and related activities for livelihood. Dalits have the highest dependence on casual labor (52%).[40]

Trainees and employers have negative perception about vocational education and training

There is a perception that TEVT is meant only for lower income strata and for excluded groups and low skilled people, and not for children of well-off and educated families. This suggests that only poorly qualified and low skilled people are available in the market.[41] The School-to-Work Transition Survey, Nepal (2008) shows that, while vocational education or training has helped the youth get into permanent or career jobs, they still consider vocational education or training less respectful. Employers also give higher level of importance to academic qualifications. The credibility of the training provided by TEVT institutes is also questioned. The trained graduates do not have the workplace level skills that employers look for, hence, the perception toward the TEVT graduates is negative (Box 4.3).[42]

36 ADB. 2018. *Skills Development Program: Quarterly Progress Report (January–March 2018)*. Kathmandu.
37 SASEC/ADB. 2018. *Fourth Quarter Reporting (as of March 2018) of South Asia Subregional Economic Cooperation-Power System Expansion Project (SASEC), Status of GESI Action Plan Implementation*. Kathmandu.
38 World Bank. 2017. *World Development Indicators: Labor Force Structure*. http://wdi.worldbank.org/table/2.2.
39 Government of Nepal, CBS/NPC. 2008. *Labor Force Survey 2008*. Kathmandu.
40 O. Gurung and M.L. Tamang. 2014. *Nepal Social Inclusion Survey 2012, Caste, Ethnic and Gender Dimensions of Socio-economic Development, Governance and Social Solidarity*. Kathmandu: Central Department of Sociology/Anthropology, Tribhuvan University. p. 17.
41 Swiss Agency for Development and Cooperation (SDC). 2018. Consultation meeting with Dr. Usha Bhandari. Kathmandu.
42 Meetings with different stakeholders. GESI Diagnostic Study. June 2018. Kathmandu.

Box 4.3: Importance of Skills Testing

The Tracer Study of Skill Test Graduates surveyed 1,498 skills-tested graduates and 43 employers in the construction and hospitality sectors. Results show that 68% of the respondents belonged to the construction sector, which had 73% men. On the other hand, women marginally led at 51% in the hospitality sector. Out of 1,498 graduates, 39.13% were found employed, either in Nepal or in a foreign country; 18% self-employed; and the remaining 42.87% unemployed. Out of 565 respondents employed in Nepal, 11.3% received less than the minimum salary specified by the Labor Law (NRs9,700). The respondents claimed that personal networking with employer was key to finding and securing employment. This was supplemented by their experience and skills certificates from the National Skill Testing Board. The employers were positive about skills certificates as it assured them that a candidate had the basic skills, job ethics, and good behavior.

Source: CTEVT/Nepal Vocational Qualifications System (NVQS) (Swiss contact). 2018. *Tracer Study of Skill Test Graduates: A Report*. Kathmandu.

Service providers show low priority and less interest in training women and excluded groups

Service providers have low commitment in building the skills of women and excluded groups because they perceive working with them as an extra burden.[43] The reluctance of employers and structural constraints (care work, safety and security, caste-based bias) deter the service providers who then take tokenistic measures but do not put intensive efforts to ensure these people are as employable as others.

Good Practices and Lessons

Special measures to promote skills training and employment of women and excluded groups

To ensure that women and excluded groups can access skills development efforts, specific measures should be in place, such as representation of women in various courses, employment in nontraditional fields, expanding access to technical education, and specific interventions that effectively caters to the marginalized groups (Box 4.4).

Strategies to encourage and prepare women for skills training and employment

Employment Fund (a project implemented by Helvetas and funded by DFID Nepal) demanded its service providers that at least a certain percentage of women trained by them (preferably in nontraditional skills) would be employed after the training. The technical education service providers learned that strategies were needed to motivate women and prepare them for employment (Box 4.5).

---

43   Meeting with GESI Adviser, Centre for International Studies and Cooperation (CECI). GESI Diagnostic Study. June 2018. Kathmandu.

Box 4.4: Measures to Increase Access of Women to Skills Training

The Skills Development Project (2013–2019) funded by ADB (grant of $20 million) and the Government of Nepal ($5 million) supported the development of a market-responsive, social, and gender-responsive technical education and vocational training (TEVT) system. The project adopted a gender equality and social inclusion (GESI) action plan, with specific GESI activities under each of the project outputs. The project aimed to ensure that women and members of excluded groups had equitable access to short-term technical education and vocational training and equal access to long-term TEVT by setting enrollment targets. In addition, service providers were mandated to provide enhanced pre- and post-training to facilitate women's and excluded group's transition into waged employment or self-employment (target of employing 40% women and 30% excluded). The project focused on the need to create opportunities for women in nontraditional industries, such as construction, where there were skill shortages, and to make up for the loss of skilled Nepalese men working overseas.

The project recruited GESI experts to provide technical support in implementing the GESI action plan. A GESI officer (whose education level is Intermediate in Commerce and gazette III class) was also nominated to lead the day-to-day management. GESI was under the responsibility of a regional monitoring officer who was trained and assigned as GESI officer. GESI elements were integrated in request for proposal, bidding, and evaluation criteria; hence GESI was mainstreamed in the service provider selection process and contract signing. The memorandum of understanding included GESI principles in all activities, particularly in trainee mobilization and selection, training operation, and training materials on supporting gainful employment of women and excluded groups. GESI training for the management staff, coordinator, and trainers was made mandatory to the school. Hence, all related staff were trained.

Source: Council of Technical Education and Vocational Training. 2019. Skills Development Project: Project Evaluation Study, Final Report. Kathmandu.

The Enhanced Vocational Education and Training (EVENT) I (2011–2015) of the Ministry of Education (funded by World Bank) aimed to expand the supply of skilled and employable labor by increasing access to quality training programs and by strengthening the TEVT system in Nepal. The project incorporated special incentives for trainers who provided training for women and excluded groups. The project also initiated the practice of having a Women Window with the aim to train women in nontraditional trades. EVENT I benefited a significant number of women—out of 73,392 trainees provided with short-term training, 41% were women. Through the Women Window, the project also trained 5,025 women in 15 different types of nontraditional skills. Majority of the women (1,071) signed up for training to become a building electrician, followed by those seeking to become junior poultry technician and junior computer hardware technician. This special focus on expanding access to technical education and vocational training of poor women, and young people from excluded groups and lagging regions, is underpinned by robust communication, outreach, engagement, and feedback strategies.

EVENT = enhanced vocational education and training, GESI = gender equality and social inclusion, TEVT = technical education and vocational training.

Source: World Bank Nepal. 2015. EVENT I Reports. Kathmandu.

Box 4.5: Strategies to Include Women in Nontraditional Trades

Situation analysis. Conduct research and analysis in each specific location before doing training in the communities and ensure that the community members will be able to continue to work in the trade.

Counseling and exposure visits. Provide a clear orientation about the training and the trade before enrolling women in nontraditional trade training. Counsel before and after the training to prepare women and their families for future employment. This should include visits to women's homes to talk to them and exposure visits to the workshops so that women and their families are more aware and can select possible options.

Life skills training before trade training. Life skills training (for 5 days) before the trade training would help women to build the confidence and awareness they need, since historical disadvantage and years of subordination psychologically constrain women's social skills of dealing with the public domain.

Family engaged in the trade. Women trained in trades which had family members find work in the same trade much easier.

Engaging business owners. Another strategy was to engage business owners on a freelance basis as trainers for the training. They would then hire women trainees as employees after completion of the training.

Workshops offered by training and employment service providers. Some training and employment service providers were companies with workshops that had trained and employed women.

On-the-job training and tools. On-the-job training was a crucial strategy to offer women with employment for 6 months and work experience after the completion of their training. Provision of tools to women encouraged them to take training in nontraditional trades.

Diversification of trades. Training in more than one trade and usually in several trades that are both traditional and nontraditional helps women in finding employment. If women are trained in only one sector of specialized trades, such as hospitality, it is challenging for them to find employment.

Source: Helvetas-Swiss Development Cooperation, Government of Nepal, Department for International Development, World Bank Group. 2015. *Learning Series: Training and Employment Service Providers Observations and Strategies regarding Women in Nontraditional Trades.* Kathmandu.

Looking Forward: Issues and Opportunities to Consider

This section highlights key learnings that merit consideration by ADB in sector and project analyses and in discussions with government counterparts.

Market feasibility studies and alignment of demand and supply requirements are essential for better employment of trained women and excluded groups

Feasibility and market studies are needed for the training to be better aligned to requirements and become more useful. Approximately 114,000 students attend long-term and short-term courses in Nepal annually;[44] but the tracer study shows that of the respondents covered in the study, almost

---

[44]   Government of Nepal, Ministry of Education. 2017. *Comprehensive TEVT Annual Report.* Kathmandu.

43% were unemployed.[45] The discrepancy between skills and labor market needs is a critical factor in preventing women and excluded groups from finding or maintaining stable employment as they tend to have less education, fewer skills, and less mobility than men and dominant social groups. A better understanding of what market exists for what types of skills is needed. A situation analysis in each specific location before doing training in the communities is essential to realize whether the training will have any impact and whether the trainees can work in the trade.[46]

Targeted courses can facilitate access of women and excluded groups to different opportunities, including in the nontraditional sector

Targeted courses for skills development provide opportunities for women and excluded groups to improve their skills and employability. Special efforts for their intake by CTEVT resulted in an increase in the number of trainees from such social background. Without explicit targets for excluded groups, not as many trainees from the groups would have benefited from skills training.

A national curriculum of vocational training for PWDs should be developed with intensive engagement of PWDs themselves. The possible training courses that could be designed and provided for PWDs include, but are not limited to, computer software operation skills (basic office package), computer maintenance (hardware and software), mobile repair and maintenance, secretarial service and reception, and graphic design.[47]

Another key learning from the projects has been that targets should not be uniform across all training areas. The nature of the trade, target beneficiaries' level of interest, training location, population density of excluded groups, and market readiness should be properly assessed before setting trade-specific targets.[48]

To facilitate the transition into waged employment or self-employment of women and excluded groups, the ADB-supported Skills Development Project (SDP) provided pre-and post-training support.[49] Opportunities were also developed for women in nontraditional industries, such as construction, where there are skill shortages due to absence of Nepalese men working overseas.

Specific support and affirmative action facilitate the involvement of women in male-dominated trades and link them with credit institutions, information, resources, and services so that they can capitalize on opportunities. Counseling and business literacy training is required to support their self-employment. According to the experience of Employment Fund, some nontraditional trades require timely counseling, including motivation and advocacy visits, which exposes women and family gatekeepers to key information that can provide them options to engage in skills development training or employment. As a result, nontraditional trades such as mobile repair and bamboo crafts-making are gradually being perceived as more acceptable for women.[50] Counseling was found essential as

45   CTEVT. 2018. *Tracer Study of Skill Test Graduates: A Report.* Kathmandu.
46   Employment Fund, Helvetas-SDC, Department for International Development, World Bank Group. 2015. *Learning Series: T&E Observations and Strategies Regarding Women in Non-Traditional Trades.* Kathmandu (Disaggregated data is unavailable).
47   M. Prasai. 2010. *Relevant Vocational Trainings for the Persons with Disabilities in Nepal.*
     https://rcrdnepa.files.wordpress.com/2011/07/relevant-vocational-trainings-for-persons-with-disabilities-in-nepal.pdf.
48   ADB. 2013. *Project Completion Report, Skills for Employment Project.* Manila.
49   The Skills Development Project was initiated on 24 October 2013 and closed on 15 January 2019.
50   The Employment Fund in Nepal provides short-term skills training to women and men aged 16–40 years. It was implemented by Helvetas and Nepal's Ministry of Energy and funded by SDC, DFID, and WBG.

a specific strategy to prepare women and their families for women's employment after the training. Motivational and advocacy visits and exposure of women and family gatekeepers were important strategies also for a more informed selection of options.

Setting targets for women and excluded groups in training courses and ensuring quality should be balanced

Setting a quota for the participation of women and excluded groups in training courses is needed, otherwise their presence is minimal or completely absent in some sectors. SDP has set enrollment targets for women and excluded groups to increase their equitable access to short-term technical education and vocational training and equal access to long-term TEVT. However, experience of SDP suggests that quality may have been compromised at times, in the attempt to fulfill required targets, with participants being enrolled without full assessment of their ability or potential to use the acquired skills (though government PCR data demonstrates that 17,082 women, representing 86.4% of the total women enrollees in Level 1, Level 2, and midlevel training courses of the SDP, were found gainfully employed).[51]

Preparation and sensitization of service providers on GESI is needed for effective training and employment of women and excluded groups

Orientation of the service providers is crucial to enhance their understanding and skills to address GESI issues in their work. The trained service providers in projects promoted GESI principles in all their operations, specifically in mobilization, training, and the incorporation of GESI in training manuals. This kind of preparation and sensitization has not been done as a routine practice in all training courses. The lack of preparation activities or in-depth, regular orientation of service providers results in inadequate attention to issues of women and excluded groups. Discriminatory values and beliefs of service providers determine their priorities and what kinds of services they provide to whom, hence it is important to orient and sensitize them.

Making the training facilities more GESI-friendly would create an enabling environment for more women and excluded groups to proactively enroll and participate in trainings. A GESI-friendly facility involves having separate toilets for women and men, provisions for childcare facilities including accommodation for child caretaker, sanitary pads for emergency use, and if possible arranging accommodation or partnering with institutions that provide short-term stay—these were undertaken in ADB-supported skills development projects. When recruiting instructors and managers, affirmative action to encourage women instructors and instructors from excluded groups would promote higher numbers of women and excluded groups to attend training courses.

Widespread communication and outreach campaigns in multiple languages and different forms of media are necessary to make information easily accessible to women and excluded groups, who many times, are unable to participate due to lack of information.[52] Information campaigns with women's associations and identity-based organizations or community stakeholders are required to increase awareness and social acceptance of the community-wide benefits achieved from skilling women and excluded groups.[53]

---

[51] Meeting with the Project Director, Skills Development Project. July 2018. Kathmandu.
[52] ADB. 2013. Skills Development Project (2004–2012). *Project Completion Report*. Kathmandu.
[53] Swiss Development Cooperation. 2006. *Gender and Skills Development Report*. Geneva.

TEVT service providers require policy directives, incentives, and systematic follow up and monitoring to ensure GESI aspects are integrated in their services

It is important to systematically work with service providers at different levels to institutionalize GESI in service delivery, GESI-related policy provisions, financial arrangements, and skills and systems strengthening. GESI should be mainstreamed in TEVT-related policies, institutional mechanisms, and training courses. Strategies such as including GESI responsibilities in provisions of agreements with service providers and basing financial arrangements or assistance on compliance with GESI provisions are needed. For example, Employment Fund pays the final installment for a training implemented by a training and employment service provider (TESP) only after it verifies the number of trainees gainfully employed (defined as a monthly income of NRs4,600) 6 months after the completion of the training.

Provisions to incentivize service providers for employment of women and excluded groups are necessary. The World Bank's Enhanced Vocational Education and Training Project (EVENT I and II) incentivized the sector through scholarships and subsidization of the cost of training and skills test.[54] SDP implemented varied placement incentives based on perceived degree of difficulty with employment generation and job placement.[55] While SDP included GESI provisions in TESP selection criteria, stricter monitoring procedures are required to ensure effective implementation by TESPs and the project implementation unit.

Dedicated staff with responsibility for GESI mainstreaming is necessary to provide technical response, and to identify and optimize emerging opportunities to achieve GESI results. Systems to program and budget with GESI aspects and to maintain disaggregated data are also needed.

Along with technical focus, it is important to do parental education and work with the society to gradually eliminate discriminatory norms

A key learning is that technical skills building is insufficient for women and excluded groups to benefit from their training. For example, Employment Fund targeted women and trained them as masons. Many women masons received the opportunity to work in the reconstruction of their villages that were affected by the 2015 earthquake. But when the work was completed, they could not market their skills and work in other areas because of gender-based constraints such as unpaid care work and mobility restrictions. Safety and security issues also constrain their ability to seek employment elsewhere.[56]

Without parental permission, it is difficult for girls and young women to select courses which are nontraditional. In SDP, some parents did not allow girls to enroll in a welding course as it would spoil their looks which was important for their marriage.[57] Skills programs need to educate young women

---

54 EVENT 1 (2011–2015), EVENT 2 (2017–2022). International Development Association project appraisal document on a proposed credit for SDR42.7 million ($60 million) to Nepal for the Enhanced Vocational Education and Training Project II. 8 September 2017.

55 Placement bonuses vary according to the perceived degree of difficulty with employment services and job placement of the following four categories: (A) women from discriminated groups, Dalit, Adivasi, disadvantaged Janajati, Madhesi, Muslims and women who are widows, physically disabled, remote rural dwellers or landless Tarai dwellers; (B) economically poor women not referred to under category A and economically active women who wish to upskill from level 1 to level 2; (C) men from discriminated groups, Dalit, Adivasi, disadvantaged Janajati, Madhesi, Muslims and women who are widows, physically disabled, remote rural dwellers or landless Tarai dwellers; (D) economically poor men not referred to under category C and economically active women who wish to upskill from level 1 to level 2. See ADB. 2013. Project Administration Manual. *Nepal Skills Development Project*. Kathmandu.

56 Meeting with a trained mason. GESI Diagnostic Study. 15 July 2018. Sindhuli, Nepal.

57 Interview with Skills Development Project team. 21 June 2018. Kathmandu.

and their families about the relative returns of different trades and encourage them to go to higher-paying fields. Young women are channeled into traditionally women-friendly trades that are less lucrative and lack sufficient market demand. The Employment Fund successfully overcame this by incentivizing the training providers to focus on employment. To address such structural constraints, project components require to integrate interventions such as advocacy with women, excluded groups, family and community gatekeepers, and service providers (Table 4.1).

Table 4.1: Tip Sheet on Integrating Gender Equality and Social Inclusion Perspectives in the Skills Development Sector

Barriers	Actions to Address the Barriers
Discriminatory gender and social norms constraining women and excluded groups from accessing sector resources and opportunities	Conduct social marketing and raise the awareness of women, families, and communities on the benefits of skills development. Prepare persons with disability (PWDs) and their families in using learned skills efficiently for income opportunities Organize exposure visits, interactive discussions, and demonstration.
Poor information access by women and excluded groups to technical educational vocational training (TEVT) courses and job prospects	Conduct information campaigns and use different mediums and appropriate languages. Request local community facilitators and groups to inform communities regarding courses, employment prospects, and other relevant information.
Limited social acceptance of women and excluded groups in nontraditional trades	Carry out advocacy, demonstration, and counselling to transform negative perceptions of "nontraditional skills" for women, Dalits, and other excluded groups.
Limited gender equality and social inclusion (GESI) mainstreaming in policy and institutional arrangements of TEVT sector	Support government at all levels (federal, provincial, and local) to review and develop policies supporting skilled employment of women and excluded groups. Mainstream gender in TEVT institutional system: policy, programs, and budgetary processes. Establish monitoring and evaluation systems for TEVT with disaggregated database.
Skills training not aligned with market needs	Conduct labor market analysis to determine training needs and opportunities for women and excluded groups.
Expensive technical and vocational courses	Provide scholarships, easy loans, and subsidized fees for women and excluded groups. Establish quotas and other affirmative measures to increase excluded groups' participation in skills training. Provide mobile training camps to ease access and reduce costs.
Limited mainstreaming of GESI aspects in training courses	Review and revise (as required) training curriculum, delivery modalities, registration procedures, and evaluation forms to incorporate GESI aspects. Train instructors and trainers on GESI so that they can recognize and respond to GESI issues during the training.

continued on next page

Table 4.1 continued

Barriers	Actions to Address the Barriers
Inappropriate training environment	Use safe, disabled-friendly accommodation and hostel facilities for students, such as separate housing facilities for boys and girls.
	Ensure availability of separate toilets, transportation systems, zero tolerance to sexual harassment, and due respect for participants and staff irrespective of their class and ethnicity.
	Provide childcare and breastfeeding facilities for women trainees who are young mothers.
	Make appropriate adjustments of methodology and timing.
Lack of interest among service providers and employers to promote women and excluded groups in the sector	Inform service providers and employers about the government's affirmative action policies and programs in TEVT.
	Incentivize service providers and employers through various strategies such as subsidization of training and skills test costs.
	Prepare and sensitize stakeholders about inequalities between social groups and how addressing gender and caste or ethnic-based bias contributes to country's progress.
Low employment prospects of women and excluded groups in higher paid sectors.	Implement systematic apprenticeship programs to provide opportunities to newly skilled trainees, especially from excluded groups, to practice their skills as interns or apprentices.
	Set up job counseling centers within all TEVT institutions with special capacity to advise students from different genders, caste, ethnicity, geographic location, and economic class.
	Introduce diversified nontraditional programs specially geared for women, Dalits, PWDs, and students of other excluded groups.
	Develop partnership with labor market key stakeholders, employers, government, and the private sector to guarantee job availability for graduates.

GESI = gender equality and social inclusion, TEVT = technical education and vocational training, PWD = person with disability.

Source: Table prepared for this study.

5

TRANSPORT

Area of collaboration	ADB assisted Nepal's transport sector through 65 projects, valued at 18.32% of its cumulative lending, grant, and technical assistance commitments from December 1966 to December 2018.
	Improvements to strategic urban and rural roads, including roads in remote regions, account for most of the investment. Areas of collaboration between ADB and the Government of Nepal also include enhanced transport connectivity within Nepal and with neighboring countries, transport policy, and capacity of transport institutions.
Sector context	The most popular modes of transport in Nepal are road transport and aviation. The nation's often difficult terrain has made a large section of the population dependent on walking. Nepal has a road network which serves as a basic road connector and requires regular maintenance, upgrading, and further connection to other districts.
Gender equality and social inclusion (GESI) considerations relevant to sector planning and outcomes	Gender and caste/ethnicity differentials in travel patterns and resources determine the use of road infrastructures and transport modalities. Gender and disabled-friendly road infrastructures are limited, constraining the mobility of these groups.
	Multiple roles and competing demands result in women minimizing their travel time and choosing work opportunities at shorter distances from home.
	Opportunities in the labor or employment market are affected by accessibility differences. Income opportunities in the transport construction sector are not equitably available to all due to differential capacities.
	Despite increased representation among women and excluded groups, their voice is still limited, and they are unable to influence decisions in transport planning.
Good practices and lessons	Policy provisions, capacity building, and institutional mainstreaming in the road transport sector facilitate effective GESI integration (e.g., training of staff, appointment of focal persons, promotion of gender- and disabled-friendly infrastructure)
	Making improved transport access increase economic opportunities for women and excluded groups requires additional measures (e.g., providing them with access to financing to open new businesses alongside improved road networks.)

Looking forward: Issues and opportunities to consider	It is essential to identify and analyze differentiated transport needs and gaps.
	Livelihood and entrepreneurial opportunities in transport services and roadside amenities need to be GESI-responsive.
	Affordable modes of transport for all, especially for women and excluded groups, should be promoted.
	Socioeconomic impacts should be analyzed and introduced in appraisal tools as alternative transport evaluation criteria for estimating benefits and costs (e.g., using accessibility, mobility, and health effects as indicators instead of travel time).
Further resources	Tip sheet on addressing barriers experienced by women and excluded groups and integrating GESI in the transport sector (Table 5.1).

GESI = gender equality and social inclusion.

Area of Collaboration

Transport has been a lead sector in the partnership between ADB and the Government of Nepal. ADB has provided assistance to the sector with 65 projects worth $1,158.92 million,[1] which is 18.32% of its cumulative lending, grant, and technical assistance commitments to Nepal from December 1966 to December 2018.[2] Improvements to strategic urban and rural roads, including roads in remote regions, account for most of the investment. Other areas of collaboration between ADB and the government include enhanced transport connectivity within Nepal and with neighboring countries, transport policy, and capacity of transport institutions.

Sector Context

The nation's often difficult terrain has made a large section of the population dependent on walking. The most popular modes of transport in Nepal are road transport and aviation. Others include ropeways and one railroad. During the past 5 years, Nepal's transport sector has grown at an average rate of 7%. Currently, the sector accounts for 11% of real GDP. The transportation industry directly provides employment to almost 20,000 people.[3] The Nepal transportation system depends largely on the road network. The country has a total road network of 80,078 kilometers (km). Out of former 75 districts, only 67 district–headquarter roads are linked with all-weather roads. Two district headquarters, Humla and Dolpa, are not yet connected by road.[4] Most of these roads work only as basic road connectors and

---

[1] ADB. 2018. Nepal by the Numbers. *ADB Data Library*. https://data.adb.org/dashboard/nepal-numbers (Data about projects and funds is cumulative from 19 December 1996 to 31 December 2017 and covers all assistance).

[2] ADB. 2018. Cumulative Lending, Grant, and Technical Assistance Commitments. *ADB Data Library*. https://data.adb.org/dataset/cumulative-lending-grant-and-technical-assistance-commitments (accessed 27 December 2019).

[3] Government of Nepal, Ministry of Industry, Office of the Investment Board, Investment Board Nepal. 2017. *Transportation Sector Profile*. Kathmandu. p. 4 (Disaggregated data is unavailable).

[4] Department of Roads, Nepal. http://dor.gov.np/home/page/ssrn-2015-16.

require regular maintenance, upgrading, and further road connection to other districts (footnote 3). The length of Strategic Road Network in FY2015–2016 was 12,898 km of which black-topped was the highest with 6,823 km and graveled the lowest at 2,044 km. Earthen roads were 4,030 km (footnote 4). Half of the population now enjoys access to paved roads. Travel time, on average, has dropped to nearly 80%.[5] In hill areas, one-third of residents walk more than four hours to reach an all-season road and this is worse in the mountain regions (Figure 5.1).

Nepal's railway line has a total length of 57 km, out of which only 5 km is currently operating. The country has one international airport and 56 domestic airports. Although comparatively expensive, air transport facilitates tourism and trade because it is safer, reliable, and cost effective.

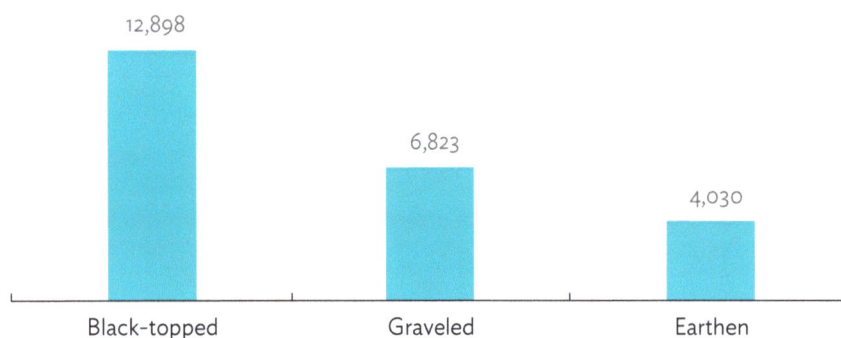

Figure 5.1: Situations of Roads in Nepal, Fiscal Year 2015–2016 (kilometer)

Source: Government of Nepal, Office of the Investment Board and Ministry of Industry. 2017. *Transportation Sector Profile.* Kathmandu. https://ibn.gov.np/uploads/files/Sector/Transportation_Sector%20Profile.pdf.

Policy and Institutional Framework

There are policies and laws regulating the sector, some of which are discussed below from a GESI perspective. The two key ministries at the policy level are the Ministry of Physical Infrastructure and Transport (MOPIT) for strategic roads and the Ministry of Culture, Tourism and Civil Aviation for air transport. The regulatory and implementation bodies are MOPIT's three departments (Roads, Railways, and Transport Management), Department of Local Infrastructure (DOLI), and Civil Aviation Authority of Nepal. The Road Board Nepal is responsible for raising funds for road maintenance.

Strategic Roads Network

MOPIT has been executing strategic roads, railways, and transport management sector programs throughout the country. Following national mandates, it approved GESI Guidelines in 2017 and is working on its implementation. Other sectoral policies do not specify GESI aspects explicitly, such as the following:

---

5   World Bank. 2017. *Strengthening Connectivity in Nepal.* http://www.worldbank.org/en/news/feature/2016/02/17/strengthening-rural-connectivity-in-nepal.

- The Public Works Directives guide the overall infrastructure development of the country. A review of the Public Works Directives indicates that GESI issues have not been specifically addressed in other sections except for social assessment. There is so limited recognition in the description of roles and responsibilities—in planning, implementation, and post-implementation stages, or of project staff and committees—that a more specific mandate of provision for effective inclusion is necessary. Aspects such as hiring of consultants or coordination with other agencies also do not reflect an understanding that different strategies or qualifications recognizing different competencies could result in a more diverse profile of consultants or partner agencies. The general and sector procedures have demanded assessment of the target group needs and social-environmental constraints which provide space for GESI related analysis. The guidance has stated that social inequalities and gender issues be assessed.

- In the Conditions of Contract for Works of Civil Engineering Construction prepared by the International Federation of Consulting Engineers, the duties and authorities of engineers and contractors and the contractual agreements are detailed but there is no mandate for GESI integration. The roles of key officers, contractors, contract agreements, the construction site provisions, and the engagement of labor are some areas that require directives for addressing GESI.

- The Public–Private Partnership Policy (2015) aims to enhance public–private sector investment for public infrastructure services through the adoption of the public–private partnership (PPP) model. It prioritizes physical infrastructures and transportation (roads, bridges, airports, railways, cable cars, ropeways, and all ports) for PPP projects.[6] The policy requires full or partial capital investment of private entities for the purpose of construction, rehabilitation or modernization of infrastructure services with responsibilities to operate, maintain and deliver infrastructure services. The public sector, on the other hand, is required to provide the legal framework and necessary support for implementation and to have the oversight responsibilities (footnote 6). There are no provisions to promote an enabling environment for addressing issues of women and excluded groups in the different stages of the PPP process.

- The Private Financing in Build and Operation of Infrastructures Act (2006) states that involvement and financing of the private sector is important in the build, operation and transfer of infrastructures in consistency with the liberal economic policy pursued by the country.[7] This act has several chapters with provisions relating to project implementation, including rights and facilities of licensee and formation of committees. The project coordination committee is mandated to work with the concerned local government unit and include a woman member for monitoring projects.

---

[6] Government of Nepal, Ministry of Finance. 2015. *Public–Private Partnership Policy, 2072 (2015)*. (Unofficial English translation). Kathmandu.

[7] Government of Nepal. 2006. *Private Financing in Build and Operation of Infrastructures Act, 2063*. Kathmandu. www.moppw.gov.np

■ The main thrust of the Public Procurement Act 2007 (which has been recently amended)[8] is to establish legal provisions to make the procedures, processes, and decisions relating to public procurement more open, transparent, objective, and reliable; and obtain the maximum returns of public expenditures in an economical and rational manner by promoting competition, fairness, honesty, accountability, and reliability in public procurement processes.[9] Furthermore, it aims to ensure good governance by enhancing the managerial capacity of public entities in procuring goods, consultancy services, and other services, and in ensuring equal opportunity for producers, sellers, suppliers, construction entrepreneurs, or service providers to participate in public procurement processes without any discrimination. However, the act does not recognize that women and excluded groups experience structural constraints in accessing procurement processes and participating as suppliers, service providers, or entrepreneurs. No provisions have been made to encourage or promote their equitable participation in public procurement processes. Similarly, the Public Procurement Regulation (2007) does not have provision on GESI issues.[10]

Rural Roads Network

The Department of Local Infrastructure Development (DOLI, previously DOLIDAR), which is under the Ministry of Federal Affairs and General Administration (Ministry of Federal Affairs and General Administration, previously Ministry of Federal Affairs and Local Development [MOFALD]), is responsible for rural transport and development in Nepal. The DOLI adopts the Local Infrastructure Development Policy which recognizes and considers GESI. The ministry has its own GESI policy, and its provisions must be effectively integrated in all local infrastructure development projects.

Environmental and Social Management Framework

The 2007 Environmental and Social Management Framework (ESMF) and its addendum of 2013 has a number of provisions for women and excluded groups such as removal of gender-biased wages, fair payment to women laborers, establishment of grievance offices, tracking of number of women employed (at least 30% employment reservation for women), and specific strategy to promote good opportunities for vulnerable groups and women. The public consultation framework has specified numerous measures to ensure the participation and inputs of women and excluded groups.[11]

---

8   The Public Procurement Act 2007 (2063) (the "PPA") and Public Procurement Rules 2008 (2064) (the "PPR") deal with the requirements and procedures relating to public procurement in Nepal. The First Amendment to the PPA has been introduced on 14 July 2016 (2073-03-30 B.S.), referred to as the "First Amendment." Subsequent to the First Amendment, certain provisions of the PPR have also been amended notably by: (i) Fourth Amendment dated 19 December 2016 (2073-09-04), and (ii) Fifth Amendment dated 9 March 2017 (2073-11-26), collectively called as the "PPR Amendments." While some processes have been relaxed and selected public entities exempted from competing with private organizations, there are no provisions addressing the specific barriers of women and excluded groups. See Pioneer Law Associates. *Legal News: Amendment to Public Procurement Law.* http://www.pioneerlaw.com/news/amendment-to-public-procurement-law.
9   Government of Nepal. *The Public Procurement Act, 2063 (2007).* http://ppmo.gov.np/image/data/files/acts_and_regulations/public_procurement_act_2063.pdf.
10 Government of Nepal. 2007. *The Public Regulation.* http://ppmo.gov.np/image/data/files/acts_and_regulations/public_ procurement_rules_2064.pdf.
11 Measures include holding separate meetings with women and excluded groups during both the environmental and the social impact assessment; at least 30% of employment reserved for women; women are adequately participating, and fairly paid for similar type of work as men, and that there is no child labor; women are fully informed of the process and procedures of resettlement, and the opportunities and rights they have from potential sources of income. Contractors need to be made liable to observe gender quota in awarding jobs to unskilled labor. See Government of Nepal. 2017. *Environment and Social Management Framework. Chapter 5: Public Consultation Framework.* Kathmandu.

Outcome level Indicators have been included, such as participation of women and excluded groups in users' committees, road construction employment contracts, employment in commercial enterprises, change in ownership over assets, and status in decision-making and mobility.[12]

Policy Provisions for Persons with Disability

Section 4 of the Constitution, which lists the government's directive principles, policies, and responsibilities, has a provision for safe, well-managed, and disabled-friendly transportation sector to ensure easy and equitable access to transportation services for all citizens. The recently promulgated People with Disability's Rights Act 2017 further establishes the rights of PWDs, including the right to mobility and the right to access all public facilities. Nepal has also signed international conventions for PWDs which require the government to provide adequate facilities for universal access. The Five-Year Strategic Plan for Road, Rail and Transport Sector (2073–2078) recently prepared by MOPIT requires all urban roads to be pedestrian and PWD-friendly. The UN Convention on the Rights of Persons with Disabilities (UNCRPD), which Nepal signed and ratified in 2010, has a provision on accessibility (Article 9).[13]

After Federal Restructuring

After federal restructuring, the Department of Roads was given authority to do procurement and construction of road infrastructure for all strategic roads. For other rural and municipal roads, the concerned municipalities have authority to procure all the works within their boundaries. For province level roads connecting more than one municipality, the provincial governments may establish infrastructure department to procure and do construction works.[14]

Gender Equality and Social Inclusion Considerations Relevant to Sector Planning and Outcomes

Situation of women and excluded groups in the sector

Inequitable access to paved and dirt roads

According to NLSS 2011, the mean travel time of 51% households to the nearest paved road was less than 30 minutes. A disaggregated analysis of NLSS data indicates that a wide disparity exists between the access of different social groups to paved roads (Box 5.1).[15]

---

[12] Government of Nepal, Ministry of Physical Infrastructure and Transport. 2017. *Environmental and Social Management Framework: A Guide to the Environmental and Social Issues Associated with New Road Construction and Upgrading (Final Version)*. Kathmandu. http://dor.gov.np/home/publication/gesu-publication/force/environmental-and-social-management-framework.

[13] Article 9 of *UN Convention for Rights of Persons with Disability* states "To enable persons with disabilities to live independently and participate fully in all aspects of life, States Parties shall take appropriate measures to ensure to persons with disabilities access, on an equal basis with others, to the physical environment, to transportation, to information and communications, including information and communications technologies and systems, and to other facilities and services open or provided to the public, both in urban and in rural areas." See UN CRPD. Article 9. Accessibility. https://www.un.org/development/desa/disabilities/convention-on-the-rights-of-persons-with-disabilities/article-9-accessibility.html.

[14] Meeting with World Bank procurement specialist. 27 April 2018. Kathmandu.

[15] LAHURNIP. 2014. A *Study on the Socio-Economic Status of Indigenous Peoples in Nepal*. Kathmandu. https://www.iwgia.org/images/publications//0712_social-economic-status-of-indigenous-peoples-of-nepal.pdf.

Box 5.1: Access to Paved Roads of Different Social Groups

Around 75% of Newar households and 61% of Hill Brahmin households have access to paved roads within 30 minutes while only 56% of Tarai Janajati and 45% of Hill Chhetri households have access to such roads within 30 minutes. About 80% households of Hill Brahmins, 70% of Hill Chhetri, and 69% of Hill Dalit can reach the nearest dirt or earthen roads within 30 minutes. People in the Tarai have better access to dirt roads. Hill indigenous peoples have the least access to dirt roads, with only 64.5% able to access a dirt road within 30 minutes from their homes. Many must spend more than 3 hours to reach the nearest dirt road. The Janajati groups, in particular, experience geographical isolation due to their remote settlements. Historically, Janajati groups, such as Magars, Limbus, Rais, and Tamangs, have lived in settlements that are remote and farthest from the district headquarters.

Source: LAHURNIP. 2014. *A Study on the Socio-Economic Status of Indigenous Peoples in Nepal.* Kathmandu. https://www.iwgia.org/images/publications//0712_social-economic-status-of-indigenous-peoples-of-nepal.pdf.

Measures enabling local communities to use constructed roads have been limited, hence a research was conducted. The study reveals that the hill regions, cash-poor subsistence farmers, and women are the least able to afford transport services or to take advantage of the access to service outlets.[16]

The road system in Nepal often lacks footpaths, and those that exist are often in poor condition, blocked by vehicles, rubbish, vendors or roadside furniture, and are lacking in ramps and other features that would assist PWDs. It is often unsafe to cross the road because of poor compliance to traffic rules, a high proportion of two- and three-wheel vehicles, and deteriorating road surfaces. These problems affect the safety and access of all people using the road, and present a significant challenge to PWDs—who may have a greater need for a smooth and continuous path and lesser speed when crossing roads, and have sensory impairments that constrain their perception and prediction of emerging traffic situations.[17]

Limited recognition in transport planning of local movement of goods and people, and differentiated needs of women, PWDs, and excluded groups

Often transport tasks in rural areas do not require people to move along the district-level road networks (e.g., to access water facilities, education, finance, health centers, and markets). Local transport links, using local paths, and relying on walking and head-loading or using intermediate means of transport is more common than using main roads and motorized transport. Conventional transport planning does not take into consideration this local movement of goods and people due to lack of recognition of the differences in the needs and interests of citizens, particularly PWDs.

---

[16]   K. Molesworth. 2005. *The Impact of Transport Provisions on Direct and Proximate Determinants of Access to Health of Women.* Basel, Switzerland: University of Basel.

[17]   Global Health Action. 2018. *Addressing Transport Safety and Accessibility for People with a Disability in Developing Countries: A Formative Evaluation of the Journey Access Tool in Cambodia.* https://www.ncbi.nlm.nih.gov/pmc/ articles/PMC6237176/.

Women's ability to use roads and other transport means is impacted by household structures, family composition and size, household roles as well as mobility and transport burden.[18] They often carry a heavier burden in terms of time and effort spent on transport, while having less access and control over resources. In some communities, existing cultural norms prohibit women from taking advantage of improved access to transportation. For example, rural Muslim and Madhesi women do not generally travel out of the village while they do so within their communities especially for household related tasks, and thus do not equally use improved road access.

The requirements of PWDs are inadequately recognized and addressed during transport planning. For instance, space and ramps for wheelchairs and facilities for the visually and hearing impaired are often unavailable, and the design of curbs and road gradients do not meet the requirements of people living with disabilities. The transport plans have not so far identified and addressed the barriers faced by PWDs in reaching and accessing a transport stop, intersections, and crossings; getting a vehicle, boarding, and arriving to the destination; and in dealing with public transport staff who are not sensitive to the needs of the disabled.

Differential capacities of women and PWDs in road construction employment opportunities

Women and PWDs are at a disadvantage in manual work required for road construction which are perceived as "heavy," as they have different physical capacities and their outputs in physically strenuous tasks are considered minimal. There is often a distinction between "heavy" versus "light" work whereby the definitions are based on cultural norms of work rather than the actual difficulty and physical exertion required for such work.[19] Additionally, contractors are reluctant to recruit women workers due to poor safety and security conditions in the work place. Work sites for road construction are far from villages, and the environment in labor camps can be at times unsafe for women.

Due to the need for daily wages, the poor are unable to benefit from short-term employment opportunities in rural road construction where payment is generally once every two weeks or monthly. Safe accessible road networks for PWDs are also underdeveloped in Nepal.[20]

Poor skills for construction related tasks result in limited opportunities for women and excluded groups. Appropriate skills that can give confidence to contractors to recruit women for specific tasks require investment in strengthening capacity, such as on-the-job training. Due to a lack of capable human resource from the target group, a gap exists between their low skills and the available employment for skilled works.[21]

[18] N. Sultana and I. Mateo-Babiano. 2017. *Transport Disadvantage and Gender Issues in South Asian Countries: A Systematic Literature Review.* Ho Chi Minh City.
[19] R. Holmes and N. Jones. 2011. *Public Works Programmes in Developing Countries: Reducing Gendered Disparities in Economic Opportunities?.* International Conference on Social Cohesion and Development. Paris. http://www.oecd.org/dev/pgd/46838043.pdf.
[20] World Bank, Asian Development Bank, and Department for International Development. 2012. *Gender and Social Exclusion Assessment 2011 Sectoral Series: Monograph 6 on a Rural Infrastructure.* Kathmandu.
[21] Meeting with Geographic and Environment Support Unit, Department of Roads. 18 June 2018. Kathmandu.

Strong challenges for women contractors

There are more than 300 women who are registered as contractors in Nepal, but only a few of them actively pursue construction as a career.[22] There are many women who are small contractors managing $5,000 to $10,000 worth of works. Their capacities need to be strengthened to manage larger scale construction. There are a range of issues women experience as contractors (Box 5.2).

Box 5.2: Issues of Women Contractors

It is a huge challenge to work as a woman contractor because of lack of support from the Federation of Contractors Association of Nepal. There is no recognition that women, along with their professional work, must manage home and care responsibilities as well as safety and security issues. For women contractors, a major challenge is to manage the financial resources required to win contracts or bids. At least $500 to $1,000 is needed to bid (depending on the size of the contract). Collateral is needed before the advance of 20% is made once bids are approved. To raise sufficient funds in order to continue work when payments are delayed is difficult, and a credible reputation has to be built before institutions forward loans to women contractors. A wide range of skills is needed from managing labor to working with senior government officials. The ability to manage site work, human resources, and financial assets is essential.

Source: Meeting notes. 19 June 2018. *Interview with Kamala Bhattarai, woman contractor*. Kathmandu.

Gender and caste and/or ethnicity differentials in travel patterns and resources determine use of road infrastructures and transport modalities

Women, especially rural women, have travel needs which require them to make short local trips, with multiple stops for various tasks such as water and fuelwood collection, dropping children to school, visiting nearby health facilities, carrying agricultural produce to local markets, and going for wage labor to neighboring areas. Global research has established that women are responsible for a disproportionate share of the household's transport burden with limited access to available means of transport.[23]

These journeys can be made more difficult if pathways or services are planned without regard to such patterns or if fares penalize short journeys or multiple stops. The transport planners have not so far addressed the structural issues of work burden and time poverty of women and the poor.[24] Transport costs are another important concern as women and the poor have lower incomes, with women having more limited claims on household resources.

PWDs experience disadvantage and marginalization due to inadequate disabled-friendly infrastructure. Designs that could support the mobility of people with different disabilities are not integrated in road infrastructure, and vehicles are not disabled-friendly.

---

[22]   Meeting with the president of Federation of Contractors Association of Nepal. 24 June 2018. Kathmandu.

[23]   World Bank. 2014. *Gender, Travel and Job Access: Evidence from Buenos Aires*. https://pdfs.semanticscholar.org/d1ee/bb650ccf4c6926d49894f200702994b4d588.pdf?_ga=2.83324950.1416792073.1591676658-46736508.1591676658.

[24]   ADB. 2015. *Sri Lanka: Gender Equality Diagnostic of Selected Sectors, Transport: National, Provincial, and Rural Roads*. Manila. p. 40.

Multiple roles and competing demands result in women and the low-income group minimizing their travel time and choosing work opportunities at shorter distances from home

Unpaid care work, subsistence agriculture, and social and cultural norms define women's time use resulting in their high work burden. These constrain their travel options and reduce their flexibility to identify and participate at different levels of transport sector activities or seek employment opportunities, which in turn, interfere with their household management tasks.

For the poor, the compulsion to earn daily wages forces them to engage in paid work that results in time poverty for other tasks. It restrains them from accessing employment opportunities which would not pay them immediately. They are unable to participate in capacity development events or decision-making forums due to the pressure of daily survival.

Opportunities in the labor or employment market are affected by accessibility differences

Due to the travel options available, women and the poor are geographically limited to a smaller number of opportunities and jobs. The mobility provided by the transportation system can increase options for employment and the ability to consider opportunities which require higher commute time. For women and the poor, this is especially significant as otherwise the selection of possible employment is constrained from the beginning of an individual's job search. A few jobs available locally with poorer remuneration are sometimes the only options available. The employment opportunities in neighboring areas are out of bounds due to the time and costs involved and, for women, the gender norms that disadvantage their mobility options.

Income earning opportunities in the transport construction sector are not equitably available to all

There are numerous income-earning opportunities in the transport sector, however, women have been mostly engaged as unskilled laborers as are men of excluded groups. Disaggregated data on people employed at different levels of skilled and unskilled construction works of projects in Nepal are unavailable. The common practice is for women and excluded groups to be mostly employed as unskilled labor. There is high wage differential between skilled and unskilled labor. Opportunities for construction work do not arise unless there are specific interventions targeting women and excluded groups.

Despite increased representation, women and excluded groups have limited voice and inability to influence decisions in transport planning

The planning of transport projects reflects limited attention to the priorities and requirements of women and excluded groups, including people of lower income groups and PWDs. The focus is on roads rather than on the network of footpaths and footbridges that many rely on, or on making the construction process PWD-friendly. The affordability and reliability of transport, which can support mobility, have not been considered in transport planning. This reflects the minimal presence of women and excluded groups in decision-making processes.

Due to policy directives, there have been efforts to increase representation of women and excluded groups in users' committees (when formed, usually only for rural roads). However, without the more substantive transformations needed to enable them to influence decisions, women and excluded groups in the user communities are often less represented; hence, their voice is limited in decision making. Nevertheless, quota for their representation in such committees is in practice and needs to be continued with additional capacity development.

Good Practices and Lessons

Measures to improve transport access can increase economic opportunities for women and excluded groups

The removal of bottlenecks, such as high transportation costs or lack of credit mechanisms, contributes to increased transport related business opportunities. Examples of good practice in transport projects include providing women and excluded groups with access to financing to pursue transport-related businesses, such as farm-related transport activities; liberalizing the provision of transport services to improve service quality and frequency that will lower transport costs for women micro-entrepreneurs; and opening of new businesses by women alongside improved road networks.[25]

Policy provisions, institutional strengthening, and capacity development can facilitate effective GESI integration in the transport sector

Projects supported by ADB, World Bank, and the Swiss Agency for Development and Cooperation (SDC) in Nepal have demonstrated that policy provisions are required to address GESI issues in transport projects. Many countries have developed gender equality policies and worked on strengthening capacities (Box 5.3).

Recently, Sajha Yatayat, a public transportation bus system in Nepal serving Kathmandu and its surrounding valley, has introduced PWD-friendly buses which are equipped with ramps, and the doors and gangways are wide enough for wheelchairs. The buses also have space for parking and strapping wheelchairs.

Box 5.3: Gender in Transport Policies and Institutional Structures

Uganda demonstrates a good practice in legal and policy provisions and a supportive institutional structure at national and district level to mainstream gender equality. Road sector programs and projects in Uganda have continuously addressed gender issues. A gender management plan was developed to mainstream gender at the Ministry of Transport. The plan focuses on building stakeholders' capacity, development of a communications strategy, and establishment of a monitoring system.

Source: World Bank. 2013. *Lessons Learned from Uganda's Gender Mainstreaming Policy in the Road Sector.* Washington DC.

At the project level, Peru's Second Rural Roads project exemplifies a good practice in gender capacity building. The *Provias Descentralizado*—the implementing agency—played an active role in developing an inclusive, demand-driven transport planning model based on participatory project design and implementation. The agency trained its staff on gender awareness and appointed regional gender focal points to help track

continued on next page

---

[25] World Bank Group. 2010. *Mainstreaming Gender in Road Transport: Operational Guidance for World Bank Staff. Transport Paper Series; No. TP-28.* Washington DC. p. 24. https://openknowledge.worldbank.org/handle/10986/17455.

Box 5.3 continued

gender-related indicators. Training and education around gender mainstreaming contributed toward increasing women's participation in roadworks and related projects. Gender quotas in rural roads committees, procurement processes, and the road maintenance system based on community-based microenterprises also significantly benefited the implementation and monitoring aspects of the project.

Source: World Bank. 2010. *Mainstreaming Gender in Road Transport: Operational Guidance for World Bank Staff, Transport Paper.* Kathmandu. p. 20.

In Nepal, the Ministry of Physical Infrastructure and Transport developed the Gender Equality and Social Inclusion (GESI) Operational Guidelines with ADB's technical support. The GESI guidelines provides guidance for mainstreaming GESI in the ministry and its sectors to ensure that a GESI-responsive approach is adopted to improve access of women and excluded groups to resources and benefits from the sector and to institutionalize GESI programmatically and institutionally. Provisions from the guidelines include hiring women contractors, allocating a certain percentage of project budget for auxiliary works targeted to women and excluded groups, promoting skilled employment of the target group, and providing GESI-friendly work environments.

Source: Ministry of Physical Infrastructure and Transport. 2017. *Gender Equality and Social Inclusion Operational Guidelines* 2017. Kathmandu.

The South Asia Subregional Economic Cooperation Road Connectivity Project has integrated GESI aspects in its design and monitoring framework. For example, output indicators demand disaggregated data regarding road safety features that are friendly to elderly people, women, children, and person with disabilities at appropriate locations. Awareness raising sessions on preventive human trafficking were conducted for about 2,000 communities with 50% women; and around 30% women participated in tree plantation programs.

GESI = gender equality and social inclusion.

Source: ADB. 2016. Project Administration Manual of the South Asia Subregional Economic Cooperation Roads Improvement Project. Manila.

Looking Forward: Issues and Opportunities to Consider

Strategic and rural roads and bridge projects implemented by the government demonstrate that it is essential to mainstream GESI in transport sector interventions, as only then efforts are made to bring about transformative changes. Examples of these efforts are ensuring that women and disadvantaged groups (i) participate in consultations on rural and strategic road and bridge construction to identify their needs; (ii) work in a conducive environment covering safety, insurance, and child care; (iii) are employed with equal wages; (iv) are proportionately represented in decision-making within user committees; and (v) are trained in construction-related activities.[26] These initiatives need to be systematically implemented in all transport sector programs.

---

[26]   Wise Nepal. 2017. *Gender Mainstreaming in Rural Transport Projects in Nepal - Policy Brief*. London: ReCAP for DFID. https://www.gov.uk/dfid-research-outputs/gender-mainstreaming-in-transport-projects-in-nepal-policy-brief. Based on research in Ramechhap and Okhaldhunga Districts in Nepal.

Identify and analyze differentiated transport needs and gaps

Gender and social impact analysis should be incorporated into all transport planning and project implementation. This will enable the sector to facilitate the movement of different modes of transport (motorized, nonmotorized) based on mobility needs of citizens of diverse social profiles. Gender-differentiated roles result in significant differences in trip purpose and distance, transport mode, and other aspects of travel behavior. In addition to accessing the labor market, women use transportation to take care of their households and families, which shapes their travel requirements. Hence, the significant role which transport plays in the lives of women and people from excluded groups must be studied and integrated into transport planning and works.

Based on such analysis, travel needs, patterns, concerns, priorities, preferences, and personal safety parameters of women and excluded groups (e.g., PWDs) need to be included in the design of transport projects and services. Transport investments that are designed with GESI dimensions can bring significant benefits to women, not only in terms of increased access to employment, markets, education, and health services, but also in terms of caretaking and household responsibilities that the majority of women hold—ultimately contributing to the wellbeing of the community at large.[27]

A multidisciplinary team from the planning stages, including engineers, sociologists, social development specialists, gender specialists, economists, and anthropologists, can provide a better representation of the infrastructure, social, and economic needs of individuals and the community, and offer a comprehensive analysis for transport planning.

MOPIT also requires formulating and enforcing urban street standards with universal designs that are applicable to all citizens and wherein PWDs can have better accessibility at the same time.

Create GESI-responsive livelihood and entrepreneurial opportunities in transport services and roadside amenities

The transport sector is key to economic activities, and the development process within the sector provides opportunities for employment. Targeted efforts are required to ensure that women and excluded groups access such benefits. Various projects have provisions for increasing employment opportunities for women (Box 5.4).

A major challenge is to improve the skills of women and excluded groups so that they can access higher paid skilled job opportunities in the transport infrastructure and management sectors. Focused capacity development interventions would support those interested to grow in the field.

---

[27]   C. Crespo-Sancho. 2015. *Why We Need Gender Strategies in the Transport Sector.* Washington DC: World Bank. https://www.weforum.org/agenda/2015/09/why-we-need-gender-strategies-in-the-transport-sector/.

Box 5.4: Employment Opportunities by Sector Projects

The World Bank's flagship Strengthening National Rural Transport Program has adopted a GESI approach (also guided by the Road Maintenance Guideline 2016) to address poverty and create employment opportunities for women and excluded groups.[a] The project employs 2,708 road maintenance workers, mainly women, who maintain 5,421 km of roads in 36 districts. The workers are recruited from the poorest households situated along the road sections to be maintained. Each road maintenance group consists of four to five workers in charge of 8 to 10 kilometers of road sections. They are specifically responsible for routine and recurrent maintenance, as well as emergency maintenance. Payments are made through bank transfers based on performance of the workers. Occupation, safety and health aspects are carefully addressed, and workers are provided with protection equipment. Additionally, the banks provide livelihood enhancement services, such as loans and skills development training, to the road maintenance group workers.

[a] The guidelines focus on generating employment opportunities for excluded groups within the program's zone of influence. Under the social criteria, it clearly mentions that preference must be given to female candidates, and states that transport infrastructures should have all-women maintenance workforce where possible. If not, at least 33% of the workforce needs to be women and 40% should come from the disadvantaged groups (e.g., Dalit and Janajati).

Source: Diagnostic study meeting notes. 2018. *Interview with project coordinator, Strengthening National Rural Transport Programme.* Kathmandu.

Nepal's Rural Access Programme, supported by the Department for International Development, is designed as a poverty and GESI-focused project. The program's geographic coverage, the midland far West of Nepal, has some of the highest poverty levels and the largest percentage of female headed households in the country due to isolation and migration. About 87,700 individuals living in the mid and far West of Nepal have better access to new roads as a result of the project. In addition, 2.1 million people have sustained income from maintenance of existing roads. Labor-based targeting ensures that all workers are poor (under the national poverty line) and come from excluded groups. As a result, among road maintenance group members, 44% are women and 68% are Dalits and Janajatis. Around 41% of workers from the road building groups are women and 25% are Dalits.

Jobs for women has been a focus under the Connect market program (a component of the Rural Access Programme) which has increased the incomes of 3,382 households. For instance, the Unilever Nepal *Hamri Didis* initiative has enabled 228 poor women to start their own small businesses, and increase their incomes by up to NRs13,000. The project is now seeking to scale up this initiative with Unilever. The team is also testing *Yuva Vayus* approach wherein lead women farmers would provide services to other farmers.

The Karnali Employment Programme (KEP) also targets the lower income and excluded groups. The DFID technical assistance has helped improve KEP systems in registering more than 18,000 workers, and enable KEP to better target work for women, introduce electronic payment, speed payment times, and increase multiyear entitlements.

DFID = Department for International Development, GESI = gender equality and social inclusion.

Source: DFID Nepal. 2017. *Rural Access Program 3: Annual Review–Summary Sheet 2017.* Kathmandu. p. 5.

Provide affordable modes of transport for women and excluded groups

Affordability and accessibility are key aspects to be considered when formulating public policies to improve equity in transport. Systematic sex-disaggregated data on modes of transport is lacking. Existing evidence suggests that in rural areas, the main transport mode of poor people, particularly women, is walking, especially where affordable public transport options are lacking. In urban areas, women are less likely to drive than men and more reliant on public transport. The number of motor vehicles registered in Nepal was reported at 45,667 units as of July 2016 (of which cars and jeeps were 28,361, and bus and minibuses were 8,978).[28] Data about women owners and drivers is unavailable but it can be safely assumed that very few women have access to private cars, increasing their dependence on others and limiting their travel possibilities. Gender differences in commute speeds and distances are reduced when women have access to a car.[29] Travel choices are determined by income and made in the context of unequal power relations within and among households and communities.

Greater investments in GESI-responsive public transportation systems and urban infrastructure (such as lanes and sufficient street lighting) are needed to reduce reliance on private passenger vehicles and to provide women and excluded groups with reliable, affordable and safe travel choices.[30]

Develop alternative transport evaluation criteria

Projects should analyze socioeconomic impacts and use them as alternative transport evaluation criteria for estimating benefits and costs (e.g., using accessibility, mobility, and health effects as outcome indicators instead of travel time). Evaluations in the transport sector focus on economic efficiency and do not measure the distributional impacts of projects and programs. A change of focus from infrastructure itself to the needs of individuals and the community, particularly those who utilize transport systems, would enable women and excluded groups to benefit more from the transport sector. Capturing the complexities and dynamics of the shifts in their lives due to the investments in the sector can provide data on project effectiveness. The results of mixed methods impact evaluations can provide examples of project design and execution that address GESI mainstreaming in transport, with the possibility of scaling up successful interventions and solutions (Table 5.1).

[28]   Census and Economic Information Center. 2017. *Nepal Number of Motor Vehicles Registered.*
       https://www.ceicdata.com/en/nepal/motor-vehicles-registration/number-of-motor-vehicles-registered.
[29]   T. Peralta-Quiros et al. 2014. *Gender, Travel and Job Access: Evidence from Buenos Aires.* Buenos Aires.
       https://pdfs.semanticscholar.org/d1ee/bb650ccf4c6926d49894f200702994b4d588.pdf?_ga=2.83324950.1416792073.1591676658-
       46736508.1591676658.
[30]   UN Women. 2018. *Turning Promises into Action.* http://www.unwomen.org/-/media/headquarters/attachments/sections/library/
       publications/2018/sdg-report-gender-equality-in-the-2030-agenda-for-sustainable-development-2018-en.pdf?la=en&vs=5653.

Table 5.1: Tip Sheet on Integrating Gender Equality and Social Inclusion Perspectives into the Transport Sector

Barriers	Actions to Address the Barriers
Transport systems do not respond to differential needs and priorities of women and excluded groups as voices of women as transport users are often not heard in consultative processes and there is no critical mass of women to influence transport planning.[a]	Analyze transport requirements of women and excluded groups based on the domestic responsibilities of women and their ability to travel in terms of distance, number of times, and monetary cost. Consult with women and excluded groups in planning and decision-making related to transport projects (e.g., selection of road alignment, physical design features, safety designs, user ticketing systems and fees). Build capacity of transport authorities and project management staff on gender equality and social inclusion (GESI). Advocate among policy makers the use of nonmotorized and intermediate modes of transport.
Nonwork travel needs are not recognized or addressed by the sector.	Provide higher quality of mobility in off-peak and off-trunk routes. Colocate retail, child and health care, and municipal services (e.g., bill payments) at transport hubs; this can lower the penalty associated with such responsibilities. Provide feeder roads, trails, and tracks for easing work burden and head-loading.
Limited skills, time flexibility, and inability to afford transport costs constrain women and excluded groups from capturing economic opportunities from improved transport.	Appropriate schemes to enable women and excluded groups to access improved transport (e.g., reduced transport costs, subsidies for transport of agriculture and other products).The ADB-funded *Pilot Border Trade and Investment Development Project in Papua New Guinea: Affordable Access to Health Services* provides cash transfers to the female head or female adult of households to cover the costs of women's bus travel to the nearest hospital on the condition that they present evidence that they accessed prenatal and postnatal care.[b] Promote capacity development measures, such as scholarships, training, and apprenticeship, for women students interested in transport-related careers.
Lack of safe, reliable transport, combined with discriminatory gender and social norms, constrains employment opportunities for women and excluded groups.	Provide social facilities (e.g., child care center, tracks/trails, market place, and storage spaces)and roadside amenities along the rural or strategic road networks. Promote gender equality and social inclusion-responsive physical designs (e.g., reserved seats, height-of-steps requirements, and panic buttons). Conduct campaigns, raise public awareness, and adopt advocacy measures to remove discriminatory norms and promote safety from sexual harassment.
Lack of required skills constrains employment opportunities.	Invest in skills strengthening of women and excluded groups with a focus on possible employment opportunities before, during, and after construction phases.
Minimal presence of women contractors in the sector	Include priority to women contractors as a criterion in contractor selection. Develop arrangements to award contracts to those who include women and excluded groups as team members.[c]

continued on next page

Table 5.1 continued

Barriers	Actions to Address the Barriers
Physical impairment may limit access to transport and activities.	Make disabled-friendly infrastructure design an integral part of planning and design.
	Ensure accessibility of transport and services so that mobility constraints of PWDs are addressed. Physical accessibility in public transportation needs improvement.
	Provide access to information and services for persons with physical, psychosocial, intellectual, neurological, and/or sensory disabilities. Train transporters on providing accessible transportation services.

[a]   ADB. 2013. *Gender Tool Kit: Transport Maximizing the Benefits of Improved Mobility for All.* Manila. p. 5.
[b]   ADB. 2009. *Papua New Guinea: Pilot Border Trade and Investment Development Project.* Manila.
[c]   Government of Nepal, Ministry of Physical Infrastructure and Transport. 2018. *Gender Equality and Social Inclusion Operational Guidelines 2017.* Kathmandu.

Source: Table prepared for this study.

6

URBAN DEVELOPMENT

Area of collaboration	Various ADB urban development projects have supported municipal infrastructure investments, urban planning, and institutional strengthening to improve the sector's service to Nepalese citizens.
	Urban infrastructure projects have supported the development of urban plans and policies that reflect greater disaster risk resilience, improved land management, and regional development.
Sector context	Nepal is one of the top ten fastest urbanizing countries in the world with a projected annual urbanization rate of 1.9%.
	Urbanization in Nepal is dominated by a few large and medium cities with an excessive population concentration in the Kathmandu Valley.
	Rapid urbanization has contributed to problems of unemployment, poverty, inadequate health care, poor sanitation, informal settlements, environmental degradation, poor infrastructure, insecure tenure, and underserviced community settlements.
	The negative consequences of urbanization are disproportionately borne by poor working women and men, young, and old. These result from high living densities, overcrowded and inadequate housing, environmentally hazardous living conditions, and rising incidences of urban violence and inadequate basic services.
Gender equality and social inclusion (GESI) considerations relevant to sector planning and outcomes	Design of urban areas and services do not reflect gender and social differentiated needs.
	Poor urban living conditions compromise the health of women and excluded groups, especially those living in informal settlements. Women are primarily responsible for all forms of waste disposal, leading to exposure to different health risks, a problem that is aggravated when no formal waste disposal services exist.
	Women and excluded groups have limited engagement in the design of urban space, waste disposal, and recycling facilities.
	There are limited interventions to address discriminatory gender and social norms.

Good practices and lessons	Project design informed by a socioeconomic and gender analysis and with GESI related project indicators has the potential to reduce barriers of women and excluded groups.

Alternative and conscious efforts are needed for women and excluded groups to benefit from urban development programs.

Strengthening the government's institutional capacity is important for mainstreaming GESI in urban development. |
| **Looking forward: Issues and opportunities to consider** | Integrate GESI in urban planning.

Create GESI-responsive legal frameworks and regulations for urban development.

Design GESI-responsive municipal infrastructure.

Enhance institutional capacity of relevant stakeholders on GESI. |
| **Further resources** | ADB tip sheet on addressing barriers experienced by women and excluded groups and integrating GESI in the urban development sector (Table 6.1). |

GESI = gender equality and social inclusion.

Area of Collaboration

As of December 2018, ADB has funded 57 projects worth $1.12 billion (which is 17.6% of its total lending, grant, and technical assistance lending) for the water and other urban infrastructure and services sector of Nepal.[1] Various ADB urban development projects have supported municipal infrastructure investments, urban planning, and institutional strengthening to improve quality of life, sustainability, economic growth, and competitiveness in Nepal (since 1989, 27 projects were specifically on urban development).[2] Urban infrastructure has improved flood management, mobility, and solid waste management, and supported the development of urban plans and policies that reflect greater disaster risk resilience, improved land management, and regional development.

[1] ADB. 2018. *Cumulative Lending Grant and Technical Assistance Commitments.* The chapters on urban development and water supply, sanitation and hygiene have the same data regarding cumulative support since ADB has WASH within its urban development sector support. The consultations in Nepal with the ADB Nepal Resident Mission and WASH experts identified the need to have separate chapters on urban development and WASH due to the significant work done in WASH in Nepal. While attempts have been made to reduce the overlap between the two intervention areas, some data and discussions have had to be repeated. See ADB. *Nepal by the Numbers.* https://data.adb.org/dashboard/nepal-numbers.
[2] ADB. 2018. *Urban Development Projects in Nepal 1989–2018.* https://www.adb.org/projects/country/nep/sector/water-and-other-urban-infrastructure-and-services-1065?terms=urban+nepal (accessed 14 February 2018).

Sector Context

Nepal is one of the least urbanized countries in Asia, however, the pace of its urbanization over the last decades has been faster and is likely to remain so. For the period 2014–2050, the country is projected to remain among the top ten fastest urbanizing countries in the world with an estimated annual urbanization rate of 2%.[3] In 2017, the share of the total population living in urban areas was 19%.[4] Urbanization is dominated by a few large and medium cities with an excessive population concentration in the Kathmandu Valley. The urban population distribution is uneven across the country. High urban growth is occurring in Kathmandu valley, Pokhara valley, inner Tarai valleys, and in market and border towns located on highway junctures between the East–West highway and the five main North–South corridors. Rapid urbanization has contributed to problems of unemployment, poverty, inadequate health, poor sanitation, informal settlements, environmental degradation, poor construction, insecure tenure, and underserviced housing plots.[5]

According to the Nepal Living Standards Survey (FY2010–2011), 16% of urban population was below the poverty line compared to 25% nationally. A higher proportion of men (compared to women) own a house or land. Urban women are more likely than rural women to own a house (9% versus 6%) and land (13% versus 9%). About 95% of urban population have access to electricity (Figure 6.1).

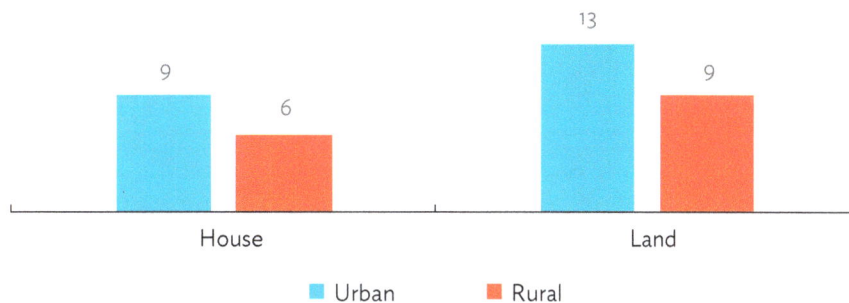

Figure 6.1: Women Ownership of House and Land in Rural and Urban Areas (%)

Source: Government of Nepal, Ministry of Health. 2016. *Nepal Demographic and Health Survey*. Kathmandu.

In the Annual Household Survey 2016, about two-third households (67%), dominantly in urban and poorest quintile group, reported to have no access to sewerage facilities. The proportion of households with access to underground drainage facility was only about 11%. About 13% had open drains. Most of the urban households (93%) as well as rural households (81%) have access to mobile phones. In urban areas, email and/or internet was used by 20%, and cable TV by 56%.

---

[3]   S. Bakrania. 2015. Urbanisation and Urban Growth in Nepal. *GSDRC Helpdesk Research Report 1294*. Birmingham, UK: GSDRC, University of Birmingham.

[4]   H. Ritchie and M. Roser. 2019. Urbanization. *OurWorldInData.org*. https://ourworldindata.org/urbanization

[5]   E. Peter and M. Roberts. 2016. Leveraging Urbanization in South Asia: Managing Spatial Transformation for Prosperity and Livability. *South Asia Development Matters*. Washington, DC: World Bank.

Urbanization can contribute to robust economic development and social mobility. However, unplanned and mismanaged urbanization results to high living densities, growth of informal settlements, environmentally hazardous living conditions, and rising incidences of urban violence. Poor urbanization also leads to inadequate access to basic services such as safe and affordable water; sanitation; drainage; electricity; solid waste management; and education, health, and social services.[6] These adverse impacts are largely and disproportionately borne by poor women and men, and the young and old.

Policy Framework

There are positive GESI provisions guiding the urban development sector in Nepal. Apart from the broader rights of equality and social justice guaranteed by the Constitution of Nepal (2015), the right to appropriate housing for all citizens has also been promised. Landless and homeless Dalits are guaranteed land and homes, respectively. House and land for livelihood or employment must be provided for the rehabilitation of bonded labors, landless people, and informal settlers. Property rights for women are also guaranteed. The 14th Three-Year Plan (FY2016–2017 to FY2018–2019) proposed the full integration of sewerage, on-site sanitation, and solid waste management in all urban schemes and specifically endorsed cost recovery from consumers.

The 2017 National Urban Development Strategy, in line with the 2007 National Urban Policy and 1996 National Action Plan on Housing and Urban Development and the National Shelter Policy, provided guidance for urban development and planning. The five guiding principles include principles about inclusivity. It calls for cities to be socially inclusive thus integrating ethnicity or caste, class, and gender in nurturing the city's social and cultural diversity, as well as for raising awareness and sensitivity of the excluded groups including the youth, elderly and PWDs, and women in general. The guidance enjoins the cities to address the poor's basic needs in education, health, housing, and transportation.

Social inclusion calls for identifying and including concerns of women and excluded groups from geographically isolated areas in infrastructure planning. Incentives and facilities are provided for the private sector to offer affordable rental housing. For effective community engagement, inclusive settlements and community-based organizations are to be promoted. Strategies for social inclusion include identification of socioeconomic issues and consideration of spatial characteristics of the urban poor, particularly in development programs and planning for the urban poor (housing, infrastructure, and transportation). For improved urban governance, GESI mainstreaming in urban institutions and social accountability through public hearing, public audit, and social audit are to be implemented. The People's Housing "Janata Awas" Program Implementation Guideline (2016) identified target groups covering 43 districts and included different models such as transitional homes (rental) and joint ownership. The GESI Operational Guidelines of the Ministry of Urban Development (MOUD) 2013 also provides guidance on mainstreaming GESI in the sectors, including urban development and building construction.

---

[6]   UN HABITAT. 2012. *Gender Responsive Urban Planning and Design.*
https://unhabitat.org/wp-content/uploads/2014/07/Gender-Responsive-Urban-Planning-and-Design.pdf. p. 1.

Institutional Arrangements

The MOUD established institutional structures and mechanisms with GESI responsibilities including the Social Coordination Unit at MOUD and its departments. GESI units were established with social development officers in regional and divisional, subdivisional, or district offices. Various training and capacity development efforts strengthened the skills of MOUD staff.[7]

After the restructuring under the new federal government, the urban development sector responsibilities have been assumed by the Ministry of Physical Infrastructure Development at the provincial level. At the urban municipality level, the urban infrastructure development division is responsible for the sector, including road and transport management, hydropower, electricity, street lighting, irrigation and water induced disasters, information and communication, facilities management and drinking water supply sections, and public–private partnership unit. GESI responsibilities are with the Ministry of Social Development in the provinces and the social development section in the municipalities.

Gender Equality and Social Inclusion Considerations Relevant to Sector Planning and Outcomes

Selected key issues impacting women and excluded groups in the urban development sector are discussed below.

Design of urban areas and services do not reflect gender- and socially-differentiated needs

The location of facilities and services and the structure of urban spaces often pose difficult challenges for women and excluded groups including people with lower mobility, such as children, older people, and PWDs. There are limited multifunctional urban spaces to accommodate the daily multitasking responsibilities of women and excluded groups. Cities and small towns in Nepal need community facilities within short travel distances to and from work, childcare, and schools such as stores and services, safe pedestrian lanes, and accessible public transportation systems. Poor women living in insecure neighborhoods are more likely to commute at late or early hours to and from work, or to and from school or training institutions. When safe, secure, and affordable options are not readily available, women and excluded groups may forego trips resulting in poorer access to services and higher unemployment because the costs of transport can be greater than the benefits of employment. The different priorities of women and excluded groups in terms of services and infrastructure are insufficiently reflected in urban policy or investments.

Informal settlers, the extremely poor, and landless people face different realities and problems, such as lack of services and subsidies, which are provided to only those with legal status or those who are formal settlers; lack of land for toilet construction; and inability to contribute 10% to 20% of the cost of a facility. These requirements need to be considered when services are planned. Due to poor public services, private suppliers are sought at a very high cost.

---

[7]   Meeting with the Ministry of Urban Development team. GESI Diagnostic Study. 20 June 2018. Kathmandu.

Poor urban living conditions compromise the health of informal settlers, especially women

Women, children, the elderly, and PWDs are all vulnerable to lack of clean and affordable water, poor sanitation, inadequate housing, and overcrowding in poorly developed urban spaces such as slums or informal settlements.[8] People living in poor urban environments have a higher risk of disease or injury and exposure to crime. This can affect their ability to sustain a livelihood. Lack of adequate and affordable housing and security of tenure results in increased vulnerability of women.[9] There is little provision to ensure that communities understand the health hazards associated with handling particular types of waste and the implications of this to the health of women and children. Women are primarily responsible for all forms of waste disposal leading to exposure to different health risks, a problem that is aggravated in the absence of proper solid waste management.

Engagement of women and excluded groups in the design of urban space, waste disposal, and recycling facilities is limited

Public engagement in urban governance and community development of women and excluded groups is still significantly hindered by lack of recognition of worth and potentials and cultural and domestic constraints. Urban planning needs to reflect the sociocultural needs of all people, including women and excluded groups. The municipal infrastructure designs are often planned without thorough consultation with women and excluded groups. Lack of needs mapping results in urban development plans and infrastructures that do not meet the specific needs and priorities of men and women from urban poor areas and communities, including those of the vulnerable groups such as children and the elderly. Lower income people living in informal settlements are further excluded from new infrastructure investments and extensions of existing service networks as their issues are not taken into consideration during construction design.

Engagement of women and excluded groups in local planning can impact the effectiveness of the design of urban cities. The plans should consider their needs particularly for transport and infrastructure for water and waste management. Women, as prime users of housing and human settlements, often have insights that can improve city plans, prevent project failures, and wastage of resources. While there have been efforts over the last decade to increase the participation of women and excluded groups in local planning processes (e.g., through social mobilization efforts, mandated settlement level consultations, and community-based forums), the quality of their participation is in question. The influence of women and excluded groups in urban planning, design, and implementation is still limited.[10]

Involvement of the social development section of the municipalities in Nepal is highly limited in the planning and budgeting processes, despite the presence of a higher number of elected representatives from diverse backgrounds after the federal restructuring. There is limited GESI responsiveness among staff and minimal number of women staff members in municipalities which also contributes to low engagement of women and excluded groups in urban development processes.[11]

---

8   UN Human Settlements Programme. 2012. *Gender and Urban Planning: Issues and Trends*. Nairobi. p. 3.
9   UN HABITAT. *Gender Responsive Urban Planning and Design*. p. 18.
     https://unhabitat.org/wp-content/uploads/2014/07/Gender-Responsive-Urban-Planning-and-Design.pdf.
10   Field work. GESI Diagnostic Study. 21–23 November 2018. Morang and Kailali.
11   Meeting notes. GESI Diagnostic Study. 20 June 2018. Kathmandu.

There are limited interventions to address discriminatory gender and social norms impacting the sector

Urban development projects in Nepal have included GESI-related activities. Examples are ADB's Regional Urban Development Project, Integrated Urban Development Project, and Secondary Town Urban Environment Improvement Project, and the World Bank's Emerging Towns Project. Many ADB and World Bank urban development projects had a community development component—implemented by a nongovernment organization—which included the construction of small infrastructure (toilets, private drinking water), and training of women and excluded groups in livelihood enhancement. Provisions for 33% representation of women in different forums are included in project documents but implementation has been a challenge, especially in getting women to assume decision-making positions. A project manager notes that "During each reporting time, we have to report the fact that targets were not met. It has been too challenging to get women engineers, supervisors, and contractors for construction works."[12] Similarly, there is still a gap in terms of meaningful engagement of women and excluded groups in forums and committees. The women who are in decision-making levels (a vital position in user groups) are unable to influence decisions as, according to views shared in the discussions, at times they are not well informed or are not listened to by men in the committees. Apart from problems in implementing existing provisions, there are limited project activities to change discriminatory gender and social norms. Activities to change social practices which constrain women and excluded groups to access project's resources and opportunities are usually not included in the project itself.

Good Practices and Lessons

There are various measures implemented in the sector to address gender and inclusion issues. Some are discussed below.

Project design informed by socioeconomic and gender analysis and with GESI related project indicators can reduce the barriers experienced by women and excluded groups

Socioeconomic and gender analysis is usually conducted to identify existing efforts and needed measures to increase project impact for excluded groups. ADB's Regional Urban Development Project (RUDP) had conducted such analysis. The World Bank's Emerging Towns Project identified the risks of elite capture of funds and projects and limited involvement of Dalits, Janajatis, and women. GESI aspects were integrated in projects with dedicated activities and indicators. For instance, the results framework of the RUDP included GESI specific targets for gender and PWD-friendly municipal offices; construction of sex segregated public, community, and school toilets; at least 33% representation of women in committees established for community development programs; women and vulnerable groups given priority in awareness-raising and skills training programs; and a GESI unit established or strengthened in project municipalities. These specific measures ensure that the project has worked to address the barriers experienced by women and excluded groups and provided some benefits to them.[13] Lessons from such efforts indicate that along with directives, internalization by staff and stakeholders about GESI is essential; otherwise, implementation gaps could be high, or project benefits could be lower than expected.

---

[12] Meeting with Bharat Neupane, Project Manager, Secondary Towns Integrated Urban Environmental Improvement Project (STIUEIP). GESI Diagnostic Study. 23 November 2018. Biratnagar.

[13] ADB. 2014. *Regional Urban Development Project: Socio-Economic Survey 2014*. Kathmandu.

Alternative and conscious efforts are needed for women and excluded groups to benefit from urban development programs

Projects have included directives for the representation of women and excluded groups in different committees and have worked through civil society organizations to increase their access to project resources and opportunities. They have allocated specific budgets for targeted activities. The World Bank's Emerging Towns Project, which ran from 2011 to 2017, had GESI-specific targets with at least 35% of the capital expenditures set aside for localized pro-poor and/or community-oriented schemes targeted at vulnerable groups, women, and children. Institutional development program for municipalities included tasks such as strengthening community and/or citizen orientation of the municipality with emphasis on vulnerable groups like Janajatis, Dalits, and women. At project closure, 55% of the beneficiaries were women and 50% were from excluded groups, which are higher than the targets of 35% and 10%, respectively.

ADB-supported projects also worked with NGOs on community development programs which enabled women and excluded groups to receive project benefits. Without a specific component for community development, households headed by women and excluded groups would not have benefited from small infrastructure works or livelihood skills development. Nepal's Janata Awas Program was clear in its targeting and had specified the target group in its guideline (Box 6.1).

Box 6.1: Janata Awas (People's Housing)

The Janata Awas (People's Housing Project) identified the following as the target group: (i) highly marginalized Dalits like Dom, Musahar, Chamar, Dusadh, Khatwe, and other Dalits; (ii) poor and marginalized Muslims; (iii) highly endangered and marginalized ethnic groups such as Chepangs, Rautes, and Kusundas; and (iv) other ethnic groups and communities. During the selection process, the guidelines recommend giving priority to the aged, single women, orphans, and physically disabled heads of households. The government's poverty card served as a reference for selecting and identifying the poor. The guideline requires 10% contribution from the beneficiaries; but in cases of the ultra-poor, single women, and the disabled, it can be waived by the decision at the district level committee. Alternative technologies and earthquake resistant technologies are to be adopted for new houses.

Source: Ministry of Urban Development. 2016. *People's Housing 'Janata Awas' Programme Implementation Guideline 2016.* Kathmandu.

A key learning from the project is the need to adopt measures that would support accurate identification of target households and the need to provide full support to extremely poor groups. Appropriation of land, which could be included in municipal maps, and additional infrastructure, such as sewerage facilities, are other aspects that should be addressed in the future.[14]

People without security of tenure have no access to basic services since government services are linked to legal ownership of land or house. To address the issues of landless people, municipalities in

---

[14]   Ministry of Urban Development. Building Consultants Pvt. Ltd. 2014. *Final Report on the Assessment of Mid and Far Western Region People's Housing Program: Implementation Challenges and Recommendations for Improved Implementation.* Kathmandu.

India and the People's Republic of China implemented various options to increase tenure security for the poor and delink land security from getting basic services (Box 6.2).

Box 6.2: Measures to Increase Tenure Security of the Poor

Municipalities in India adopted the following measures to increase house or land tenure security of the poor:

- The government has recognized temporary occupancy rights of informal settlements through notification of slums (Andhra Pradesh in India).

- Madhya Pradesh (India) has offered legal ownership of land to all slum dwellers residing in cities prior to a certain date but not allowing sale of property.

Meanwhile, the People's Republic of China used equity grants (as a mortgage) to get leases on cheap housing built by developers and by giving developers special tax rates to encourage development of cheap homes.

Source: ADB. 2016. Gender and Social Development Consultant, Project Preparation Technical Assistance, Regional Urban Development Project. *Gender Equality and Social Inclusion Assessment of Regional Urban Development*. Kathmandu.

Strengthening the government's institutional capacity is important for mainstreaming GESI in urban development

The GESI project of the MOUD demonstrates the significance of strengthening institutional capacity of government agencies and the larger impact of such efforts (Box 6.3).

Box 6.3: Gender Equality and Social Inclusion Project of Ministry of Urban Development, Nepal

The Ministry of Urban Development (MOUD) received grant support from ADB under the Integrated Urban Development Project to implement the gender equality and social inclusion (GESI) project. The project aimed to mainstream GESI and enhance GESI mainstreaming capacity of the MOUD and the departments, regional directories, and divisional or subdivisional offices under the ministry. Also, a GESI section (now known as the Social Coordination Section) was created at the ministry level. It was headed by a senior sociologist, and accompanied by an engineer, a section officer, and an assistant officer. A GESI consultant team was recruited to assist the section. The MOUD endorsed its own GESI Operational Guidelines (2013) and formed a GESI steering committee to provide guidance to the section for the implementation of the guidelines. More than 200 officials from the ministry and two departments, as well as regional and local officials, were trained to use the guidelines.

continued on next page

Box 6.3 continued

Both the Department of Urban Development and Building Construction and the Department of Water Supply and Sewerage (this department was moved to the new Ministry of Water Supply and Sanitation in 2016) also established GESI desks under senior sociologists. They developed annual GESI action plans in fiscal year 2014–2015 and received government funding for implementation. Actions by the ministry's GESI section to implement the GESI guidelines included reviewing policies, strengthening mechanisms for GESI mainstreaming into planning and monitoring activities, supporting the capacity development of staff, developing GESI training modules and toolkits, and monitoring and measuring GESI performance against targets.

GESI = gender equality and social inclusion, MOUD = Ministry of Urban Development.

Source: MOUD. 2017. Social Coordination Section Reports 2017. Kathmandu.

Looking Forward: Issues and Opportunities to Consider

This section highlights key issues and opportunities that merit consideration by ADB in sector and project analyses and in discussions with government counterparts.

Integrate GESI in urban planning

Urban planning not only identifies land uses but also ideally integrates employment with transport and housing to make places work for everyone.[15] Hence, it is essential that GESI aspects are well thought out and integrated in urban planning especially as Nepal is a rapidly urbanizing country.

GESI analysis and sex, caste, and ethnicity disaggregated data should inform the planning processes for urban development. Consultations with different social groups to identify their priorities and capacities would enable the urban space to be more responsive to their needs. Including women and excluded groups in infrastructure decision-making processes and giving them the opportunity to participate in governance can improve the way in which water, sanitation, and solid waste are managed.

Nepal has adopted participatory planning processes. Some urban projects are using participatory methodologies and socioeconomic surveys to identify priorities of women and excluded groups (e.g., under physical infrastructure and market center, roads and water supply were prioritized in different municipalities; under social infrastructure priorities, birthing center and agriculture collection centers were identified during consultations).[16] The priorities identified through such participatory methods need to be part of the planned investments with appropriate budget and skilled staff to ensure implementation. Only when the diverse experiences and needs of women and men are integrated into urban planning and design will it be possible to form inclusive urban planning procedures, public spaces, and land management (footnote 15).

---

[15]   UN HABITAT. 2012. *Gender Responsive Urban Planning and Design*. p. 4.
       https://unhabitat.org/wp-content/uploads/2014/07/Gender-Responsive-Urban-Planning-and-Design.pdf.
[16]   MOUD. 2015. *Socio Economic and Gender Analysis*. Second Integrated Urban Development Project. Kathmandu.

Training of government and municipal officials, engineers, and contractors on universal design of urban facilities would assist them to make cities and services friendly for all citizens including women, PWDs, and other excluded groups.[17]

Create GESI-responsive legal frameworks and regulations for urban development

Legal frameworks and regulations are needed at federal, provincial, and local levels to: (i) facilitate economic opportunities for women and men engaged in the urban informal sector; (ii) foster safe and secure environments for all residents, including women and excluded groups; (iii) provide GESI-inclusive land management tools for security of tenure and housing, and secure the right to the city facilities of slum dwellers and informal settlers; (iv) incorporate GESI features in the design of municipal infrastructure; (v) provide staggered utility connection costs and tariffs, subsidies for the poorest households, and equitable resettlement and compensation plans; and (vi) promote the development of policies and programs that will address violence against women and girls in public and private spheres, which impacts their access to urban services and resources.

Ensuring that women and the landless have legal status for their tenure is an important factor in obtaining basic services. Regulations are also required to ensure that women's unpaid work in the care economy is supported through appropriate mixed-land use planning and relevant municipal services, such as childcare.

The importance of positive policies is demonstrated by India's Street Vendors Bill 2012 (Protection of Livelihood and Regulation of Street Vending), which is one of the pivotal efforts in the world to protect street vendors' rights at the level of national law (footnote 15).

Design GESI-responsive municipal infrastructure

The constructed infrastructure should promote the active participation in social and economic activities and encourage employment of women and excluded groups, including PWDs, the elderly, and individuals with limited mobility. Proper drainage and solid waste management reduces environmental contamination and contributes to better health for all. These facilities need to be accessed by slum and poorer settlements of urban spaces also, not only by the elite of the cities. No garbage and better-managed wastewater in the streets of a town promote better mobility. Safe and secure places for walking or playing; well-lit roads and lanes; adequate potable water and toilets; safe, frequent, and affordable transportation; and health, school, and recreation services can decrease caregiving responsibilities of families, especially of women, and improve their safety and security. Adequately sized and designed dwellings (with at least one bedroom, toilet and bathroom, and well-ventilated kitchen) can reduce exposure of household members, especially women and girls, to indoor air pollution from cooking, and exposure of children to sexual abuse. A GESI-friendly city therefore takes into consideration the housing design; pedestrian-friendly design and child, women, and disabled-friendly public transport; positioning of public water taps for ease of use by elders and smaller persons; disabled-friendly, smooth and even paths; parks with seats and benches; clearly visible signages; safe restrooms; and projects geared to specific needs of women and excluded groups.

---

[17] National Federation of Disabled—Nepal.
https://nfdn.org.np/article/access-to-transport-services-for-people-with-disabilities-in-kathmandu/.

Enhance institutional capacity on GESI

As illustrated by the GESI project of MOUD, for urban development to be more responsive to the needs of women and excluded groups, it is essential to strengthen the institutional capacities of government agencies—especially the recently restructured local government units—and relevant stakeholders. To benefit excluded groups, GESI needs to be integrated into planning, budgeting, management, implementation, monitoring, and evaluation of urban development projects. Skills and capacities of relevant staff and decision makers to identify and respond to GESI issues of urban development should be enhanced. For instance, extending piped water supply and sewerage networks into informal and unplanned settlements poses physical and technical challenges. Technical teams need to identify innovative solutions that can be accessed by women and excluded groups in those areas. Institutional policies and strategies should be implemented to ensure women and excluded groups can directly participate in and benefit from urban development programs (Table 6.1).

Table 6.1: Tip Sheet on Integrating Gender Equality and Social Inclusion Perspectives into Urban Development

Barriers	Actions to Address the Barriers
Gender and social differentiated needs are not reflected in the design of urban areas and services.	Conduct gender equality and social inclusion (GESI) analysis and produce sex, caste and ethnicity, and disability disaggregated data to inform the design and planning processes for urban development.
The location of facilities and services and the structure of urban spaces often pose difficult challenges for women and excluded groups.	Use participatory methodologies and socioeconomic surveys to identify the priorities and needs of women and excluded groups, including persons with disability (PWDs).
Urban policy or investments on services and infrastructure that have been identified by women and excluded groups as their top priority are inadequate.	Incorporate priorities identified through participatory methods into the planned investments with appropriate budget and skilled staff to ensure implementation.
Women and excluded groups have poor access to services; and safe, secure, and affordable options are not readily available and are not elderly- or disabled-friendly.	Develop safe and secure places for walking or playing; well-lit roads and lanes; adequate potable water and toilets; safe, frequent, and affordable transportation; and health, school, and recreation services.
Poor urban living conditions compromise the health of women and excluded groups.	Ensure access of proper drainage and solid waste management by informal and poorer settlements of urban spaces also, not only by the elite of the cities.
Private suppliers provide services at high cost as alternative to poor public services.	Provide temporary occupancy rights for informal settlers and give developers special tax rates to encourage cheaper services.
Public engagement in urban governance is still significantly hindered by unequal regard, cultural, and domestic constraints.	Formulate legal frameworks and regulations at federal, provincial, and local levels to facilitate participation of women and men of excluded groups in the urban informal sector and to provide them with economic opportunities.

continued on next page

Table 6.1 continued

Barriers	Actions to Address the Barriers
Poor, women, and excluded groups, particularly those living in informal settlements, are not sufficiently consulted on municipal infrastructure designs and planning, and housing programs for the poor.	Adopt participatory and consultative approaches, increasing participation of poor, women and excluded groups, in municipal planning. Prioritize women, elderly, differently abled and children's needs when designing housing programs for the poor.
The involvement of social development section of the municipalities in Nepal is highly limited in the planning and budgeting processes.	Strengthen institutional capacities of local governments/municipalities, especially the social development sections, for urban development to be more responsive to the needs of women and excluded groups in the planning and budgeting processes.
There is limited GESI responsiveness among staff and minimal number of women staff members in municipalities.	Adopt strategies toward increasing staff diversity and strengthening the capacity of municipal staff on GESI.
Inclusion of women in policy provisions is challenging.	Include social mobilization and awareness programs as project components to increase understanding of women, families, and communities about the importance of their participation in decision-making. Invest in capacity strengthening of women to increase their influence in the meetings.
Projects have limited activities that intend to change discriminatory gender and social norms.	Incorporate in the project's design and monitoring framework and GESI action plan, activities which can further reduce discriminatory practices and improve social norms or behaviors toward women and excluded groups.

GESI = gender equality and social inclusion.

Source: Table prepared for this study.

7

WATER, SANITATION, AND HYGIENE

Area of collaboration	Since 2000, ADB has been working with the Government of Nepal to improve water, sanitation, and hygiene (WASH) in the country's small urban centers through a series of Small Town Water Supply and Sanitation Support Programs.
	ADB has contributed in strengthening Nepal's urban sector policy, regulation, and institutional framework for water and sanitation service delivery; and supported municipalities in improving infrastructure and services, including water supply, septage management and sanitation, and solid waste management.
	ADB has also supported rural communities in developing water supplies and community-based organizations for subsequent operations and maintenance.
Sector context	Access to drinking water and sanitation is a fundamental right of citizens according to the Constitution (2015). Around 64% of Nepal's population uses safely managed sanitation services, and 95% uses safely managed drinking water services (Nepal Demographic Health Survey 2016).
	A large percentage of the population suffers from waterborne diseases due to low quality drinking water and inadequate sanitation facilities. A large segment of the Tarai population depends on shallow groundwater and wells, with arsenic contamination as a major issue.
	Drinking water is inadequate. Sewer drains are directly discharged into rivers without any prior treatment. Sludge is also discharged into public drains. Solid waste management is an increasing problem in urban areas. Water supply systems in rural and semi-urban towns are more community managed than central water supply systems.
	Water sector institutions struggle to achieve operational and financial sustainability because of low tariffs, poor asset management, and inadequate institutional capacity.

Gender equality and social inclusion (GESI) considerations relevant to sector planning and outcomes	Inability to pay for construction or sanitation services or use assets to build toilets negatively impact low income communities and informal settlers. There is limited recognition of gender, child and disability differentiated requirements of WASH services. Issues in pit emptying and fecal sludge treatment services have significant impact on poor urban communities. Lack of access to appropriate water, sanitation, and hygiene services increases vulnerabilities of women and girls to violence of varying forms. Gender and social norms constrain access of women and excluded groups to information and employment opportunities in the sector.
Good practices and lessons	Subsidized connections to piped water supply and output-based aid for sanitation infrastructure support coverage of poor and vulnerable households. It is essential to effectively incorporate gender and social analysis and actions in projects, along with disaggregated indicators.
Looking forward: Issues and opportunities to consider	WASH must be viewed as a service to all, including women and excluded groups, rather than just an infrastructure. Discriminatory gender, caste, and ethnicity- differentiated labor as well as access to resources and decision-making authority need to be addressed. An adaptive, process-oriented approach that is empowering and responsive to the needs of women and excluded groups is important. GESI-supportive policies, institutional arrangements, programming, and monitoring are essential. Ensure meaningful and equal participation in leadership among women and excluded groups.
Further resources	ADB tip sheet on addressing barriers experienced by women and excluded groups and integrating GESI in the WASH sector (Table 7.3).

GESI = gender equality and social inclusion, WASH = water, sanitation, and hygiene.

Area of Collaboration

The water and sanitation sector, including in urban areas, has been a major focus of collaboration between ADB and the government. As of December 2018, ADB has funded 57 projects worth $1.12 billion in Nepal (which is 17.6% of its total lending, grant, and technical assistance lending) for the water and other urban infrastructure and services sector.[1] Improved access to drinking water has been the lead area of investment. Since 2000, ADB has been working with the government to improve WASH in the country's burgeoning small urban centers through a series of Small Towns Water Supply and Sanitation Support Projects (STWSSSPs). The goal is, by the end of the third project in 2021, more than 1.24 million people in 69 urban centers across the country would have benefited from the program. The project also aims to strengthen Nepal's urban sector policy, regulation, and institutional framework for water and sanitation service delivery.[2] The approaches and lessons learned from the small-towns model are also being institutionalized through the government's cofinancing (*Sahalagani*) program currently implemented by the Department of Water Supply and Sewerage using the government's internal financial resources.[3]

ADB worked with the Ministry of Urban Development (which included drinking water and sanitation department before a separate Ministry of Drinking Water Supply and Sanitation was formed) to develop and implement GESI Operational Guidelines. ADB has supported municipalities in improving infrastructure and services, including water supply, septage management and sanitation, and solid waste management. Rural communities have been supported in developing water supplies and community-based organizations for subsequent operations and maintenance.

Sector Context

Policy and Institutional Framework

Policy commitments

There are strong national and international mandates for inclusive WASH services in Nepal. Access to drinking water and sanitation is a fundamental right of citizens, according to the Constitution (2015), stated in Article 35 (4), "Every citizen shall have the right of access to safe water and sanitation." The goal is to ensure sustainable delivery of water supply and sanitation services for which payment, through taxes and transfers or directly through affordable tariffs, would be necessary.[4] The 15th Periodic Plan (2019/2020–2024/2025) aims to provide basic drinking water and sanitation services to 99% of the population, and expand medium- and high-quality services in the Plan period. The plan commits to implement (i) improve public health through safe, secure, and accessible drinking water and sanitation services; (ii) maintain environmental sanitation by providing access to basic sanitation services to all citizens by managing

1 ADB. 2018. *Cumulative Lending Grant and Technical Assistance Commitments*. The chapters on urban development and WASH have some overlap as the data regarding ADB support for WASH is within the urban development sector. See ADB. Nepal: By the Numbers. https://data.adb.org/dashboard/nepal-numbers.
2 ADB. 2017. *Tapping the Unreached—Nepal Small Towns Water Supply and Sanitation Sector Projects: A Sustainable Model of Service Delivery*. Kathmandu. p. 1.
3 Sahalagani Karyakram (Joint Investment Program) is one in which there is 50:50 cost-sharing between local consumers and the government. See GWP Nepal, Jalsrot Vikas Sanstha (JVS). 2018. *Water Nepal: A Historical Perspective*. September. Kathmandu.
4 Constituent Assembly Secretariat. 2015. *Constitution of Nepal* (Unofficial translation). Kathmandu.

high levels of human waste and sewage, (iii) ensure climate change and disaster management friendly WASH services; and (iv) strengthen capacity of the federal, state and local governments for sustained provision of water and sanitation services.

Since 2009, various policies have directed for increased participation of women and excluded groups in water and sanitation user groups in planning, implementation, ownership of systems, and operation of services. Some of these policies are the National Urban Water Supply and Sanitation Sector Policy (2009), the Sanitation and Hygiene Master Plan (2011), and the National Urban Water Supply and Sanitation Policy (2014). The policies aim to address the rights and needs of women and excluded groups through proportional representation and increasing their role in decision-making, and to identify urban poor and vulnerable groups requiring special assistance through social mapping. Strategies such as output-based aid (OBA), financing for poor and marginalized settlements, connection costs for poor and disadvantaged groups built into the total scheme costs, and consultations during tariff setting were implemented. As a step toward addressing equity in access to WASH services, four disadvantaged groups are identified in WASH plans: (i) poor populations, (ii) indigenous populations, (iii) ethnic minorities, and (iv) PWDs, including people living with PWDs.

The 15-year Water Supply, Sanitation and Hygiene Sector Development Plan (2016–2030) mandates that child, gender and disabled (CGD)-friendly facilities be available as part of improved services, with sufficient supply of water, separate toilets for boys and girls, handwashing with soap, and menstrual hygiene management (MHM).[5] It directs that priority should be given to women and excluded groups in cross subsidy mechanisms and to projects that mainstream GESI in large and medium systems. Under this plan, 0.065% (NRs597,000) of the total cost (NRs915,383,910) has been allocated to GESI interventions.[6] It emphasizes the importance of strengthening facilities for water security, sanitation, waste collection, and sanitary landfill sites; adoption of 3R (reduce, reuse, and recycle); and establishment of a dedicated solid waste management unit in municipalities.

In addition to national policies, international commitments such as the 2030 Agenda for Sustainable Development and New Urban Agenda have emphasized the need for water and sanitation services in urban areas. Sustainable Development Goal (SDG) 6 includes achievement of universal access to sanitation and emphasizes that special efforts are required to address the needs of women and girls and those in vulnerable situations. Urban WASH has a strong policy mandate for GESI, but field level implementation has been a challenge. Some key issues include unavailability of disaggregated data; deep-rooted biased attitudes of some policy makers and implementers; lack of meaningful participation of women who can influence decision-making processes; and lack of user-friendly, GESI-compliant structural design of WASH facilities.[7]

---

[5] Child, gender, and differently abled (CGD) friendly features:(i) Child friendly features include water taps, knobs and latches of toilet doors and windows at suitable heights and convenience for children at different ages. (ii) In gender friendly features, the toilet should be located in a safe and secure place and the door, windows and ventilation should safeguard privacy. In addition to water in schools and other public institutions, the toilet should have facilities for maintaining menstrual hygiene management. For example, a bucket with cover or lid inside the toilet or an incinerator attached just outside the toilet is essential. (iii) Disabled-friendly toilet should include a ramp up to toilet, sufficient space for a wheelchair in the passage, hand railing in the passage and, within the toilet cubicles, appropriate types of seating arrangements and support on the toilet.

[6] Government of Nepal, Ministry of Water Supply and Sanitation. 2016. *15-year Water Supply, Sanitation and Hygiene Sector Development Plan (2016–2030)*. Kathmandu.

[7] Meeting notes. 2018. *Meeting with Department of Water Supply and Sanitation, July 12, 2018*. Kathmandu

Institutional Structure for WASH

The Constitution of Nepal has envisaged complete decentralization of all aspects of planning, implementation, operation, and maintenance of WASH projects to the federal, provincial, and local tiers of government. Water supply systems in Nepal are managed by the water users' and sanitation committees both in the rural and semi-urban areas. Systems in large towns are managed either by the Nepal Water Supply Corporation (NWSC) or management board in line with Water Supply Management Board Act 2006. Small-towns are managed by the Water Users and Sanitation Committees (WUSCs). The collected tariff should be adequate to operate and maintain the systems. The progressive tariff system is helping to give value to water and addressing the needs of the urban poor.[8]

Table 7.1: Urban Water and Sanitation Service Providers Institution Models in Nepal

Urban Areas	Current Service Area	Legislative/ Institutional Framework	Functions Planning	Construction	Tariff Setting	Operations
Municipalities	Kathmandu Valley, Bharatpur, Hetauda, Kavre, Dharan, Butwal	WSMB Act (2006)	WSMB and municipality	Contractor/ WSMB	WSTFC Act (2006)	Service Providers
Large to medium-sized towns	21 towns	NWSC Act (1989, 2007 amendment)	NWSC	NWSC	WSTFC Act (2006)	NWSC
Small-towns	69 STWSSSP towns plus others supported by cofinancing program of the Government of Nepal and other funding partners	Updated 15-year plan for small-towns water and sanitation	Local bodies	Contractor/ WUSCs	WUSCs	WUSCs

NWSC = Nepal Water Supply Corporation, STWSSSP = Small Towns Water Supply and Sanitation Sector Project, WSMB = Water Supply Management Board, WSTFC = Water Supply Tariff Fixation Commission, WUSC = Water Users and Sanitation Committees.

Source: Government of Nepal, Ministry of Water Supply and Sanitation. 2016. *Draft National WASH Sector Development Plan*. Kathmandu.

The Ministry of Water Supply and Sanitation with its various institutions are responsible for WASH related service delivery.[9] The former WASH-Coordination Committees (WASH-CCs) became defunct with the introduction of the federal governance structure, and projects and programs now have to establish linkages with the new WASH-CCs formed by the ward and the municipalities. As ward level WASH-CCs are yet to be formed by many ward offices, the existing projects work in coordination with municipalities to implement and sustain ongoing WASH initiatives. Water sector institutions struggle to achieve operational and financial sustainability because of low tariffs, poor asset management, and

---

[8]   Government of Nepal, Ministry of Water Supply and Sanitation, Sector Efficiency Improvement Unit (SEIU). 2016. *Nepal Water Supply, Sanitation and Hygiene Sector Development Plan (2016–2030)*. Kathmandu.

[9]   Department of Water Supply and Sewerage, Melamchi Water Supply Development Board, Project Implementation Directorate, Kathmandu Valley Water Supply Management Board, Nepal Water Supply Corporation, Kathmandu *Upatyaka Khanepani* Limited, Rural Water Supply and Sanitation Fund Development Board, Water Supply Tariff Fixation Commission.

inadequate institutional capacity.[10] All municipalities may not have a WASH section, but the component is monitored by the Environment Section. They do not have a GESI focal person. GESI is a responsibility of the municipality either through the Environment Section or Women Development Section.

Gender Equality and Social Inclusion Considerations Relevant to Sector Planning and Outcomes

Situation of women and excluded groups in the sector

Despite significant progress, there are income, gender, caste, ethnicity, and locational disparities in the level of access to WASH services by people from different social groups in Nepal, including in urban areas.[11] Approximately 15% of the population in Nepal have no access to improved water sources. Sector figures show generally high coverage rates for all groups in accessing drinking water but disparities in sanitation service delivery exist, particularly between income levels and across social groups.

There is a high correlation between access to toilets and poverty levels. The Annual Household Survey 2016 states that 99% of the richest quintile have access to toilets while 43.5% of the poorest group have no toilet facilities. Poverty is a strong barrier as poorer households have limited access to project information and resources, and limited time for project construction and attending meetings. As financial contributions are challenging for them, the poor often contribute the bulk of the labor. There are inadequate data to assess the exact number of PWDs who face water scarcity and lack of access. However, there is evidence that points to the relative marginalization and invisibility of this population in water sector development programs.[12]

Nepal Living Standards Survey (NLSS) 2011 shows that 56% of the population has access to toilets in Nepal. About 90% Newars and 85% Hill Brahmans have this access while only 28% Madhesi "other backward castes" and 11% Madhesi Dalits have access to toilets. Piped water supply systems coverage is 52.3%. There is high income disparity as 63.4% of the richest quintile households and 28.5% of the poorest have access to piped water supply systems. There are high disparities between urban and rural areas too. In 2016, around 95% of the population used safely managed drinking water services while 65% used safely managed sanitation services, including a handwashing facility with soap and water (Figure 7.1).

The 2018 data from the Department of Water Supply and Sanitation (DWSS) shows that about 99% of the total population have access to basic sanitation facilities and 88% have access to basic water supply facilities. By the end of 2018, a total of 63 districts of Nepal achieved status of Open Free Defecation zones. Almost all people living in hill and mountain belts have access to basic sanitation facility. Coverage of sanitation facility in Tarai is at 93% which is 6% below the national coverage. Disparity in sanitation exists within Tarai districts with eight districts having less than 30% coverage to basic sanitation while people in other districts have more than 62% coverage.[13]

10   ADB. Nepal: Third Small Towns Water Supply and Sanitation Sector Project. Sector Assessment (Summary): Water and Other Urban Infrastructure and Services. Unpublished.
11   On 30 September 2019, Nepal was declared an open defecation free (ODF) country.
12   World Bank. 2017. *Including Persons with Disabilities in Water Sector Operations: A Guidance Note.* https://openknowledge.worldbank.org/handle/10986/27542.
13   The Himalayan Times, Nepal. *Water Supply, Sanitation Coverage Remains Stagnant.* Kathmandu. https://thehimalayantimes.com/kathmandu/water-supply-sanitation-coverage-remains-stagnant/.

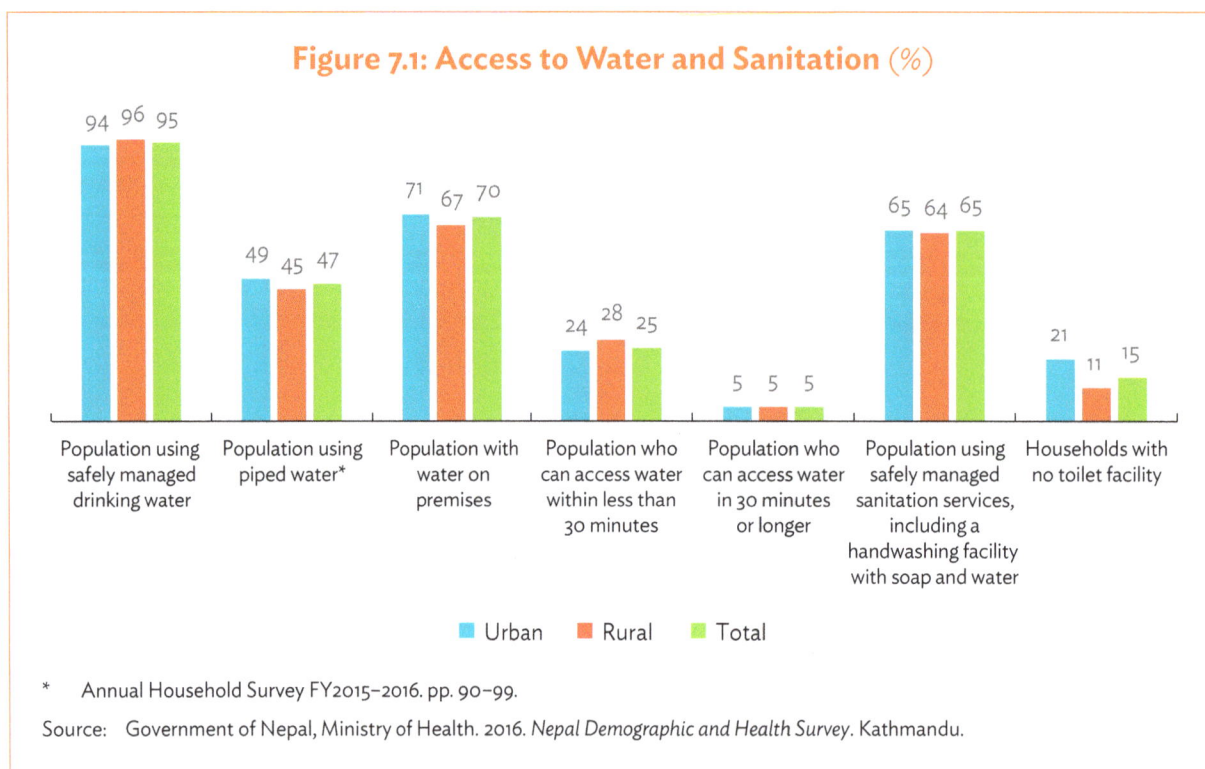

Figure 7.1: Access to Water and Sanitation (%)

*   Annual Household Survey FY2015–2016. pp. 90–99.

Source: Government of Nepal, Ministry of Health. 2016. *Nepal Demographic and Health Survey*. Kathmandu.

Disparity exists in water supply facility of the seven provinces of Nepal (Table 7.2). The coverage of water supply facility is lowest (70.45%) in Province 6, which is mainly composed of remote and mountain districts. The population of Province 3 with access to basic water supply service is 90%. Twenty-four districts have water supply coverage of more than 90%, and only four districts have coverage below 80%. Almost all households in three districts like Kailali, Dadeldhura, and Manang have access to basic water supply facility.[14]

Table 7.2: Water Supply and Sanitation Coverage in Seven Provinces of Nepal (%)

Province	Water Supply	Sanitation
Province 1	85.55	95.11
Province 2	87.86	88.19
Province 3	91.01	98.83
Province 4	89.68	100.00
Province 5	88.20	98.97
Province 6	70.45	100.00
Province 7	87.39	96.62
Nepal	87.39	96.62

Source: Government of Nepal, Ministry of Water Supply and Sanitation, Department of Water Supply and Sewerage, Environmental Sanitation Section. 2018. *Sanitation Status of Nepal: Factsheet*. Kathmandu.

[14]   C. B. Budhathoki. 2019. Water Supply, Sanitation, and Hygiene Situation in Nepal: A Review. *Journal of Health Promotion*. Kathmandu.

The School Sector Development Plan (SSDP) 2016 highlights the lack of disabled-friendly WASH facilities as a barrier for children with disabilities to enroll and remain in school. Hence, SSDP 2016 mandated sex-disaggregated and disabled-friendly WASH facilities in schools.

The current state of menstrual health and hygiene management (MHM) constrains women in Nepal in more than just physical ways. It also generates significant psychological burdens extending from embarrassment in front of peers, hindering them from living a life free from shame. Adolescent girls view menstruation and menstrual blood as "impure" and "dirty," thus they feel ashamed of it.[15] Apart from the social, cultural, and religious aspects, the severe health impacts associated with the taboos and stigmas of menstrual huts is ignored. Due to the practice of *chhapaudi* (menstrual exclusion in which women and girls during their menstruation cycle are isolated in huts), particularly in the far west Nepal, women suffer from pneumonia, diarrhea, and other respiratory tract infections. Additionally, there is an absence of strategic plans on how to identify and address the barriers faced by groups who experience multiple levels of marginalization (e.g., income poor and Dalit women living in remote areas).

Majority of the population still suffers from waterborne diseases due to low quality drinking water and inadequate sanitation facilities. Piped water is only intermittently available in most areas of the country (urban: 35%; rural: 30%), and most systems need repair. A large segment of the Tarai population depends on shallow groundwater and wells; arsenic contamination of the shallow groundwater, first reported in 2003, has become a major issue. Drinking water is extremely inadequate. Sewer drains are directly discharged into rivers without any prior treatment. Sludge is also discharged into public drains. Water conservation is not a priority. Solid waste management is an increasing problem in urban areas. Only a few small-towns have formal solid waste collection, usually weekly or biweekly, by a mini-tractor and trailer. None of the small-towns has sanitary landfill (footnote 10). These sectoral deficits impact negatively on all citizens but more so on women and excluded groups as they are forced to manage with scarce resources. Women, due to traditional work division, are responsible for household management and hence are burdened with managing water for drinking, cooking, and cleaning, and for waste management that has no proper systems. With poor hygiene, illnesses increase, resulting in higher care burden of women. Landless people (who are mostly Dalits) do not have space for toilet construction and are forced to use unhygienic sanitation measures.

Water supply provisions have largely been for domestic demands, such as drinking, cooking, washing, and other personal hygiene. Nonetheless, planning for water supply services includes municipal uses of water such as for firefighting, street cleaning, city greeneries, recreation, public drinking, and washing facilities. Other institutional and industrial water demands especially of hospitals, schools, hotels, and housings are also incorporated in the planning. However, the provision of water for these purposes highly depends on water availability. Storage of abundantly available rainwater locally for distribution in dry weather is difficult because of high land prices and difficult terrains. Provision of basic water supply and sanitation services for informal settlers and slum dwellers and for the lower income and marginalized groups have largely been neglected due to legality issues.[16] If such facilities are provided, informal settlements may acquire permanent possession of land that they have encroached upon which for many years has deprived these groups from basic amenities.

[15] PSI/Nepal, MIRA, and Maverick Collective. 2017. *Peer Ethnographic Study on Menstrual Health and Hygiene Management in Nepal.* Kathmandu.
[16] Government of Nepal. 2011. *Sanitation and Hygiene Master Plan 2011.* Kathmandu. p. 9.

With such wide gaps in the sector, gender disparities exist in access, design, construction, and maintenance of water supply and sanitation (WSS) systems. These disparities highlight a pressing need to address the urban sanitation challenge comprehensively, with emphasis on slum dwellers and poor communities that have typically been neglected. Without concerted interventions, the prospects of cholera, diarrhea, and worm infections will increase, jeopardizing education, productivity, and the quality of life of all urban dwellers.

Social equality, child, gender and disabled (CGD)-friendly facilities, menstrual hygiene management (MHM), and financial feasibility are key issues in WASH regarding GESI. The WASH services need to move beyond technical solutions and adopt a more GESI-oriented approach that considers the existing power relations between men and women, and between social groups, and how these influence access to resources and participation in decision-making process.[17]

Gender and caste or ethnicity-based barriers

Generally, women and girls continue to bear the brunt of the responsibility of water collection and maintaining sanitation facilities. It is therefore they who suffer the most from limited or no access to adequate WASH services. They are also often put at risk when they need to use or access these services. Deficiencies in services result in high costs for excluded groups, especially for women. Women are disproportionately affected by poor water supply because it forces them to spend more time fetching water and fulfilling their household role of caring for those who fall ill from contaminated water. This leaves less time for income-generating activities and, in the case of school-aged girls, for study. Disposal of sanitation materials is also a challenge in urban areas. Proper disposal mechanisms are not available in offices and other public places, which limits girls' and women's mobility during their menstruation.

Caste-based barriers and prejudices exist at public water sources, where the "low caste" people are frequently subjected to insults and emotional abuse. In fetching water, Dalit women need to queue and wait for their turn until the "high caste" people have fetched water. They must use a separate water source. They are denied access to the source of water meant for the general public on the grounds of their caste which is a gross violation of Dalits' right to water, as well as violation of their fundamental and human rights. While there has been a decrease in this practice with the increase of household level drinking water sources, it still exists in rural areas.[18]

Another barrier for women and Dalits is their inability to influence decisions regarding WASH. Even when projects ensure that Dalits are included, their time poverty and low self-esteem constrain the quality of their participation and influence in key discussions on water access and development. Language, distance, and mobility are key constraints especially for Janajatis living in remote areas. They all face significant extra difficulties in gaining access to information about projects and benefiting from them. Sanitary conditions for poor people in urban areas are aggravated by high-density living, inadequate septage and solid waste management, and poor drainage. Some key issues experienced by women and excluded groups are discussed below.

---

[17]   Government of Nepal. 2016. *Water Supply, Sanitation and Hygiene SDP (2016–2030)*. Kathmandu. p. 55.
[18]   Meeting notes. Meeting with WASH experts. GESI Diagnostic Study. 12 July 2018. Kathmandu.

Inability to pay for construction or sanitation services or use assets to build toilcts negatively impacts low income communities and informal settlers

Access to sanitation facilities is tied with land space, and therefore limited for certain vulnerable groups such as those in informal settlements and low income communities. The government is hesitant to provide WASH facilities to the informal settlers because it would give them permanent residence which would be illegal since they do not have land ownership rights.[19] There can be marginalization of specific infrastructure requirements in sanitation and solid waste management services for low-income communities. People from marginal low-lying land unsuitable for formal urban development experience delay or unfinished infrastructure. Households and settlement clusters at a distance from headquarters tend to be excluded from scheme support because of the higher project costs entailed in reaching those clusters.

There is limited recognition of gender, child, and disability differentiated requirements of WASH services

There is minimal recognition of the gender differentiated requirements of women and men, children, and PWDs for WASH facilities and services. Women and men have different requirements from facilities due to biological factors, including menstruation and pregnancy, and social and cultural factors such as expectations around maintaining "dignity" and "modesty." Women are the main caregivers for children, the sick and elderly and hence they need bigger spaces to manage them while using toilets. They also remain at greater risk of harassment and sexual violence than men near public and community toilets if precautions are not undertaken. Usually, design of services and toilets do not consider the needs of children and PWDs, which increases their difficulty in using these facilities. Lack of separate and disabled-friendly toilets impacts women and PWDs who are forced to somehow manage without the facility for long hours. Access to sanitation services is also impacted by inability to pay the use of public toilets by transient or homeless populations; barriers to the access and use of latrines by individuals within households, especially by the disabled or elderly people; and exclusion from the use of community or public facilities such as by transgender individuals.

Inadequate pit emptying and fecal sludge treatment services impact poor urban communities

Poor fecal sludge management, which is prevalent in poor communities, can result in serious health problems including bladder inflations, stomach aches, kidney stones, skin problems, urinary tract infections, jaundice, nausea, anxiety attacks, and feelings of social shame. Apart from affecting the health of all, the care work of women also increases. Despite the role of women in hygiene and sanitation at household level, toilet construction programs that provide income-generation opportunities often presume that only men will be interested in or suited for those tasks. In semi-urban areas and small-towns, the use of tractors to clean the fecal sludge is usually handled by male contractors. It is important to ensure that the supply chain for sanitation does not fail to meet the excreta disposal needs of other groups. It should not reach only the richer, sewer-based wards.

---

[19]   However, the National Water Supply and Sanitation Sector Policy 2014 aims to ensure access of women, poor and marginalized groups, informal settlers, and the disabled to water supply and sanitation services. Project implementing agencies and service providers will be required to prepare social maps to adequately identify poor communities and informal settlers requiring special assistance to avail the services so that the poor and marginalized people get and remain connected to water supply and sanitation services.

Lack of access to appropriate water, sanitation, and hygiene services increases vulnerabilities of women and girls to violence of varying forms

When women and girls access public toilets, their safety and sense of privacy is threatened by a number of factors: poor design (e.g., open roofs where men can peek in), poor maintenance (e.g., broken latches and doors), men and boys loitering around public toilet complexes, and inadequate lighting and power failure. Safety concerns limit the mobility of women and guide their behavior and ability to access essential services in their communities and even determine their timing to relieve themselves.[20]

Gender and social norms constrain access of women and excluded groups to information and employment opportunities

Gendered norms and roles of women, and caste, ethnicity, and disability-based disadvantage restrict the access of women and excluded groups to information, limit their active engagement in social and community work, and limit their opportunity for paid technical work in the WASH sector. The percentage of women, excluded groups, and PWDs engaged in technical jobs is lower than that of men. Women do not always receive equal wages, while men (of advantaged social groups) are more involved in higher paying, specialized tasks. The stereotypical division of work restricts options for women in the sector and their involvement in sanitation development and planning.

Multiplicity of policies and lack of coordination in the sector causes confusion

The WASH sector lacks a strategic and unified plan that expresses the vision of the government in both subsectors. The multiplicity of policies that exist to guide the sector reflects the fragmented institutional setup. Coordination has also been a challenge, with multiple actors continuing to work according to project-driven modalities. Attempts have been made to coordinate efforts across different actors—government, nongovernment organizations, international NGOs, and donors—by establishing national and regional coordination committees. However, these do not meet regularly or subscribe to a schedule of coordination. The absence of coordination and clear leadership leads to overlapping responsibilities and institutional gaps. While this is a general problem, it can have specific implications on inclusion.

Good Practices and Lessons

Subsidized connections to piped water supply and output-based aid for sanitation infrastructure support coverage of lower income and excluded group households

The ADB-assisted Small Towns Water Supply and Sanitation Support Projects (STWSSSP) of DWSS have implemented the output-based aid modality and facilitated the outreach to lower income and excluded groups (Box 7.1). The subsidy enabled the lower income group to purchase the materials required for toilet construction and pay for the technician. A woman claims, "We would never have

---

20   Women in Cities International (Montréal, Canada; Jagori, New Delhi, India), IDRC Canada. 2011. *Gender and Essential Services in Low-Income Communities: Report on the Findings of the Action Research Project Women's Rights and Access to Water and Sanitation in Asian Cities.* Montréal.

been able to construct the toilets if the NRs10,000 support was not provided. We had to add some resources but now we do not need to wait to relieve ourselves or go to the forest."[21] For piped water connections, connection charges were covered. Illnesses have been reduced in the communities, with women having more time to invest in productive tasks; they use piped water for drinking and tube well water for other tasks, including vegetable farming. According to a resident: "Earlier, the line in front of the health post was always so long. Diarrhea, stomach pain, and other such diseases plagued us. Now the lines are very

---

Box 7.1: Water and Sanitation for the Poor through Output-Based Aid

The Small Towns Water Supply and Sanitation Sector Projects (STWSSSP) have successfully used a strategy for explicit performance-based grants to deliver last mile connectivity and toilets primarily to poor and vulnerable groups. Under the output-based aid (OBA), grants are given to service providers (i.e., water users' and sanitation committees) after delivery of the household connections or after the construction of toilets has been verified by an independent agent. Based on the success of the OBA scheme used by the STWSSSP, the government through its Urban Water Supply and Sanitation Sector Policy 2009 has included OBA as one of the recommended models to facilitate the access of poor people to water supply and sanitation services. Around 10,000 and 4,800 latrines were provided during the first and second project, respectively, to households living below the poverty line. Based on lessons from first, second, and third projects, water connections are mandatory for all households, with no connection charges for those below the poverty line. Households headed by women account for about 18% of connections on average.

OBA = output-based aid, STWSSSP = Small Towns Water Supply and Sanitation Sector Project.

Source: ADB. 2017. *Tapping the Unreached: Nepal Small Towns Water Supply and Sanitation Sector Projects: A Sustainable Model of Service Delivery*. Manila.

---

short—a benefit of clean drinking water."[22]

It is essential to effectively incorporate gender and social analysis and actions in projects along with disaggregated indicators

An ADB topical paper *Leading Factors of Success and Failure in ADB Urban Sanitation Projects,* revealed that of 63 projects reviewed, only seven had gender-specific targets for the sanitation components. More projects should have monitored the gender-specific socioeconomic impacts of ADB's support for urban sanitation. Performance indicators on gender should be incorporated and traced during project implementation. According to the study, projects with a gender action plan (GAP)—a tool used by ADB to ensure gender mainstreaming—have facilitated more effective gender integration because the project design has adopted explicit gender objectives.[23]

---

[21]   Focused group discussion with Tharu women. GESI Diagnostic Study. 2018. Shaktinagar, Dhangadi, Nepal.
[22]   Focused group discussion with mixed group. GESI Diagnostic Study. 2 December 2018. Sitapur, Dhangadi, Nepal.
[23]   ADB. 2018. Leading Factors of Success and Failure in Asian Development Bank Urban Sanitation Projects. *Executive Summary: Independent Evaluation*. Manila. p. 31.

ICIMOD's Koshi Basin Program in partnership with Helvetas Nepal has piloted water use master plans (WUMPs) in the mountains, hills, and floodplains of the Koshi basin since 2013 to increase the participation and role of women and excluded groups in local water planning and decision-making. The participatory and inclusive approach of WUMPs has helped make the water planning process more inclusive. In the absence of such an approach, local water planning is controlled by political elites. Affirmative action adopted by WUMP to ensure participation of women and excluded groups has increased their confidence to a large extent. However, integrating GESI in the WUMP process remains a challenge because of the sociocultural barriers faced by women and excluded groups.

The Rural Water Supply and Sanitation Project in Western Nepal Phase II (RWSSP-WN II), a bilateral development cooperation project funded by the Governments of Nepal and Finland, integrates and mainstreams the principles of GESI in all its activities as a crosscutting objective. The document *Human Rights Based Approach (HRBA) and GESI Strategy and Action Plan—Operationalizing HRBA and GESI Principles in the Water and Sanitation Sector* provides useful guidance for GESI mainstreaming. The joint RWSSP-WN and RVWRMP (Rural Village Water Resources Management Project) HRBA and GESI Strategy and Action Plan merge both GESI and human rights-based approach as one comprehensive strategy that provides practical steps in translating policies and principles into meaningful action with tangible results. ADB and World Bank adopted strategies in preparing the GESI Action Plan and Vulnerable Communities Development Plan, respectively, to ensure that specific focus is maintained and activities targeting women and excluded groups are implemented within a project (Box 7.2).

Box 7.2: Gender Equality and Social Inclusion Strategies in Small Towns Water Supply and Sanitation Sector Project

Gender equality and social inclusion strategies adopted by the Small Towns Water Supply and Sanitation Sector Project include the following:

Situational analysis
- Socioeconomic survey, profile, and roster: sex-disaggregated data according to Dalit, ethnic and caste groups.

Approaches
- Selection of service area through participatory and inclusive approaches.

- Participation of women in decision-making on location and design of water points and latrines.

- Recruitment of women and men hygiene promoters. At least 15% of project staff are either women or from excluded groups.

- Equal employment opportunities and equal wages to poor women and men. Employment records disaggregated by sex.

- Women and vulnerable groups to participate in project orientation, consultations in each tole and ward, and focus group discussions.

- One separate public toilet with disabled-friendly design installed in strategic places in each town, with women's toilets designed to ensure privacy and safety.

continued on next page

Box 7.2 continued

Policies
- Pro-poor and gender-sensitive guidelines in the constitution of water users and sanitation committee (WUSCs).

Structures
- Involve women, Dalit, and Janajati in district level coordination committees for social audits.

- One of the community mobilizers must be either a woman or from vulnerable groups.

- Provision of at least 33% women in the WUSC and at least one woman in key positions. Vulnerable groups appropriately represented in general and key positions at WUSC.

- Project management office is given the responsibility to ensure integration of environmental and social safeguards, including land acquisition and gender aspects, as required in all documents, particularly in tender documents.

Capacity Development
- Gender equality and social inclusion training for WUSC members.

- Women-only project orientation seminars.

- Sanitation strategy developed as part of the water, sanitation, and hygiene campaign, including girls' menstrual health.

WUSC = Water Users and Sanitation Committee.

Source: ADB.2014. *Project Administration Manual, Nepal: Third Small Towns Water Supply and Sanitation Sector Project.* Kathmandu. p. 33.

The Framework for Inclusion of Poor and Vulnerable was adopted under the Third Small Town Water Supply and Sanitation Sector Project, and subsequently in Urban Water Supply and Sanitation Sector Project. It outlines the strategy for free water supply connections to 100% of poor and vulnerable households in the project-towns and provides the identification process and eligibility criteria for beneficiaries and fund flow mechanisms.[24]

Looking Forward: Issues and Opportunities to Consider

This section highlights key issues and opportunities that merit consideration by ADB in sector and project analyses, and in discussions with government counterparts, especially for improving service delivery.

---

[24]   ADB. 2019. *Project Administration Manual Nepal: Third Small Towns Water Supply and Sanitation Sector Project Appendix 5: Framework for Inclusion of Poor and Vulnerable Households.* Kathmandu. pp. 78–81.

WASH must be viewed as a service to all, including women and excluded groups, rather than just an infrastructure

Investments in urban sanitation infrastructure can be more effective if they are planned and managed as part of a service delivery chain to all, including women and excluded groups—supported by enabling policies. This means that small-towns or municipalities need effective urban sanitation systems, consisting of sustainable processes and service providers that will ensure the safe capture, storage, transport, and treatment of excreta in a managed and coordinated way—not just investments in hardware. The focus should be on GESI-responsive outcomes rather than inputs, which has been the pattern in most projects. The effective and safe management of excreta, rather than the construction of toilets or sewers *per se*, should be the objective of the service delivery chain. Without effective management of the wider sanitation service chain (containment, emptying, transport, treatment, and waste conversion or disposal), a sizeable percentage of waste still ends up contaminating the environment. This causes a major public health hazard which has a higher impact on women and excluded groups.

Often, the specific requirements of women and excluded groups are overlooked. Menstrual hygiene management (MHM) facilities need to be integrated and promoted as part of child, gender, and disability-friendly toilets and WASH interventions. Specific MHM facilities should be provided (i.e., lockable doors, waste management, accessible water for washing, and a maintenance plan). It is critical that establishing toilets and other facilities be accompanied with proper orientation on use and maintenance, so people would know how to use and care for such facilities. Having safe, well-sited water collection points and well-lit, women- and girl-friendly sanitation facilities, with provision for MHM, would help advance girls' secondary education and prevent gender-based violence.

Discriminatory gender, caste, and ethnicity differentiated labor; access to resources; and decision-making authority need to be addressed

The focus on providing better facilities like toilet and piped water has improved the condition of life, especially of women. However, structural issues on gender and social inequalities were not addressed substantively in the projects. There have been limited interventions with household heads or advantaged social groups on division of toilet and water related tasks. The discriminatory practices burdening Dalits and other excluded groups (e.g., responsibility given to them to fetch water) constrain their progress. Development interventions, including potential subsidy components, are important to address structural issues of unequal treatment and subordination of Dalits. Even women's water needs for home-based productive tasks are often overlooked, such as cooking food to sell, running tea shops, petty trading, and handicraft production. The focus is on reproductive roles of cooking, cleaning, and childcare and not on productive roles which can contribute to a shift in the existing power relations.

An adaptive, process-oriented approach that is empowering and responsive to the needs of women and excluded groups is important

Women and excluded groups are empowered when they have control over resources to meet their WASH needs and participate in the provision of WASH services. If they are part of the planning process and are empowered to identify uses of WASH services, they can recognize and respond to issues constraining their progress. Various efforts of engaging the community and working with municipal governments in Nepal have indicated that a process-oriented collaborative approach is effective in identifying needs and capacities of women and excluded groups, and enables them to work in coordination with their service providers (Box 7.3).

Box 7.3: Methodologies Used During Program Implementation

As part of a community-led urban environmental sanitation (CLUES) program, data about the extent of water contamination in Nala at each of the key water sources around the community was posted on a public signboard, both shocking participants and motivating them to take action. The community has around 400 households. Following the participatory CLUES methodology, the community opted for simplified sewers, together with a small local treatment plant using an anaerobic baffle reactor and a horizontal-flow, gravel-bed filter. A users' committee was made responsible for the long-term operation and maintenance of the system.

Source: Practical Action. 2016. *Urban Community-Led Total Sanitation: A Potential Way Forward for Co-Producing Sanitation Services*. Kathmandu.

In Gulariya, Nepal, Practical Action worked through the municipal government to implement community-led total sanitation (CLTS) in a peri-urban context. They engaged municipal leadership through the project management committee and invested considerable effort in informing and engaging a wide range of stakeholders through training and workshops to ensure they fully understood the CLTS process. Pressure from national government to deliver on national sanitation goals complemented their local efforts and open defecation free (ODF) status was achieved in a population of 60,000—more than 50% of whom were practicing ODF in just six months.

CLTS = community-led total sanitation, CLUES = community-led urban environmental sanitation, ODF = open defecation free.

Source: Practical Action. 2015. *Innovations for Urban Sanitation Adapting Community-led Approaches: Case Study 4*. Gulariya, Nepal.

GESI supportive policies, institutional arrangements, programming, and monitoring are essential

Specific institutional arrangements are necessary to ensure that GESI is considered an integral part of efficient and effective planning and implementation. This includes the development of GESI policies and procedures, commitment at all organizational levels, and the availability of GESI expertise and funds for targeted and supportive activities. It is important to promote diversity among service providers as there are very few women in the WSS sector. Simple measures to create a supportive working environment, such as provision of child care and flexible work schedule, can be very effective in attracting and retaining women professionals.

To ensure a more systematic and inclusive approach, GESI-sensitive interventions and monitoring and evaluation indicators disaggregated by sex, caste, ethnicity, regional identity, and location are needed. A rigorous GESI analysis should support effective programming with adequate financial resources. Guidelines and tools for addressing GESI in all aspects of a project cycle should be available as technical support for stakeholders.

The Local Government Operation Act 2017 has entrusted municipalities with the responsibility for water supply and sanitation (WSS) services. Water users' associations (WUAs) and water users' and sanitation committees (WUSCs) are key bodies for service delivery. At all these levels, GESI mainstreaming must be a key strategy and competencies of staff and officers should be strengthened to recognize and respond to the barriers experienced by women and excluded groups. Dedicated to the sanitation campaign of Nepal, the National Water Supply and Sanitation Training Center Department of Water Supply and Sewerage has developed a manual, *Options on Household Toilet Facilities for People with Disabilities and Difficulties 2017*.[25]

Meaningful and equal participation in leadership of women and excluded groups should be ensured

The WUSCs are required to have women (at least 33%) and representatives of ethnic groups among their members, and for a woman to occupy at least one of the key posts (chair, vice chair, or treasurer). Women generally dominate the position of the treasurer, although they have little or no knowledge on formal accounting and management.[26] Strengthening the capacity of women and excluded groups in these positions is important to ensure that leadership roles are not merely tokenistic or another source of dependency. It is important to identify and address gender, caste and ethnicity related barriers and issues faced by those in leadership roles to enable them to make meaningful contributions. For instance, the time poverty of women needs to be explicitly acknowledged at the beginning of the project and advocacy measures with family members should be adopted.

Equal representation and engagement of key stakeholders in decision-making, particularly in matters related to planning, implementation, and operation and maintenance, are key factors that can contribute to bridging the gap between high-level decision makers, community leaders (from advantaged groups), and women and excluded groups. Collaboration among these stakeholders can provide targeted information and communication opportunities for all the parties involved.

Given the federal restructuring in the country, there are 6,743 new wards replacing 32,358 previous wards. In the new structures, the ward WASH coordination committee chairperson can be represented in the municipality or rural municipality. The WASH coordination committee and chairpersons of municipality and rural municipality may be represented in the district WASH coordination committee. In the current scenario, the chairperson of local government structures comprised mostly of men (from advantaged groups), therefore there is probability of reduced number of women and excluded groups (who reflect the true nature of the community, with each gender, caste, and disadvantaged ethnic group represented) in these WASH coordination committees. Thus, it will be important to promote women and excluded groups for other leadership positions, especially chairperson, rather than confining them to insignificant posts (Table 7.3).

[25] National Water Supply and Sanitation Training Centre, DWSS. 2017. *Options on Household Toilet Facilities for People with Disabilities and Difficulties.* Kathmandu. https://snv.org/cms/sites/default/files/explore/download/handbook-disabilities-toilet-option-nepal.pdf.

[26] ADB. 2017. *Tapping the Unreached: Nepal Small Towns Water Supply and Sanitation Sector Projects: A Sustainable Model of Service Delivery.* Manila. p. 9.

Table 7.3: Tip Sheet on Integrating Gender Equality and Social Inclusion Perspectives in the Water, Sanitation, and Hygiene Sector

Barriers	Actions to Address the Barriers
Limited recognition of gender, child, and disability differentiated requirements of water, sanitation, and hygiene services.	Conduct assessment and consultations with women, Dalits, Janajatis, PWDs, and other excluded groups to identify priorities and prepare project designs that are GESI-responsive.
Lack of access to appropriate water, sanitation, and hygiene services by women, urban poor, and excluded groups.	Improve accessibility of women, the urban poor, and PWDs to water, sanitation, and hygiene services. Provide sex-segregated toilets, regular water supply, better solid waste management services, and assistive technologies, such as specially designed handles for water pumps or toilets, ramps and handrails, and wider doors to fit wheelchairs.
Inability to pay for construction or sanitation services.	Promote strategies, such as output-based aid, subsidies, and other creative measures, to address immediate barriers. Incentivize willingness to pay by improving water quality and regularity of supply, providing measures to reduce waterborne illnesses, and efficiently managing water fetching time.
Vulnerabilities of women and girls to violence of varying forms while using water, sanitation, and hygiene facilities.	Design facilities with features to increase safety and security of women and girls; promote awareness and strengthen capacity of women in recognizing and resisting violence; and advocate with men and boys to change mindsets regarding gender-based violence.
Local power relations and geographical inequalities are critical barriers.	Identify measures based on mapping of power relations and assessment of geographical barriers. Provide subsidies and other financial measures to reduce costs due to distance or rough terrains.
Discriminatory gender and social norms constraining women and excluded groups from accessing sector resources and opportunities.	Conduct social marketing and raise awareness of women, families, and communities on reducing discriminatory social practices. Organize exposure visits, interactive discussions, and demonstrations to provide opportunities for learnings regarding shifts in social practices.

GESI = gender equality and social inclusion, PWDs = persons with disabilities.

Source: Table prepared for this study.

APPENDIX: DATA ON SELECTED ISSUES

Table A.1: Literacy—Women

| Province | SLC and Above | No Schooling, Primary or Secondary School | | | | | Total | Literate* (%) | Number of Women |
		Can Read a Whole Sentence	Can Read Part of a Sentence	Cannot Read at All	No Card with Required Language	Blind/ Visually-Impaired			
Province 1	27.0	40.8	9.8	21.8	0.4	0.2	100.0	77.7	2,173
Province 2	12.2	18.5	7.8	61.4	0.1	0.1	100.0	38.5	2,563
Province 3	36.8	37.4	7.8	18.0	0.0	0.0	100.0	82.0	2,732
Province 4	29.0	48.8	8.6	13.6	0.0	0.0	100.0	86.4	1,249
Province 5	22.2	39.4	11.0	27.4	0.0	0.0	100.0	72.6	2,274
Province 6	19.6	36.4	10.2	33.8	0.0	0.0	100.0	66.2	724
Province 7	19.7	39.9	7.3	33.0	0.0	0.0	100.0	67.0	1,145

SLC = School Leaving Certificate.

* Refers to women with an SLC or higher and women who can read a whole sentence or part of a sentence.

Note: Percent distribution of women aged 15 to 49 by level of schooling attended, level of literacy, and percentage literate, according to background characteristics.

Source: Government of Nepal, Ministry of Health. 2016. *Demographic and Health Survey*. Kathmandu (Table 3.4.1, p. 54).

Table A.2: Literacy—Men

| Province | SLC and Above | No Schooling, Primary or Secondary School | | | | Total | Literate* (%) | Number of Men |
		Can Read a Whole Sentence	Can Read Part of a Sentence	Cannot Read at All	Blind/ Visually-Impaired			
Province 1	35.6	46.3	9.8	8.3	0.0	100.0	91.7	691
Province 2	29.7	37.4	11.0	21.9	0.0	100.0	78.1	795
Province 3	50.5	36.1	7.3	5.9	0.1	100.0	94.0	1,009
Province 4	38.6	51.0	5.2	5.2	0.0	100.0	94.8	376
Province 5	26.7	51.6	8.6	13.1	0.0	100.0	86.9	658
Province 6	35.3	45.9	10.3	8.2	0.2	100.0	91.5	203
Province 7	33.9	51.0	6.7	8.3	0.1	100.0	91.6	330

SLC = School Leaving Certificate.

* Refers to men with an SLC or higher and women who can read a whole sentence or part of a sentence.

Note: Percent distribution of men aged 15 to 49 by level of schooling attended, level of literacy, and percentage literate, according to background characteristics.

Source: Government of Nepal, Ministry of Health. 2016. *Demographic and Health Survey*. Kathmandu (Table 3.4.2, p. 55).

Table A.3: Literacy Rates by Ethnic or Caste and Religious Groups (Selected) and Gender

Ethnic/Caste and Religious Group	Population 6 Years and Older (%)			Population 15 Years and Older (%)		
	Male	Female	Total	Male	Female	Total
Hill Brahmins	89.06	70.61	79.02	88.85	65.23	75.64
Hill Chhetris	80.22	59.92	68.92	79.17	50.54	62.88
Tarai Castes	58.48	30.92	43.92	61.27	24.97	41.76
Hill Dalits	69.15	49.87	58.24	63.58	38.84	48.93
Other Hill Dalits	70.33	51.35	59.41	65.77	38.63	49.42
Tarai Dalits	47.73	16.46	31.01	49.17	11.03	28.66
Indigenous Peoples	73.96	55.47	63.87	71.63	48.53	58.64
Newar (Hill Indigenous Peoples)	85.39	66.72	75.28	85.02	61.65	72.2
Other Hill Indigenous Peoples	72.51	55.44	63.23	68.7	47.76	56.89
Other (Muslims, etc.)	59.03	35.53	46.29	61.25	28.37	42.79
Total	72.21	51.41	60.85	71.64	44.55	56.45

Source: World Bank. 2018. *Country Level Gender Equality and Social Inclusion Assessment (Annex 2)*. Kathmandu.

Table A.4: Employment Status—Women

Province	Employed in the 12 Months Preceding the Survey (%)		Not Employed in the 12 Months Preceding the Survey (%)	Total	Number of Women
	Currently Employed*	Not Currently Employed			
Province 1	59.1	7.9	33.1	100.0	2,173
Province 2	38.5	12.3	49.1	100.0	2,563
Province 3	61.5	9.0	29.5	100.0	2,732
Province 4	61.3	8.9	29.8	100.0	1,249
Province 5	59.1	9.9	31.0	100.0	2,274
Province 6	63.2	9.9	26.9	100.0	724
Province 7	70.1	12.2	17.7	100.0	1,145

* "Currently employed" is defined as having done work in the past 7 days; includes persons who did not work in the past 7 days but who are regularly employed and were absent from work for leave, illness, vacation, or any other reason.

Note: Percent distribution of women aged 15 to 49 by employment status, according to background characteristics.

Source: Government of Nepal, Ministry of Health. 2016. *Demographic and Health Survey*. Kathmandu (Table 3.8.1, p. 62).

Table A.5: Employment Status—Men

Province	Employed in the 12 Months Preceding the Survey (%)		Not Employed in the 12 Months Preceding the Survey (%)	Total	Number of Men
	Currently Employed*	Not Currently Employed			
Province 1	82.1	8.9	9.0	100.0	691
Province 2	76.4	9.3	14.3	100.0	795
Province 3	79.1	7.9	13.0	100.0	1,009
Province 4	75.6	6.2	18.2	100.0	376
Province 5	76.4	4.5	19.1	100.0	658
Province 6	76.7	11.5	11.8	100.0	203
Province 7	75.4	7.8	16.8	100.0	330

*   "Currently employed" is defined as having done work in the past 7 days; includes persons who did not work in the past 7 days but who are regularly employed and were absent from work for leave, illness, vacation, or any other reason.

Note: Percent distribution of men aged 15 to 49 by employment status, according to background characteristics.

Source: Government of Nepal, Ministry of Health. 2016. *Demographic and Health Survey*. Kathmandu (Table 3.8.2, p. 63).

Table A.6: Employment of Currently Married Women

Caste and Ethnicity	Respondent Worked in Last 12 Months (%)			
	%	In the Past Year	Currently Working	Have a Job, But on Leave Last 7 Days
Hill Brahmin	27.2	6.7	63.9	2.3
Hill Chhetri	23.6	5.8	69.4	1.2
Tarai Brahmin/Chhetri	62	2.8	35.1	0
Other Tarai Caste	51.3	11.1	37.2	0.4
Hill Dalit	21.8	10.2	66.2	1.8
Tarai Dalit	36.7	15.4	47.1	0.8
Newar	27.2	8.8	62	2
Hill Janajati	25.2	8.6	64.7	1.5
Tarai Janajati	20.9	14.4	64.4	0.3
Muslim	60.5	9.9	29.4	0.2
Other	56.5	13.5	26.7	3.3
Total	31.8	9.3	57.7	1.2

Source: World Bank. 2018. *Country Level Gender Equality and Social Inclusion Assessment (Annex 2)*. Kathmandu.

Table A.7: Cash Earnings of Currently Married Women

Ethnicity	Type of Earnings from Respondent's Work (%)			
	Not Paid	**Cash Only**	**Cash and In-Kind**	**In-Kind Only**
Hill Brahmin	49.2	43.5	5.9	1.4
Hill Chhetri	62.3	28.9	5.7	3.1
Tarai Brahmin/Chhetri	27.4	61.3	3.4	7.9
Other Tarai Caste	48.4	28.4	13.4	9.8
Hill Dalit	59.7	33.6	4.5	2.2
Tarai Dalit	17.6	36.6	32	13.8
Newar	35.3	61.1	3.1	0.5
Hill Janajati	56.1	36.7	5.8	1.4
Tarai Janajati	52.6	32.3	10.3	4.8
Muslim	31.6	42.5	18.9	7
Other	15.1	74.7	3.9	6.3
Total	51.7	35.9	8.5	3.9

Source: World Bank. 2018. *Country Level Gender Equality and Social Inclusion Assessment (Annex 2)*. Kathmandu.

Table A.8: Type of Employment—Women

Employment Characteristic	Agricultural Work (%)	Nonagricultural Work (%)	Total (%)
Type of earnings			
Cash only	13.8	89.3	36.6
Cash and in-kind	10.1	2.7	7.9
In-kind only	4.7	0.4	3.4
Not paid	71.4	7.6	52.2
Total	100.0	100.0	100.0
Type of employer			
Employed by family member	86.8	27.9	69.0
Employed by non-family member	9.4	38.1	18.0
Self-employed	3.9	34.0	12.9
Total	100.0	100.0	100.0
Continuity of employment			
All year	34.5	79.2	48.0
Seasonal	57.0	10.4	43.0
Occasional	8.5	10.4	9.1
Total	100.0	100.0	100.0
Number of women employed during the last 12 months	6,011	2,592	8,603

Note: Percent distribution of women aged 15 to 49 employed in the 12 months preceding the survey by type of earnings, type of employer, and continuity of employment, according to type of employment (agricultural or nonagricultural).

Source: Government of Nepal, Ministry of Health. 2016. *Demographic and Health Survey*. Kathmandu (Table 3.10.1, p. 66).

Table A.9: Type of Employment—Men

Employment Characteristic	Agricultural Work (%)	Nonagricultural Work (%)	Total (%)
Type of earnings			
Cash only	34.2	95.4	75.3
Cash and in-kind	9.7	1.9	4.5
In-kind only	3.4	0.1	1.2
Not paid	52.6	2.6	19.1
Total	100.0	100.0	100.0
Continuity of employment			
All year	53.0	83.0	73.1
Seasonal	38.9	12.7	21.3
Occasional	8.0	4.3	5.5
Total	100.0	100.0	100.0
Number of men employed during the last 12 months	1,144	2,333	3,482

Note: Percent distribution of men aged 15 to 49 employed in the 12 months preceding the survey by type of earnings, type of employer, and continuity of employment, according to type of employment (agricultural or nonagricultural).

Total includes men with missing information on type of employment who are not shown separately.

Source: Government of Nepal, Ministry of Health. 2016. *Demographic and Health Survey*. Kathmandu (Table 3.10.2, p. 66).

Table A.10: Employment and Cash Earnings of Currently Married Women and Men

Age	Among Currently Married Respondents		Percent Distribution of Currently Married Respondents Employed in the Past 12 Months, by Type of Earnings				Total	Number of Women
	% Employed in past 12 months	Number of respondents	Cash only	Cash and in-kind	In-kind only	Not paid		
Women								
15–19	49.1	704	22.1	3.3	1.8	72.7	100.0	346
20–24	59.4	1,684	32.0	4.3	3.6	60.0	100.0	1,001
25–29	65.5	1,957	42.0	7.6	3.5	46.8	100.0	1,281
30–34	73.4	1,726	39.4	7.9	4.0	48.7	100.0	1,266
35–39	74.1	1,1510	37.8	10.3	4.8	47.1	100.0	1,120
40–44	75.5	1,283	35.2	12.5	4.4	48.0	100.0	969
45–49	74.2	1,011	28.9	11.2	3.8	56.1	100.0	750
Total	68.2	9,875	35.9	8.5	3.9	51.7	100.0	6,733
Men								
15–19	93.6	60	66.1	1.3	5.1	27.5	100.0	56
20–24	97.6	284	81.0	1.7	1.0	16.2	100.0	277
25–29	97.4	423	79.9	5.9	1.4	12.7	100.0	412
30–34	97.8	513	80.3	3.3	1.0	15.5	100.0	502

continued on next page

Table A.10 continued

| Age | Among Currently Married Respondents | | Percent Distribution of Currently Married Respondents Employed in the Past 12 Months, by Type of Earnings | | | | Total | Number of Women |
	% Employed in past 12 months	Number of respondents	Cash only	Cash and in-kind	In-kind only	Not paid		
35–39	97.7	528	78.8	5.5	1.1	14.6	100.0	516
40–44	97.8	461	75.7	7.8	0.9	15.6	100.0	450
45–49	95.7	407	68.6	6.5	1.7	23.2	100.0	390
Total	97.3	2,675	77.2	5.2	1.3	16.4	100.0	2,602

Note: Percentage of currently married women and men aged 15 to 49 who were employed at any time in the past 12 months and the percent distribution of currently married women and men employed in the past 12 months by type of earnings, according to age.

Source: Government of Nepal, Ministry of Health. 2016. *Demographic and Health Survey*. Kathmandu (Table 15.1, p. 311).

Table A.11: Occupation—Women

Province	Professional/ Technical/ Managerial	Clerical	Sales and Services	Skilled Manual	Unskilled Manual	Agriculture	Other	Total	Number of Women
Province 1	5.3	2.8	12.4	4.2	2.5	72.5	0.4	100.0	1,455
Province 2	3.8	1.1	5.6	7.0	3.9	78.7	0.0	100.0	1,303
Province 3	10.8	3.6	25.0	9.0	4.7	46.7	0.2	100.0	1,927
Province 4	4.8	2.1	15.7	4.2	2.8	70.5	0.0	100.0	877
Province 5	4.1	1.5	9.8	6.1	2.5	75.8	0.2	100.0	1,569
Province 6	4.3	0.3	8.6	2.1	2.6	82.1	0.0	100.0	529
Province 7	2.5	0.4	6.8	2.4	4.2	83.7	0.0	100.0	943

Note: Percent distribution of women aged 15 to 49 employed in the 12 months preceding the survey by occupation, according to background characteristics.

Source: Government of Nepal, Ministry of Health. 2016. *Demographic and Health Survey*. Kathmandu (Table 3.9.1, p. 64).

Table A.12: Occupation—Men

Province	Professional/ Technical/ Managerial	Clerical	Sales and Services	Skilled Manual	Unskilled Manual	Agriculture	Other	Don't Know	Total	Number of Men
Province 1	12.8	7.3	14.2	11.0	7.3	45.7	1.3	0.3	100.0	629
Province 2	6.4	5.2	23.0	19.9	18.7	26.8	0.0	0.0	100.0	681
Province 3	13.2	7.4	33.2	14.4	8.4	21.6	1.5	0.2	100.0	877
Province 4	8.7	8.0	21.2	12.3	8.5	41.3	0.0	0.0	100.0	308
Province 5	6.4	6.1	19.8	16.2	20.3	31.2	0.0	0.0	100.0	533
Province 6	5.7	1.5	21.9	6.3	15.2	49.3	0.0	0.0	100.0	179
Province 7	8.8	1.7	23.1	13.7	14.3	37.4	0.8	0.1	100.0	274

Note: Percent distribution of men aged 15 to 49 employed in the 12 months preceding the survey by occupation, according to background characteristics.

Source: Government of Nepal, Ministry of Health. 2016. *Demographic and Health Survey*. Kathmandu (Table 3.9.2, p. 65).

Table A.13: Women's Control Over Their Own Earnings and Over Those of Their Husbands

Women's Earnings Relative to Husband's Earnings	Person Who Decides How the Wife's Cash Earnings are Used				Total[a]	No.	Person Who Decides How the Husband's Cash Earnings are Used				Total[a]	No.
	Mainly Wife	Wife and Husband Jointly	Mainly Husband	Other			Mainly Wife	Wife and Husband Jointly	Mainly Husband	Other		
More than husband	56.7	31.3	9.5	2.4	100.0	223	25.8	41.0	30.8	2.4	100.0	223
Less than husband	54.9	31.8	10.5	2.9	100.0	2,192	19.4	48.1	26.8	5.7	100.0	2,192
Same as husband	30.6	52.3	16.6	0.5	100.0	409	12.1	62.9	25.0	0.0	100.0	409
Husband has no cash earnings or did not work	54.2	35.4	8.4	2.0	100.0	142	NA	NA	NA	NA	NA	0
Women worked but has no cash earnings	NA	NA	NA	NA	NA	0	14.0	40.4	33.3	12.4	100.0	3,665
Women did not work	NA	NA	NA	NA	NA	0	13.8	42.4	26.3	17.5	100.0	3,058
Total	51.8	34.5	11.2	2.5	100.0	2,986	15.3	43.7	29.2	11.8	100.0	9,568

NA = Not Applicable.

[a] Includes cases where a woman does not know whether she earned more or less than her husband.

Note: Percent distribution of currently married women aged 15 to 49 with cash earnings in the last 12 months by person who decides how the wife's cash earnings are used and percent distribution of currently married women aged 15 to 49 whose husbands have cash earnings by person who decides how the husband's cash earnings are used, according to the relation between wife's and husband's cash earnings.

Source: Government of Nepal, Ministry of Health. 2016. *Demographic and Health Survey*. Kathmandu (Table 15.3, p. 314).

Table A.14: Household Food Security

Province	Food Secure	Mildly Food Insecure	Moderately Food Insecure	Severely Food Insecure	Total	Number of Households
Province 1	52.6	20.3	18.0	9.2	100.0	2,004
Province 2	43.1	26.4	19.8	10.7	100.0	2,014
Province 3	55.0	16.4	20.0	8.5	100.0	2,521
Province 4	56.0	16.9	21.1	6.0	100.0	1,173
Province 5	48.4	19.2	22.2	10.2	100.0	1,793
Province 6	22.5	17.8	42.2	17.5	100.0	619
Province 7	37.7	18.0	31.2	13.0	100.0	915

Note: Percent distribution of households by level of food insecurity, according to background characteristics.

Source: Government of Nepal, Ministry of Health. 2016. *Demographic and Health Survey*. Kathmandu (Table 2.11, p. 42).

Table A.15: Migration Status

Province	Women	Men	Total
Province 1	20.4	19.0	19.6
Province 2	20.2	20.4	20.3
Province 3	20.4	17.0	18.3
Province 4	11.7	12.5	12.2
Province 5	14.8	16.8	15.9
Province 6	4.3	5.1	4.8
Province 7	8.7	9.2	9.0
Total	100.0	100.0	100.0

Note: Percentage distribution of women and men who migrated within 10 years before the survey, by selected background characteristics.

Source: Government of Nepal, Ministry of Health. 2016. *Demographic and Health Survey*. Kathmandu (Table 2.11, p. 30).

Table A.16: Ownership of Assets—Women

Province	Owns a House (%)					Owns Land (%)					Number
	Alone	Jointly	Alone and Jointly	Do Not Own a House (%)	Total	Alone	Jointly	Alone and Jointly	Do Not Own Land (%)	Total	
Province 1	9.3	1.1	0.8	88.8	100.0	12.9	0.5	0.3	86.2	100.0	2,173
Province 2	6.1	0.3	0.6	93.0	100.0	11.9	0.2	0.2	87.7	100.0	2,563
Province 3	7.3	1.3	0.3	91.1	100.0	9.5	3.0	0.9	86.6	100.0	2,732
Province 4	8.6	0.6	0.1	90.8	100.0	11.3	0.8	0.3	87.7	100.0	1,249
Province 5	5.6	0.3	0.4	93.7	100.0	9.4	0.4	0.2	90.0	100.0	2,274
Province 6	5.7	0.2	0.3	93.8	100.0	7.3	0.1	0.1	92.5	100.0	724
Province 7	2.8	0.3	0.2	96.8	100.0	3.1	0.2	0.2	96.5	100.0	1,145

Note: Percent distribution of women aged 15 to 49 by ownership of housing and land, according to background characteristics.

Source: Government of Nepal, Ministry of Health. 2016. *Demographic and Health Survey*. Kathmandu (Table 15.4.1, p. 315).

Table A.17: Ownership of Assets—Men

Province	Owns a House (%)					Owns Land (%)					Number
	Alone	Jointly	Alone and Jointly	Do Not Own a House (%)	Total	Alone	Jointly	Alone and Jointly	Do Not Own Land (%)	Total	
Province 1	21.8	1.0	0.0	77.2	100.0	25.7	0.6	0.4	73.3	100.0	691
Province 2	16.8	0.3	0.0	83.0	100.0	15.3	0.4	1.3	83.0	100.0	795
Province 3	16.7	1.8	0.8	80.7	100.0	19.2	2.6	0.4	77.8	100.0	1,009
Province 4	15.1	1.4	1.1	82.4	100.0	16.6	1.4	1.1	80.9	100.0	376
Province 5	18.2	0.6	0.2	81.0	100.0	19.6	0.2	1.1	79.2	100.0	658
Province 6	19.2	0.1	0.5	80.2	100.0	20.3	0.1	0.3	79.3	100.0	203
Province 7	19.3	0.2	0.1	80.4	100.0	18.2	0.2	0.4	81.3	100.0	330

Note: Percent distribution of men aged 15 to 49 by ownership of housing and land, according to background characteristics.

Source: Government of Nepal, Ministry of Health. 2016. *Demographic and Health Survey*. Kathmandu (Table 15.4.2, p. 316).

Table A.18: Ownership of Assets—Women
(House)

Ethnic/Caste/Religious Groups	Owns a House Alone or Jointly (%)			
	Does Not Own	Alone Only	Jointly Only	Both Alone and Jointly
Hill Brahmin	89	9.7	0.9	0.3
Hill Chhetri	91	7.6	0.9	0.4
Tarai Brahmin/Chhetri	87.6	11	1.4	0
Other Tarai Caste	93.8	5.3	0.3	0.7
Hill Dalit	93.6	5.9	0.3	0.2
Tarai Dalit	95.2	4.6	0.2	0
Newar	90.5	7.8	1.4	0.3
Hill Janajati	92.5	6.8	0.4	0.3
Tarai Janajati	94.4	4.2	0.6	0.7
Muslim	91.6	6.6	1.1	0.7
Other	95.3	2.3	2.3	0
Total	92.2	6.7	0.6	0.4

Source: World Bank. 2018. *Country Level Gender Equality and Social Inclusion Assessment (Annex 2)*. Kathmandu.

Table A.19: Ownership of Assets—Women
(Land)

Ethnic/Caste/Religious Groups	Owns Land Alone or Jointly (%)			
	Does Not Own	Alone Only	Jointly Only	Both Alone and Jointly
Hill Brahmin	84.4	13.5	1.7	0.5
Hill Chhetri	86.9	11.2	1.1	0.8
Tarai Brahmin/Chhetri	87.3	10.6	1.3	0.8
Other Tarai Caste	87.7	11.9	0.2	0.2
Hill Dalit	93.4	6.2	0.1	0.2
Tarai Dalit	93.8	6.2	0	0
Newar	86.9	10.5	2.6	0
Hill Janajati	89.1	9.6	0.9	0.4
Tarai Janajati	92.5	6.4	0.8	0.3
Muslim	89.3	9.7	0.6	0.3
Other	81.4	6.4	12.1	0
Total	88.7	10	0.9	0.4

Source: World Bank. 2018. *Country Level Gender Equality and Social Inclusion Assessment (Annex 2)*. Kathmandu.

Table A.20: Participation in Decision-Making

Decision	Mainly Wife	Wife and Husband Jointly	Mainly Husband	Someone Else	Other	Total	Number of Women
WOMEN							
Own Health Care	23.3	34.5	29.1	12.8	0.4	100.0	9,875
Major Household Purchase	35.2	17.8	21.8	24.5	0.7	100.0	9,875
Visits to Her Family or Relatives	26.8	28.8	23.2	20.6	0.6	100.0	9,875
MEN							
Own Health Care	7.3	32.3	52.8	7.6	0.1	100.0	2,675
Major Household Purchases	23.4	25.0	30.9	20.7	0.0	100.0	2,675

Note: Percent distribution of currently married women and currently married men aged 15 to 49 by person who usually makes decisions about various issues.

Source: Government of Nepal, Ministry of Health. 2016. *Demographic and Health Survey*. Kathmandu (Table 15.9, p. 324).

Table A.21: Women's Role in Final Decisions on How to Use Remittances

Ethnic/Caste/Religious Groups (Selected)	Wife	Husband	Both	Other	Total
Hill Brahmins	29.42	14.62	35.35	20.62	100
Hill Chhetris	23.66	10.99	44.37	20.97	100
Tarai Castes	9.55	8.53	55.17	26.75	100
Hill Dalits	35.77	11.43	34.96	17.84	100
Other Hill Dalits	37.64	8.2	29.28	24.89	100
Tarai Dalits	1.84	3.26	63.15	31.75	100
Indigenous Peoples	23.56	9.3	45.16	21.97	100
Newar (Hill Indigenous Peoples)	32.51	7.05	50.53	9.91	100
Other Hill Indigenous Peoples	23.71	10.39	41.38	24.52	100
Tarai Indigenous Peoples	17.94	7.1	54.25	20.72	100
Other (Muslims, etc.)	2.52	1.73	49.85	45.9	100
Total	22.2	9.94	44.71	23.15	100

Source: World Bank. 2018. *Country Level Gender Equality and Social Inclusion Assessment (Annex 2)*. Kathmandu.

Table A.22: Women's Participation in Decision-Making (%)

Ethnic/Caste/Religious Groups	Respondent Alone	Respondent and Husband/Partner	Husband/Partner Alone	Someone Else
Person Who Usually Decides on Respondent's Health Care				
Hill Brahmin	27.2	36	28.8	7.9
Hill Chhetri	28.7	29.1	32.4	9.1
Tarai Brahmin/Chhetri	24.5	43.5	22.6	8.7
Other Tarai Caste	8.9	41	25.2	24.4
Hill Dalit	31.7	25.1	33.7	9.5
Tarai Dalit	12.8	37.2	25.3	23.6
Newar	28.4	36.5	29.6	5.4
Hill Janajati	31.1	30.8	29.6	8.4
Tarai Janajati	16.2	42.3	30.1	11.2
Muslim	15.4	36.3	24	23.4
Other	10	38.5	41.6	6.4
Total	23.3	34.5	29.1	12.8
Person Who Usually Decides on Large Household Purchases				
Hill Brahmin	39.5	20.5	19.4	19.6
Hill Chhetri	38.1	17.8	21.9	21.2
Tarai Brahmin/Chhetri	34.4	23.8	21.4	18.7
Other Tarai Caste	21.5	18.1	25.2	34.7
Hill Dalit	47.4	13.5	20.7	18.3
Tarai Dalit	30.1	16.2	20	32.7
Newar	37.6	15.7	17.3	28.9
Hill Janajati	42.2	16.7	21.3	19.3
Tarai Janajati	29.8	21.4	21.5	26.7
Muslim	25.9	15.5	25.3	32.5
Other	30	22.7	29.1	14.7
Total	35.2	17.8	21.8	24.5
Person Who Usually Decides on Visits to Family or Relatives				
Hill Brahmin	30.5	31.6	20.4	16.9
Hill Chhetri	30.3	22.3	27.9	18.7
Tarai Brahmin/Chhetri	24.4	38.2	21	15.8
Other Tarai Caste	12	35.4	20.1	32.2
Hill Dalit	33.1	21.4	29.3	16
Tarai Dalit	15.4	35.7	18.9	28.6
Newar	37.1	29.3	16.1	16.8
Hill Janajati	37	25.5	22.7	14.5
Tarai Janajati	23.1	31.4	25.5	19.6
Muslim	12.9	33.4	22.8	29.8
Other	26.9	38.4	16.1	15.2
Total	26.8	28.8	23.2	20.6

Source: World Bank. 2018. *Country Level Gender Equality and Social Inclusion Assessment (Annex 2)*. Kathmandu.

Table A.23: Attitude Toward Wife Beating—Women

Province	Husband is Justified in Hitting or Beating His Wife if She (%)					Agrees with at Least One Specified Reason (%)	Brings Less or No Dowry (%)	Number
	Burns the Food	Argues with Him	Goes out without Telling Him	Neglects the Children	Refuses to Have Sexual Intercourse with Him			
Province 1	3.1	6.8	12.1	23.4	2.5	27.5	0.8	2,173
Province 2	8.1	17.1	14.6	25.9	5.2	32.6	2.2	2,563
Province 3	2.2	4.7	10.7	23.7	2.2	26.3	0.8	2,732
Province 4	0.9	3.4	7.2	21.0	1.6	23.4	0.5	1,249
Province 5	1.7	10.1	11.2	23.9	2.2	27.7	0.5	2,274
Province 6	2.8	6.4	11.7	24.2	2.7	28.4	0.2	724
Province 7	2.9	9.5	12.6	29.3	4.5	34.3	0.7	1,145

Note: Percentage of all women aged 15 to 49 who agree that a husband is justified in hitting or beating his wife for specific reasons, by background characteristics.

Source: Government of Nepal, Ministry of Health. 2016. *Demographic and Health Survey*. Kathmandu (Table 15.11.1, p. 327).

Table A.24: Attitude Toward Wife Beating—Men

Province	Husband is Justified in Hitting or Beating His Wife if She (%)					Agree with at Least One Specified Reason (%)	Brings Less or No Dowry (%)	Number
	Burns the Food	Argues with Him	Goes out without Telling him	Neglects the Children	Refuses to Have Sexual Intercourse with Him			
Province 1	1.0	5.9	10.7	19.2	2.3	24.0	0.4	691
Province 2	2.9	15.6	11.9	18.1	4.9	22.2	0.5	795
Province 3	1.0	6.1	8.6	17.9	3.5	21.9	0.6	1,009
Province 4	0.4	1.7	6.8	13.6	2.1	18.4	0.3	376
Province 5	1.0	7.3	5.6	14.1	3.3	17.4	0.4	658
Province 6	3.1	11.6	13.8	29.3	8.3	33.9	0.8	203
Province 7	2.8	15.5	11.0	28.9	5.4	35.3	0.3	330

Note: Percentage of all men aged 15 to 49 who agree that a husband is justified in hitting or beating his wife for specific reasons, by background characteristics.

Source: Government of Nepal, Ministry of Health. 2016. *Demographic and Health Survey*. Kathmandu (Table 15.11.2, p. 328).

Table A.25: Attitude Toward Wife Beating—Women (%)

Ethnic/Caste/Religious Groups	No	Yes	Don't Know
Beating Justified if Wife Burns the Food			
Hill Brahmin	98.8	1.2	0
Hill Chhetri	97.4	2.4	0.2
Tarai Brahmin/Chhetri	95.3	4.7	0
Other Tarai Caste	94	6	0
Hill Dalit	95.2	3.9	0.8
Tarai Dalit	92.3	7.7	0
Newar	99.2	0.8	0
Hill Janajati	98.2	1.8	0
Tarai Janajati	96.6	3.4	0
Muslim	91.1	8.7	0.2
Other	97.4	2.6	0
Total	96.5	3.4	0.1
Beating Justified if Wife Argues with Husband			
Hill Brahmin	95.7	4.3	0
Hill Chhetri	93.5	6.3	0.2
Tarai Brahmin/Chhetri	94.5	5.5	0
Other Tarai Caste	83.8	16.1	0.2
Hill Dalit	91.3	8.7	0.1
Tarai Dalit	82.7	17.3	0
Newar	97.4	2.6	0
Hill Janajati	94.2	5.6	0.2
Tarai Janajati	91.1	8.9	0
Muslim	77.9	22.1	0
Other	97.4	2.6	0
Total	91	8.9	0.1
Beating Justified if Wife Goes out without Telling Husband			
Hill Brahmin	92.6	7.3	0.1
Hill Chhetri	87.2	12.6	0.1
Tarai Brahmin/Chhetri	91.6	8.4	0
Other Tarai Caste	87.2	12.7	0.1
Hill Dalit	87.6	12.3	0.1
Tarai Dalit	81.6	18.4	0
Newar	93.3	6.5	0.2
Hill Janajati	89.1	10.7	0.1
Tarai Janajati	88.9	11.1	0
Muslim	79.5	20.5	0
Other	95.2	4.8	0
Total	88.2	11.7	0.1

continued on next page

Table A.25 continued

Ethnic/Caste/Religious Groups	No	Yes	Don't Know
Beating Justified if Wife Neglects the Children			
Hill Brahmin	79.8	20	0.2
Hill Chhetri	74.3	25.7	0.1
Tarai Brahmin/Chhetri	78.6	21.4	0
Other Tarai Caste	77	23	0
Hill Dalit	72.2	27.6	0.2
Tarai Dalit	71.9	28.1	0
Newar	84	15.6	0.4
Hill Janajati	75.1	24.8	0.1
Tarai Janajati	74.1	25.8	0.1
Muslim	68.2	31.8	0
Other	89.3	10.7	0
Total	75.5	24.4	0.1
Beating Justified if Wife Refuses to Have Sex with Husband			
Hill Brahmin	98.8	0.9	0.3
Hill Chhetri	96.3	3.1	0.6
Tarai Brahmin/Chhetri	97.8	1.5	0.6
Other Tarai Caste	95.7	4.2	0.1
Hill Dalit	95.6	4.3	0
Tarai Dalit	95.4	4.6	0
Newar	97.7	1.5	0.8
Hill Janajati	98.1	1.7	0.2
Tarai Janajati	96.4	3.2	0.4
Muslim	92.1	7.8	0.1
Other	97.4	2.6	0
Total	96.7	3	0.3

Source: World Bank. 2018. *Country Level Gender Equality and Social Inclusion Assessment (Annex 2)*. Kathmandu.

Table A.26: Spousal Physical Violence Against Men

Ethnic/Caste/Religious Groups	Female Respondent Ever Physically Hurt Husband/Partner When He Was Not Hurting Her (%)	
	No	Yes
Hill Brahmin	99.7	0.3
Hill Chhetri	98.9	1.1
Tarai Brahmin/Chhetri	100.0	0.0
Other Tarai Caste	98.7	1.3
Hill Dalit	98.4	1.6
Tarai Dalit	99.2	0.8
Newar	97.7	2.3
Hill Janajati	96.5	3.5
Tarai Janajati	98.2	1.8
Muslim	98.1	1.9
Other	100.0	0.0
Total	98.3	1.7

Source: World Bank. 2018. *Country Level Gender Equality and Social Inclusion Assessment (Annex 2)*. Kathmandu.

Table A.27: Indicator of Women's Empowerment

Empowerment Indicator	Participates in All Decision-Making (%)	Disagrees with All of the Reasons Justifying Wife Beating	Number of Women
Number of Decisions in Which Women Participate[1]			
0	NA	71.6	2,713
1–2	NA	70.9	3,440
3	NA	72.8	3,722
Number of Reasons for Which Wife Beating is Justified[2]			
0	38.2	NA	7,091
1–2	37.3	NA	2,122
3–4	35.0	NA	563
5	23.8	NA	99

NA = not applicable.

[1] See Table 15.10.1 of Ministry of Health's Demographic and Health Survey for the list of decisions. Excludes decisions on children's education and use of her inherited asset (*pewa*).

[2] See Table 15.11.1 of Ministry of Health's Demographic and Health Survey for the list of reasons. Excludes the reason bringing less or no dowry.

Note: Percentage of currently married women aged 15 to 49 who participate in all decision-making and the percentage who disagree with all of the reasons justifying wife beating, by value on each of the indicators of women's empowerment.

Source: Government of Nepal, Ministry of Health. 2016. *Demographic and Health Survey*. Kathmandu (Table 15.14, p. 331).

Table A.28: Provincial Poverty Index (%)

Province	Population under absolute poverty	Multi-dimensional poverty rate
Province 1	12.4	19.7
Province 2	19.8	47.9
Province 3	15.3	12.2
Province 4	15.5	14.2
Province 5	18.2	29.9
Province 6	28.9	51.2
Province 7	33.9	33.6
Nepal	18.7	28.6

Source: Ministry of Finance. *Economic Survey 2018/19*. Table 2(a). p. 13. Kathmandu, Nepal.
https://mof.gov.np/uploads/document/file/compiled%20economic%20Survey%20english%207-25_20191111101758.pdf.

Table A.29: Population by Caste and Ethnicity, and Religion by Province (%)

Province	Khas Arya	Hill Janajati	Tarai Janajati	Dalit	Madhesi	Muslim	Other
Province 1	27.84	39.77	11.03	9.31	7.54	3.59	0.92
Province 2	4.88	6.45	8.49	16.30	51.80	11.58	0.51
Province 3	37.10	52.68	1.77	5.66	1.65	0.67	0.45
Province 4	36.10	39.26	2.27	17.62	3.45	1.17	0.14
Province 5	30.03	19.58	14.88	14.07	14.5	6.65	0.29
Province 6	60.96	14.76	0.51	22.92	0.00	0.00	0.85
Province 7	60.02	3.50	17.25	12.94	1.73	0.23	4.32
Nepal	31.25	27.28	7.70	12.94	15.37	4.39	1.07

Source: Governance Facility. 2018. *Federal Nepal: The Provinces, Socio-Cultural Profiles of the Seven Provinces*. Kathmandu (Table 3.5, p. 79).

Table A.30: Human Development Index Values by Province

Province	HDI	Life Expectancy	Adult Literacy	Mean Years of Schooling	Per Capita Income (PPP $)
Province 1	0.504	68.45	65.33	4.25	1,184
Province 2	0.421	70.41	40.88	2.73	922
Province 3	0.548	69.70	69.30	5.14	1,767
Province 4	0.516	69.79	61.24	2.73	1,206
Province 5	0.467	67.65	59.18	5.14	1,013
Province 6	0.426	66.57	52.30	4.50	784
Province 7	0.431	66.89	54.95	3.61	767
Nepal	0.49	68.80	59.57	3.90	1,160

HDI = human development index, PPP = Purchasing Power Parity.

Source: Governance Facility. 2018. *Federal Nepal: The Provinces, Socio-Cultural Profiles of the Seven Provinces*. Kathmandu (Table 3.6, p. 79).

Table A.31: Area and Population by Province

Province	Area (km²)	Population 2011	Female Population (%)	Literacy Rate Total	Literacy Rate Female	Literacy Rate Male	Government Expenditure (NRs billion, 2017)
Province 1	25,905	4,534,943	52.23	65.30	63.94	79.27	206.00
Province 2	9,661	5,404,145	49.71	40.90	38.88	60.09	149.10
Province 3	20,300	5,529,452	50.31	69.30	67.04	82.82	962.90
Province 4	21,504	2,478,258	54.39	55.60	67.72	83.54	142.60
Province 5	22,288	4,473,576	52.51	59.40	58.33	75.50	191.90
Province 6	27,984	1,521,613	51.08	53.00	53.21	72.88	109.50
Province 7	19,539	2,552,517	52.29	54.90	51.93	76.37	129.90
Nepal	147,181	26,494,504	51.50				1891.90

km² = square kilometer, NRs = Nepalese rupees.

Source: Bikas Udhyami. 2017. *Nepal in Data*. Lalitpur, Nepal. https://www.nepalindata.com/data/analytics/.

Table A.32: Caste or Ethnic and Religious Groups

Classification of 125 Social Groups in the 2011 Census

3 Broad Categories	5 Social Groups	11 Disaggregated Social Subgroups	205 Caste/Ethnic/Religious Groups Within 11 Groups
Adivasi Janajati (Ethnic Groups)		Hill Janajati	Aathpariya,* Bahing,* Bantaba,* Bhote, Bote, Brahmu/Baramo, Byasi/Sauka, Chamling,* Chepang/Praja, Chhantyal/Chhantel, Danuwar, Darai, Dolpo,* Dura, Ghale, Gharti/Bhujel, Gurung, Hayu, Hyolmo, Jirel, Khaling,* Kulung,* Kumal, Kusunda, Lepcha, Lhomi,* Lhopa,* Limbu, Loharung,* Magar, Majhi, Mewahang Bala,* Nachhiring,*Pahari, Rai, Raji, Raute, Samgpang,* Sherpa, Sunwar, Tamang, Thakali, Thami, Thulung,* Topkegola, Walung, Yakkha, Yamphu*
		Newar	Newar
		Tarai Janajati	Dhanuk, Dhimal, Gangai, Jhangar/Dhagar, Khawas,* Kisan, Koche, Meche, Munda, Pathharkatta/Kusbadiya, Rajbanshi, Satar/Santhal, Tajpuriya, Tharu
Hindu Caste Groups	Brahman/ Chhetri	Hill Brahman	Brahman-Hill
		Hill Chhetri	Chhetri, Thakuri, Sanyasi/Dasnami
		Madhesi Brahman	Brahman-Tarai, Kayastha, Nurang, Rajput
	Madhesi Caste	Madhesi Other Caste	Amat,* Badhaee, Baniya, Baraee, Bin, Dev, Dhandi,* Dhankar/Dharikar,* Gaderi/Bhediyar, Hazam/Thakur, Haluwai, Kahar, Kalwar, Kanu, Kathabaniyan,* Kewat, Koiri/Kushwaha, Kori,* Kumhar, Kurmi, Lodh, Lohar, Mali, Mallaha, Natuwa,* Nuniya, Rajbhar, Rajdhob,* Sarbaria,* Sonar, Sudhi, Teli, Yadav
	Dalit	Hill Dalit	Badi, Damai/Dholi, Gaine, Kami, Sarki (5)
		Madhesi Dalit	Bantar/Sardar, Chamar/Harijan/Ram, Chidimar, Dhobi, Dom, Dushad/ Paswan/Pasi, Halkhor, Khatwe, Musahar Tatma/Tatwa
Muslim			Madhesi Musalman, Churaute
Other			Marwari, Jain, Bengali, Punjabi/Sikh

* Additional subgroups identified after 2001 census.

Source: Central Department of Sociology/Anthropology, Tribhuvan University. 2014. *Social Inclusion Atlas of Nepal, Ethnic and Caste Groups*. Volume 1. Kathmandu: Tribhuvan University.

www.ingramcontent.com/pod-product-compliance
Lightning Source LLC
Chambersburg PA
CBHW041120280326
41928CB00061B/3466